# TRUST

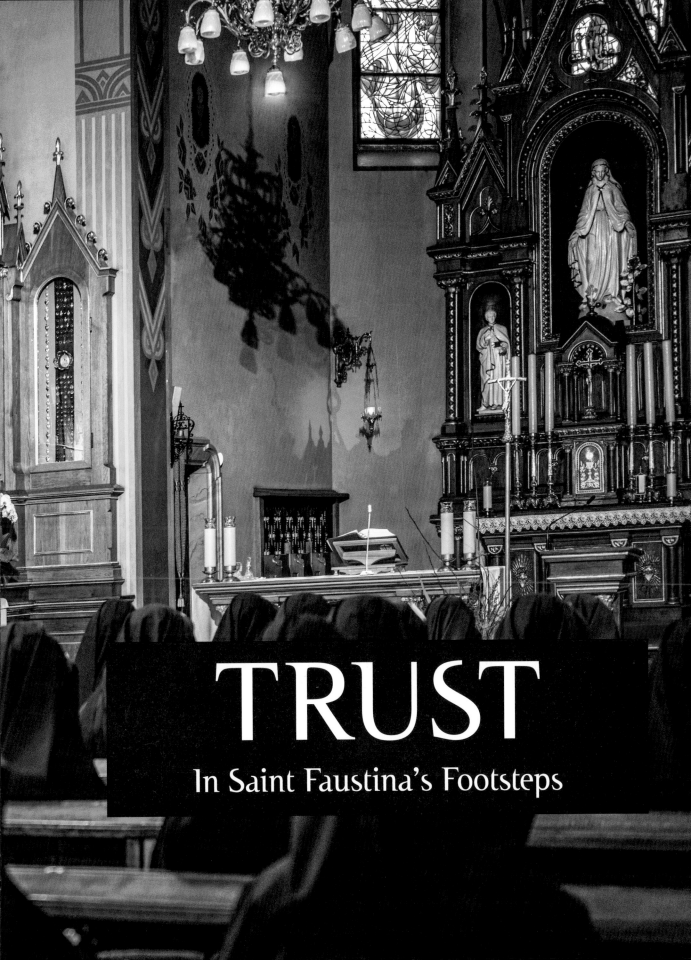

# TRUST
## In Saint Faustina's Footsteps

During the consecration of the Divine Mercy Basilica in Kraków, in 2002, Holy Father John Paul II said: "The world will find peace in God's mercy, and man—happiness." Today there is little peace in the world, and many are unhappy. That is precisely why mankind needs to turn to God's mercy.

The global and rapid spread of the devotion to the Divine Mercy throughout the world is the best testimony to this need. It satisfies man's deepest yearnings and desires, written into the human soul, and, at the same time, it is at the center of Christian revelations that proclaim a loving and merciful God, Who is solicitous about every being.

St. Faustina Kowalska, an unassuming nun from Poland and Karol Wojtyla's compatriot, was a singular advocate of this truth in the twentieth century. Her whole life bore witness to God's mercy, while the work she left behind her is, and will remain, a source of inspiration for the Church.

This book tells of the saint's experiences. It leads the reader in her footsteps to the principal places with which she is associated. Primarily, however, it is concerned with the history and the essence of the devotion that Sr. Faustina advocated. After all, she never put any emphasis on herself; instead she always pointed to the Holy Trinity, the Creator of man's existence, the Guarantor of our freedom, and most importantly the Source of love. I hope that this book will not only be an occasion to meet an extraordinary mystic, but also be an invitation to delve deeply into the infinite mystery of God's mercy.

**POPE JOHN PAUL II** not only consecrated the basilica in Łagiewniki (August 17, 2002) during his visit to Kraków, but he also entrusted the world to God's mercy.

José Cardinal Saraiva Martins

*Prefect of the Congregation for the Causes of Saints*

*(1998–2008)*

**ST. FAUSTINA KOWALSKA**
(1905–1938).
Like Christ, she
lived for 33
years.

# PROLOGUE

The work that St. Faustina Kowalska, of the Congregation of the Sisters of Our Lady of Mercy, bequeathed to posterity is of exceptional value, not only for the Church in Poland, but also for the universal Church. Through this unassuming nun, sometimes known as the Secretary of the Divine Mercy, the Christian world of the twentieth century has been enriched with new means for proclaiming the salvific message.

It is precisely through Sr. Faustina's bequest that countless people have truly been able to experience the action of God's mercy in their lives. They have been able to discover the presence of God, the only Guarantor of the meaning of our existence.

The Church is continuously being renewed through her saints, who all draw inspiration from the same divine Source.

Sr. Faustina is an eloquent example. Because of her, the devotion to the Divine Mercy, which is to many people the greatest attribute of our Creator and Savior, has spread rapidly throughout the world. Millions worldwide recite the Divine Mercy Chaplet, a short propitiatory prayer that Jesus dictated to the Polish nun (September 1935, Vilnius). Today, in many Catholic churches and homes, Christ is venerated and adored in the image of the Merciful Jesus that our Lord enjoined Sr. Faustina to paint (February 22, 1931, Płock). It is impossible to count all the faithful who venerate Jesus at the Hour of Mercy, as Christ instructed the Polish mystic to do (October 1937, Łagiewniki, Kraków).

These specific dates and places are very important, for they show that God comes to us at specific times and in specific places, just as He did two thousand years ago in Palestine. He is not an abstract God, but a loving, forgiving, and ever affectionately present Father. It is untrue that He cares nothing for us. On the contrary, He knows of our problems, our wounds, and our sufferings, and He wants us to invite Him into our lives. Seized by "the madness of love", He yearns to come to us with His mercy. He wants us only to open ourselves to His action. And that is precisely what Sr. Faustina advocated: that we open our hearts to Christ.

It was no coincidence that Pope John Paul II's call, during the first homily of his pontificate, harmonized with this: "Do not be afraid! Open the door to Christ!" God's providence so decreed that the destinies of Helen Kowalska and Karol Wojtyla would be closely interwoven. As the archbishop of Kraków, Karol Wojtyla initiated the informative process relating to the life and virtues of Sr. Faustina. Two years later in 1970, he forwarded its findings to the Sacred Congregation for the Causes of Saints, which in turn inaugurated her beatification process. Finally, when all the documents relating to her cause were submitted to the Holy See, he requested a formal review in March 1978. It was after the intervention in 1978 of Karol Wojtyla, then metropolitan of Kraków, that the Vatican Congregation for the Doctrine of the Faith withdrew its earlier charges and reservations with regard to the writings of Sr. Faustina Kowalska. Thanks to this, the devotion gained new vitality throughout the world. In time, the Polish nun's *Diary: Divine Mercy in My Soul* became the world's most published work of twentieth-century Christian mysticism. Cardinal Wojtyla himself was a discerning reader of this work as clearly came to light after he assumed the Chair of St. Peter. His encyclical on the Divine Mercy, *Dives in Misericordia,* was published in 1980. It is not difficult to perceive between St. Faustina's *Diary* and the encyclical an inner link, that is, the truth about merciful love, which is more powerful than any evil.

But the mystical relationship that linked these two people, both of whom were very closely connected with the spiritual circles of Kraków—the city with the oldest church dedicated to Divine Mercy—did not end there. For the Holy Father beatified Sr. Faustina in 1993 and canonized her seven years later. Moreover, John Paul II fulfilled the instructions that were directed to her seven decades earlier, and in 2000 he established the Divine Mercy Feast, which has ever since been celebrated on the first Sunday after Easter.

In 2002, the Holy Father went to his homeland on his farewell pilgrimage. It was no coincidence that the climax of that pilgrimage was the act of entrusting the world to God's mercy, which took place at the Divine Mercy Shrine in Łagiewniki (Kraków). Pope John Paul II's address to his compatriots may be regarded as a peculiar spiritual testament. He called upon Poles to proclaim that God's mercy can lead man out of every sin, misfortune, and suffering and will give him true happiness.

This book is a response to Pope John Paul II's call. In presenting the experiences of St. Faustina Kowalska, it shows that which was of greatest importance in her life: her intimate relationship with God, Who was—we are not afraid to say this—in love with her, just as He is in love with each one of us. Our problem lies in the fact that this "love is not loved", as St. Francis of Assisi put it; we do not reciprocate God's love or trust sufficiently in His love. However, this biography shows that it is possible to cleave to the Savior with our whole being.

Through this book's photographs and narrative we are able to accompany the Polish nun on her spiritual pilgrimage through life. God revealed Himself to her in specific places, and she was capable of seeing His presence in all of life's circumstances. Perhaps this book will become an occasion for us to see that our lives are also pervaded by God's mercy and that we can invite Jesus into our innermost selves—anywhere and at any time.

**"JESUS, I TRUST IN YOU."** So wrote Sr. Faustina in her diary when describing her vision in Płock of Merciful Jesus on February 22, 1931.

**A LITTLE PICTURE OF MARY**, which Sr. Faustina received (February 15, 1935) from Sr. Petronela Basiur. She gave it to her brother Stanisław two days later.

Dziewico Święta! zmiłuj się nad
temi co się trwożą i płaczą, wyproś
wszystkim ufność i pokój.

*(Ojciec Perreyve)*

MADE IN FRANCE, PARIS

9

# CONTENTS

10

POLAND before World War II

EUROPE

POLAND

GERMANY

Kiekrz

# ST. FAUSTINA'S SOJOURNS

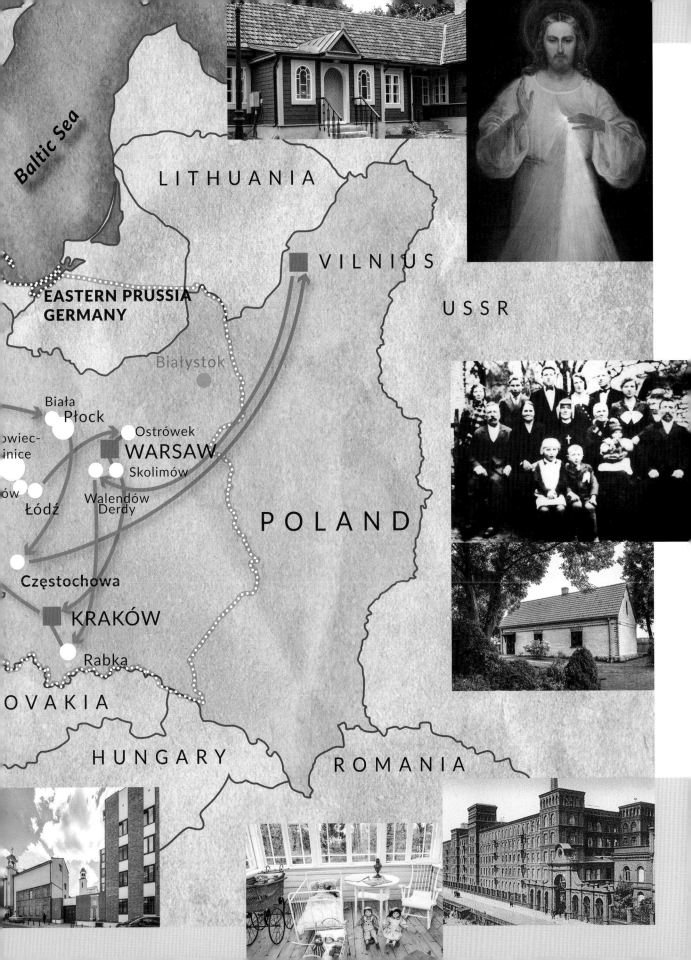

Baltic Sea

LITHUANIA

VILNIUS

EASTERN PRUSSIA
GERMANY

USSR

Białystok

Biała
Płock

owiec-
inice

Ostrówek

WARSAW

Skolimów

ów

Walendów

Łódź

Derdy

POLAND

Częstochowa

KRAKÓW

Rabka

OVAKIA

HUNGARY

ROMANIA

PRUSSIA

RUSSIA

■ Warsaw

AUSTRIA

# Poland

# CHAPTER 1

# Poland

"In Poland, that is, nowhere"— it is there that the French writer Alfred Jarry set his well-known play *King Ubu* (a non-existent king, an allusion to a non-existent Poland). Critics include this 1896 play among those of the so-called theater of the absurd. For Poles of that time, however, the situation was not at all absurd, but very real: Poland was nowhere. Quite simply, such a state did not exist on any world map. It had been divided between the absolutist Russian, Prussian, and Austrian governments one hundred years earlier.

**POLISH FOLK TRADITION** is pervaded by Catholic customs and piety. The Rosary has a special place.

Helen Kowalska came into the world in 1905, born in a country that did not exist. She was born in a village that did not figure on any detailed

17

# THREE PARTITIONS
# AND **EIGHT UPRISINGS**

**PRUSSIA, AUSTRIA,**
and **RUSSIA** partitioned the
Polish-Lithuanian state in 1772,
1793, and 1795. Poles repeatedly
attempted to regain their
independence by successive
uprisings. The first, led by Tadeusz
Kościuszko, in 1794, failed. They
were closest to freedom in the
years 1807 to 1815, when, thanks
to Napoleon Bonaparte, the Duchy
of Warsaw arose. That makeshift
Polish state, subordinated to
France, fell with the defeat of
Napoleon.

The next two attempts at
independence also failed: the
November Uprising of 1830 and
the January Uprising of 1863, both
largely in the Russian Partition. The
rebellion in the Austrian Partition
was even more quickly suppressed,
that is, the Kraków Uprising in 1846.
Because failed attempts resulted in
repression by the occupiers, Poles
returned to work and awaited a
favorable moment to again fight for
freedom.

The moment came with World
War I, which weakened all three
partitioning powers. Poles then
proclaimed independence in
1918. They started four revolts –
concerning borders – against the
German occupiers: the Greater
Poland Uprising of 1918 and three
Silesian uprisings (1919, 1920,
and 1921).

map of the Russian Empire; a village to which there was no paved road and whose inhabitants for the most part were illiterate. She lived in a home where she and her sisters had to share one Sunday dress; a home where the death of a cow raised the specter of famine for the whole family.

Pope John Paul II said that it was to precisely this poor girl, a girl from nowhere, that God had entrusted the mission of announcing to the whole world the most important message of the twentieth century. Were the most outstanding contemporary specialists in information strategy, mass communication, or promotion campaigns to have decided on how to go about such a task, they would have chosen Paris, London, New York, or another of the world's important cities, and they would have chosen a child from an aristocratic, bourgeois, or at least educated family. The one who was to have spread such an exceptional message all over the globe would have been appropriately educated and have proven himself to be the right person for the task.

**POZNAŃ, DECEMBER 27, 1918**. The inhabitants enthusiastically welcome Ignacy Paderewski. His arrival was the spark that caused the Greater Poland Uprising.

19

**PARTITIONS
OF POLAND.**
The Prussians
occupied 7 percent
of Poland
(including Poznan
and Gdansk),
the Austrians,
11 percent
(including Kraków
and Lviv), while
the Russians
occupied as much
as 82 percent
(including Warsaw
and Vilnius).

But God's logic differs from human logic. St. Paul, in his First Letter to the Corinthians, wrote: "God chose what is foolish in the world to shame the wise, God chose what is weak in the world to shame the strong, God chose what is low and despised in the world, even things that are not, to bring to nothing things that are, so that no flesh might boast in the presence of God" (1 Cor 1:27–29). In 1846, near the hamlet of La Salette, our Lady chose two illiterate cowherds—fourteen-year-old Melanie Calvat and ten-year-old Maximin Giraud—to announce her message. In 1858, in the Pyrenean village of Lourdes, our Lady entrusted her message to a poor country girl, fourteen-year-old Bernadette Soubirous. And in 1917, in the hamlet of Fatima, Portugal, Mary conveyed news for the whole world through three simple shepherds: ten-year-old Lucia, eight-year-old Francisco, and seven-year-old Jacinta.

The choices turned out to be extraordinarily apt. In all three cases the news conveyed by the country children, juvenile illiterates from remote places, reached the farthest corners of the globe. And what is more, it was not the sort of news that flashed across the front pages of newspapers like a meteor, to be forgotten the next day. The messages from La Salette, Lourdes, and Fatima do not cease to fascinate to this day. Despite the passage of decades, many people all over the world are still faithful to these extraordinary messages.

A similar logic with regard to propagating the salvific message was hidden in Jesus' coming into the world. Palestine was the most accursed province in Octavian's empire. Every Roman official shuddered at the very thought of being sent to that land of fanatics; Judea was regarded as the largest hotbed of extremists, and Bethlehem was reputed to be its poorest town. There were many miserable stables in that town. In those days stables, full of animal excrement, were used as toilets. Such was the setting for the event that divided human history into two parts—B. C. and A. D. The Creator of the universe, of galaxies and of genes, of interplanetary and intercellular spaces, took on a body, not disdaining sweat and tears—the setting full of dung and stench, buzzing flies, and wriggling maggots.

If one says that he is humbling himself, it just means that he is in the right place. God alone truly humbled Himself.

It was not by chance that St. Paul wrote that Christianity is a scandal, and not just to people of those times. How does one explain God's scan-

**SUCH SIGHTS** were impossible in the Russian and Prussian Partitions, where the majority of religious orders were suppressed.

# SUPPRESSION OF RELIGIOUS ORDERS
# A CATACOMB CHURCH

The occupiers suppressed religious orders in Poland, but Catholics formed others to replace them.

**THE OCCUPIERS,** knowing that the Catholic Church was the mainstay of Polish identity, attempted to subordinate the clergy to themselves and to weaken **their** patriotic influence. One method was the suppression of religious orders. The first occurred in the Austrian Partition in 1782 at the order of the emperor, Joseph II. As a result of his reforms, over half of the religious orders there, male and female, disappeared, and their possessions were given to Germans **who** had settled on Polish land.

In the Prussian Partition the suppression of religious orders occurred in two stages. The first, in 1810, mainly affected Silesia. The second stage was in 1875, when all the religious orders in the Kingdom of Prussia were suppressed.

Religious orders were also gradually suppressed in the Russian Partition. The first suppression decree was issued in 1819, when twenty-five male and fourteen female orders were closed. The next two suppressions were in 1832 and 1864, after the failure of two national uprisings. Of the several hundred convents and monasteries in the Russian Partition, barely a dozen or so remained. The authorities thus wanted to punish the Church for supporting Polish aspirations for independence. Historians have shown that wherever convents and monasteries were suppressed, social ties began to break down, religiousness crumbled, and cultural life deteriorated. But repression by the authorities did not destroy religious life, which began to develop secretly. A phenomenon of Polish Catholicism was religious orders without habits, which carried out underground evangelization. This phenomenon was of a significant scale, particularly in the Russian Partition, where Fr. Honorat Kozminski alone founded as many as twenty-six new religious orders.

**MARIAN APPARITIONS** in 19th-century Poland often foretold Poland's independence. Tomasz Kłossowski (a Polish soldier in Napoleon's army, wounded at the Battle of Leipzig) had such visions in 1813. They gave rise to the largest church in Poland – Our Lady of Licheń Sanctuary.

dalous behavior? St. Francis said that there could be but one answer— "the madness of love". The Incarnation revealed God as One Who takes on Himself the human condition—the joys, but also the pains and cares; He is prepared to sympathize and to suffer with people. Contemplating this mystery, the Columbian thinker Nicolas Gomez Davila addressed his readers thus: "You are irreplaceable in God's eyes alone." The certainty that God is not indifferent to man—rather, that man is loved by Him unto madness, even unto death—gave people a totally new view of their own lives and pushed civilization in a new direction, infused by faith, hope, and charity.

Over the centuries, many Christians followed the road that Christ Himself had marked out. Sr. Faustina did not have a curriculum vitae to be proud of: she had hardly completed but two years of primary school, knew no foreign languages, and had never been abroad. She had been a

housemaid, helped in a kitchen, worked as a shop assistant and also as a gardener; she was referred for psychiatric examination, to remove suspicion of mental illness for her mystical visions. She was from a place that many thought of as forsaken by God: on August 23, 1905 (two days before her birth), the Russian press reported cases of cholera in the Vistula and Warta watershed areas (the region where she was born). Newspapers warned people not to go to those areas unnecessarily. In short, Faustina was born in an accursed place.

God, however, chooses such surprising places. His mercy pursues man to the furthest areas, the darkest recesses, the gloomiest corners, where there appears to be no way out. There are no circumstances that might discourage Him. Sr. Faustina's life shows that God can personally enter a person's life anywhere and everywhere—even in Poland.

Poland, that is, everywhere.

**BARBARA SAMULOWSKA**
had a vision of our Lady in Gietrzwałd when she was 12. She later entered the Congregation of the Sisters of Mercy.

23

Głogowiec · Świnice Warckie

POLAND

# Home

# Home

Glogowiec is 93 miles from
Poznań and 118 miles
from Warsaw. The nearest larger
town, Łęczyca, is 14 miles away.
In this modest, insignificant
village, on August 25,1905,
at eight o'clock in the morning,
Helen Kowalska, whom the
world would come to know
years later as St. Faustina,
the Apostle of Divine Mercy,
was born.

**ST. FAUSTINA'S
BIRTHPLACE**.
The house built
by Faustina's
father around
1900 is made
of white-yellow
limestone,
characteristic of
the Glogowiec
region.

**FR. JANUSZ KOWALSKI**, parish priest of St. Casimir's, Świnice Warckie, showing the baptismal register with the entry concerning Helen Kowalska.

She was born in the house her father, Stanislaw Kowalski, had built; he was then a thirty-seven-year-old farmer with fourteen acres of land. His wife was thirty-year-old Marianna Kowalska, née Babel. (Some Polish surnames end in "i" for a man and "a" for a woman). Helen was their third child. In all, the couple had ten children.

At one o'clock in the afternoon on August 27, 1905, Stanislaw Kowalski brought his barely two-day-old daughter to St. Casimir's Church in Świnice Warckie; the child's mother was at home, still in bed after the delivery. Two witnesses—Franciszek Bednarek and Jozef Stasiak, farmers from Glogowiec—accompanied them to the church. The parish priest, Fr. Jozef Chodynski, baptized the girl and named her Helen. Her godparents, Marianna Szewczyk and Konstanty Bednarek, were neighbors.

When St. Faustina was born, Świnice Warckie was in the Russian zone (of the then-partitioned Poland). All the entries in the baptismal register had to be in Russian. The parish priest, though a native Pole, was also obliged to make entries in Russian—even his own name. The entries in the parish register of 1900–1908

**HELEN KOWALSKA'S** baptism was attested to by the signatures of Fr. Jozef Chodynski (in Russian) and Stanislaw Kowalski (in Polish).

**THE CHAPEL**
is dedicated to
the sponsors of
the church. The
confessional at
which the future
saint confessed as
a child was moved
to the chapel in
2004.

**INTERIOR**
of St. Casimir's
Church, Świnice
Warckie.

indicate that the majority of parishioners were illiterate, as were little Helen's witnesses. Apart from Wojciech Berezinski, Stanislaw Kowalski was the only person in Glogowiec who could read and write. Not only did he sign his own name in the parish register, but he was also one of the few who did so in Polish.

Stanislaw Kowalski had met Marianna Babel in nearby Dabie. They were married at St. Nicholas's Church, Dabie, on October 28, 1892. The date on the marriage certificate is according to the Julian calendar, as this was binding in the Russian zone. According to the Gregorian calendar, it was November 9, 1892. Stanislaw was twenty-four, and Marianna was just seventeen. Shortly after the wedding the newlyweds bought a small property—with a ramshackle dwelling—in Glogowiec. They decided to build a new house, which was finished about 1900. It was made of limestone and red bricks, and it had a thatched roof. Stanislaw personally supervised the building work; he also did the joinery, making the doors and windows himself.

He not only knew a lot about farming, carpentry, and bricklaying, he could also operate a steam engine, as he had worked in the nearby brewery in Dabie. He had accumulated an impressive collection of books, which in those days was a great rarity in that vicinity. The Bible and books on the lives of saints occupied a privileged

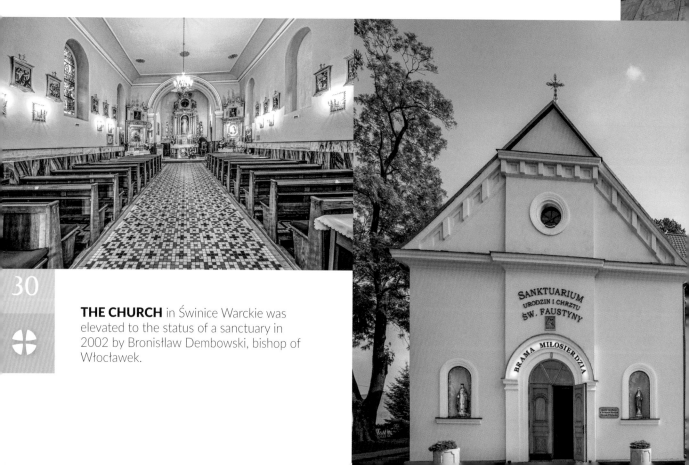

30

**THE CHURCH** in Świnice Warckie was elevated to the status of a sanctuary in 2002 by Bronisław Dembowski, bishop of Włocławek.

# ŚWINICE **WARCKIE**

**HELEN KOWALSKA** was born in the parish of Świnice Warckie. This place was first mentioned in 1301, when according to a legend the archbishop of Gniezno, Jakub Swinka (in the above illustration), established it. Documents from 1458 mention it as a town, though in decline. At present, it is a large village of about six hundred inhabitants. Its name has changed repeatedly over the centuries: Świnie, Śwince, Świńcze, Świeńce, Świeńcze, Swence, Świenie, and from 1757 Świnice. The word "Warckie" was added on account of a the nearby River Warta. The village belonged to successive families: the Świniecki, Byszewski, Kawowski, and Rembieski families.

Today there is a Divine Mercy center there. The Church of St. Casimir, built in 1859, is the Sanctuary of the Birth and Baptism of Saint Faustina.

place in the Kowalskis' own library. Stanislaw introduced the daily custom of reading books aloud, which he initially did himself, and later his children followed suit.

The inhabitants of Glogowiec remembered Marianna Kowalska as an extremely warm, sincere, and obliging woman. The neighbors emphasized that she was very hard-working and organized. No one in the whole village could make tastier bread.

Though ten years had passed since their wedding, Marianna and Stanislaw were childless and were therefore very unhappy. It was not until 1902 that they had a daughter, Jozefa, and Ewa a year later. "Both births nearly cost me my life", recalled Marianna. "Hence, as I was thirty, I anxiously awaited my third child, but she was born without any complications, as were my next seven children. This blessed child sanctified my womb."

Neither Glogowiec nor Świnice Warckie had a primary school until 1917, when the first primary school in Świnice was built, after the liberation of regions under

**AS A NUN**, Sr. Faustina visited her family home only once—in February 1935. It was such a momentous occasion for Mr. and Mrs. Kowalski that they hired a photographer to take photographs of the whole family.

Russian rule. Thus, Helen was twelve when she went to school for the first time. Yet she was not illiterate; her father had taught her to read and write from an early age. The world of the written word absorbed her more and more, and as a little girl she read books aloud at night to the whole family.

Stanislaw Kowalski introduced little Helen to the Faith. As his wife, Marianna, recalled: "The Faith was very important to him, which is what I liked about him. Though I could not read or write, I taught my daughters and sons the truths of the Gospel, taking care that they not only knew the precept of love of neighbor, but, primarily, that they observed it. Stanislaw was an example to them of daily prayer and obligatory participation in Sunday Mass. We both instilled Christian morality in our children and demanded respect for the affairs of God."

Singing resounded in the Kowalskis' home beginning at dawn each day. Stanislaw fervently sang, among other things, the Little Office of the Immaculate

**NATALIA KOWALSKA,** Helen's younger sister.

33

# THE KOWALSKI FAMILY

**STANISLAW KOWALSKI** was born on May 6, 1868, in the village of Kraski, near Świnice Warckie. Marianna Babel was born seven years later in the village of Mniewo, near Koło. They met in 1891 in Dąbie, where he worked as a carpenter in the local brewery, and where she lived with her father and stepmother. They married on November 9, 1892, at St. Nicholas' in Dąbie, where they settled for the first few years of their marriage.

After several years they moved to Głogowiec. Ten years passed before they had a child. Their first child, a girl, was born in 1902, and over the next eight years Marianna gave birth to seven more children. In all they had six daughters and two sons, but two girls died in infancy.

The Kowalski family, like most of the peasants in the Russian Partition, lived very modestly. Over half of the farms in their vicinity were so-called small holdings (up to 12 acres) or diminished farms (up to 5 acres). The Kowalskis bought about 12 acres of land in Głogowiec, of which five were meadow and seven were long strips of land. The soil was not very fertile, hence they mainly cultivated potatoes and rye.

Because the house they had bought with the land was dilapidated, Stanislaw Kowalski built a new limestone house with a thatched roof. It had two rooms divided by a large hallway, with a bedroom on the left, and a kitchen and a carpentry workshop on the right.

The farm was the family's main source of support. The children worked from an early age, helping their parents to feed the hens and to graze the cows. Most of the work was done by hand, for example, the grain was harvested using a sickle and threshed with a flail. In time the family acquired a horse, but when it was requisitioned during World War I they had to use a cow to plough the land.

Stanislaw Kowalski died in July 1946, age seventy-eight, his wife in February 1965, age ninety. Both were buried in a cemetery near the church in Świnice Warckie. Sister Faustina's mother did not live to see her daughter's beatification process, which began eight months after her death. She did, however, swear an oath for the process. Being illiterate, she "signed" it with her thumb print.

**SR. FAUSTINA'S FAMILY HOME IN GLOGOWIEC** is now a museum. It houses domestic furnishings from the first half of the 20th century, collected from the parish of Świnice Warckie and from the neighboring parishes of Wielenin and Grodzisko. There are also a few items that belonged to the Kowalski family.

**HEART OF JESUS** pictures from the original house furnishings – little Helen Kowalska prayed in front of these pictures.

**A LITTLE PICTURE OF OUR LADY** and a prayer to the Immaculate Heart of Mary, which Sr. Faustina gave to her brother Stanislaw, with the dedication "to Staś".

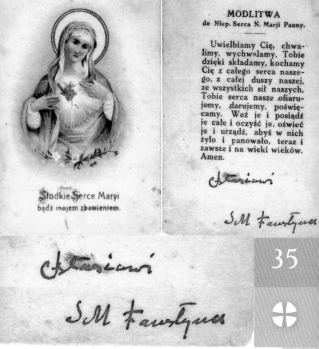

MODLITWA
do Niep. Serca N. Marji Panny.

Uwielbiamy Cię, chwalimy, wychwalamy, Tobie dzięki składamy, kochamy Cię z całego serca naszego, z całej duszy naszej, ze wszystkich sił naszych. Tobie serca nasze ofiarujemy, darujemy, poświęcamy. Weź je i posiądź je całe i oczyść je, oświeć je i urządź, abyś w nich żyło i panowało, teraz i zawsze i na wieki wieków. Amen.

Słodkie Serce Maryi bądź mojem zbawieniem.

Nr. **36936**

Nazwisko *Kowalska*

Imię *Helena Faustyna*

Data urodzenia *25 sierpnia 1905*

Miejsce urodzenia *w. Głogowice p. Turecki*

Imię ojca *Stanisław* matki *Marjanna*

Zawód *Zakonnica Zgrom. Sióstr Najś.*
*Marji Panny Miłosierdzia.*

Miejsce zamieszkania *m. st. Warszawa*

Wzrost *średni*

Twarz *owalna*

Włosy *blond*

Oczy *szare*

Znaki szczególne *brak*

Wydany dnia *5 marca 1931*

(własnoręczny podpis osoby wyszczególnionej w dowodzie)

Stosownie do art. 19 rozp. Prezydenta R. P. z dnia 16 marca 1928 r.
o ewidencji i kontroli ruchu ludności (Dz. U. R. P. Nr. 32, poz. 309)
zaświadczam, że wymieniony(a) w niniejszym dowodzie

p.

jest obywatelem(ką) polskim(ą), co zostało stwierdzone

na podstawie

Urząd

Nr.

Conception and Lenten psalms. Marianna was annoyed by this at times and insisted that he stop, as his singing awakened the children too early in the morning. But Stanislaw was resolute and said that he was doing it for the children: "Woman! After all, I want to give them a good example, so I must serve God above all and only then think about you all."

When, after many years—in February 1935—Sr. Faustina visited her family in Glogowiec, the one and only time as a nun, she was impressed by how her father prayed. When she saw him kneeling, deep in conversation with God, she was ashamed of herself; despite having spent so many years in a convent, she could not pray so fervently.

At the age of five, little Helen made miniature altars and spent time praying before a metal crucifix that her father had bought in Czestochowa. She talked to her brothers

37

**MINIATURE ALTAR.** Helen Kowalska prayed before this crucifix and these figures of the Sacred Heart of Jesus and the Immaculate Heart of Mary. This altar can be found at the convent in Łagiewniki.

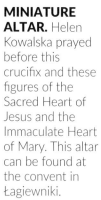

and sisters about our Lady, whom she had frequently seen in dreams in a very beautiful garden. Though she did not know any monks or nuns personally, she tried to convince her neighbors that she would one day go to the "pilgrims", the hermits who lived in the forest. She often did not sleep at night. When her mother asked her why, she said that her guardian angel woke her in order that she might pray.

She was seven when she first heard God's voice in her soul. This was in 1912, in the parish church of Świnice Warckie, about a mile from Glogowiec. It was at Vespers, during the exposition of the Blessed Sacrament. She felt her heart overflow with God's love, while she began to understand that another reality existed, hidden from one's eyes, a reality more important than the visible one. The little girl had felt God's extraordinary closeness, but she did not as yet understand her spiritual state, all the more so because she did not know anyone who could have explained it to her.

In 1914, at the age of nine, Helen received First Communion from Fr. Roman Pawloski. When returning home, she kept apart from her friends. When one of her neighbors, the elderly Mrs. Berezinska, asked her why she was walking alone, little Helen replied: "I am not walking alone; I am with the Lord Jesus."

Despite the best of intentions, Helen could not participate in Mass every Sunday. There was only one Sunday dress at home, so the girls could not go to church together. When Helen had to stay at home, she always took up a book of devotions and prayed in solitude.

She occasionally had unusual ideas. Once, dressed as a beggar, she went around the whole village begging alms. She gave the alms to the parish priest in Świnice to distribute to the poor. She also organized a raffle, whose proceeds were for the poorest in the parish. Her brothers and sisters laughed at her for seeing the needy all around. But this did not dissuade her.

The poverty at home made life a misery. Two girls, her classmates, clearly made her feel it; they did not want to sit on the same bench with her, as she was too poorly dressed. However, the sight of her overworked father worried her far more. He worked from morning until night, but the family barely made ends meet. Although Helen was the best pupil in her class, there was not enough room in the school for all the children of the area. The oldest were forced to leave to make room for younger children. She gave up school after two years and begged permission to take up gainful employment to lighten her parents' burden. Her parents gave her their consent. They decided that their daughter should go into service with someone. Helen was fourteen at the time.

**MUSEUM EXHIBITS IN GŁOGOWIEC** – leather bags from the beginning of the 20th century.

**MARIANNA KOWALSKA,** Sr. Faustina's mother, with her daughter Gienia.

39

Ostrówek ❖ Warsaw

Aleksandrów ❖ Łódź
Łódzki

POLAND

# Domestic Service

# CHAPTER 3

# Domestic Service

During a family meeting it was decided that Helen was to work as a domestic. Stanislaw and Marianna did not want to send their daughter to a complete stranger, so they asked for help from their good friend Marcin Lugowski, who had well-to-do friends.

It turned out, Mr. Lugowski's sister-in-law needed a trusted person to help her. So Helen found herself at the place of Leokadia and Kazimierz Bryszewski, who had a shop and bakery at 30 Parczewska Street (now 1 May Street) in the little town of Aleksandrów, near Łódź.

Helen Kowalska spent almost a year in Aleksandrów. She helped Mr. and Mrs. Bryszewski to run their house and also looked after their six-year-old son, Zenon. Years later, he recalled that time: "Mother served the customers in the shop, while Helen did the cleaning and the tidying up and helped with the cooking. She had to do the dishes and dispose of rubbish, as well as bring water because there was no water supply. She also served food to the bakery workers—whose meals were provided by my parents—and entertained me when time allowed. She must have had a lot of work to do, as there were four rooms in the house, as well as the shop and bakery."

**LEOKADIA AND KAZIMIERZ BRYSZEWSKI**, Faustina's first employers in Aleksandrów, Łódź.

**CONTEMPORARY PAINTING** of Faustina Kowalska, painted by Ewa Mika on the basis of a photograph from 1923.

43

**THE GATE** of the house where the future nun worked for the Bryszewski couple.

**ALEKSANDRÓW ŁÓDZKI** was a multi-cultural town. Its inhabitants were largely descendants of German Protestant weavers, Jewish merchants and shopkeepers, and Polish Catholic workers and artisans.

44

✠

The girl lived in the kitchen, where she had her cot. One night, an extraordinary bright light, shining through the backyard window, awakened her. Convinced that a fire had broken out in the bakery, she ran out of the house, shouting: "There is a fire in the backyard!" A crowd formed, and the bakers appeared, along with the roused household. But it turned out to be a false alarm. From that time on, the hosts and the neighbors began to treat the girl with suspicion. They even called a doctor to see why she had delusions. Surrounded by mistrust, looked at strangely, Helen decided to give notice. The Bryszewskis were pleased with her work and urged her to stay, but she was steadfast. On being asked why she was resigning, she said: "I shall not say why I am leaving; I just cannot stay."

After leaving Aleksandrów, she first headed for home. She fell at her parents' feet and begged them to let her enter a convent. In those days a young girl who had decided

THE INNER courtyard of the Bryszewski house. A box indicates the window of the kitchen where Helen Kowalska lived.

CHURCH OF SAINTS Archangels Raphael and Michael in Aleksandrów Łódzki, where Helen received the sacrament of confirmation.

45

**THE HOUSE**
at 9 Krośnieńska Street in Łódź, where Helen's uncle Michał Rapacki lived. It is from here that they both started for the train station to go to Warsaw. A chapel dedicated to Helen is in the room on the ground floor where she stayed.

to enter a convent had to have an appropriate dowry. But the Kowalskis were too poor; they had no savings, only debts. They would have had to sell a cow, but Stanislaw would not agree to that. Helen tried to convince him that she did not need money, as God Himself would see to the dowry. But her father stubbornly repeated: No!

The girl did not want to enter a convent without her parents' consent, so she decided to go back to work. This time, the first in her life, she went to a big city. Łódź, known as the Polish Manchester, was a large industrial center. Wladyslaw Reymont had portrayed the phenomenon of Łódź's chequered development at the turn of the nineteenth and twentieth centuries in his novel *The Promised Land*, which Andrzej Wajda captured on film many years later. At that time, strangers were drawn to Łódź from all directions. They counted on making a fortune, a career,

Лодзь. Фаб. Акц. Общ. Познанскаго.
Łódź. Fabryka Tow. Ak. Poznańskiego.
Lodz. Ansicht d. Fabrik Ac. Gesel. v.
J. K. Poznanski.

**IZRAEL POZNANSKI'S** factory, Łódź. It was the largest factory in the Kalisz-Mazovia region. It has housed the Manufaktura Shopping Center since 2006.

# ŁÓDŹ, THE **POLISH MANCHESTER**

**HELEN KOWALSKA** lived in Łódź for two years (1922–1924). It then had over five hundred thousand inhabitants and was the second largest city in Poland, though there had barely been two hundred fifty inhabitants at the beginning of the nineteenth century. However, the Russian authorities decided to make it into a textile center. The town's population grew rapidly: to four thousand in 1830, forty thousand in 1865, and three hundred thousand in 1900. Large textile complexes arose, and factory owner fortunes grew: the Grohman, Scheibler, Poznanski, and Geyer fortunes. The population was a mixture of Poles, Russians, Germans, and Jews. But the town did not develop evenly. Palaces arose, but so did poverty-stricken districts. The Russians did not invest in the city infrastructure, while Łódź itself was ruled by a governor who

lived in the much smaller Piotrkow Trybunalski. It was not until Poland had gained independence in 1918 that the city ceased to be a district administrative center and became a province. When Sr. Faustina was there, Łódź was going through an economic crisis as the Russians had closed their own markets.

**ŁÓDŹ** was the first place in the Russian Partition to have an electric tramway (1898).

**29 ABRAMOWSKI STREET, ŁÓDŹ**, where Marcjanna Sadowska (Wieczorek - after her second husband) lived in the first block of flats on the right. Helen Kowalska worked for her as a domestic (1923-1924).

**STASIA AND BOLEK WIECZOREK**, Marcjanna Sadowska's stepchildren, who were looked after by Helen Kowalska in Łódź from 1923 to 1924.

and good connections. Helen Kowalska appeared there too, but the city was not "the promised land" to her—she dreamed of a convent.

She stayed with her uncle Michal Rapacki, at 9 Krosnienski Street, and worked as a domestic for three female Franciscan tertiaries. In negotiating her work conditions, she reserved the right to have access to their confessor, free time for daily Mass, and time to visit the sick and the dying. Helen worked for the tertiaries for almost one year, sending almost all her earnings home.

When she was eighteen, she went to Głogowiec again to ask for her parents' consent to enter a convent. But again she met with a decisive refusal. She was aware of the inner call of vocation, but she decided to drown it out. She threw herself into the hustle and bustle of daily life, completely engrossing herself in work and in having fun in her free time, but she could not find contentment in anything. The call in her soul did not cease, but she ignored it.

**THREE SISTERS**.
From left to right: Helen, Natalia, and Gienia Kowalska. They all lived and worked in Łódź at the same time.

49

Helen began to attach greater importance to her appearance. But when, on February 2, 1923, she appeared at an address she had received from an employment agency, she did not make a good impression. Marcjanna Sadowska-Wieczorek, the owner of a grocery shop at 29 Abramowski Street, Łódź, was looking for someone to do her housework and to tend her three small children. Meanwhile a smiling, determined, fashionably dressed teenager stood at her door. "A girl who dresses up in that way, and so self-confident, surely cannot be good at housework", thought Mrs. Sadowska-Wieczorek. So, to discourage the would-be worker, she immediately reduced the remuneration she had proposed earlier. But, not put off, the girl accepted the conditions.

Helen worked at Marcjanna Sadowska-Wieczorek's home for almost eighteen months. Her employer later recalled her domestic thus: "She was good-natured and somewhat of a giggler. In the evenings, when she sat down on a stool, my three children would immediately gather around her. They liked her because she told them fairy tales and played with them at whatever they wished. Whenever I left the house, I was confident that she would do everything better than I would. She was so foresighted and loving. Moreover, she was pleasant, polite, and hard-working. I cannot say anything bad about her—she was just so good."

**THE BUILDING** of the present Łódź Cathedral began in 1901, when Archbishop Wincenty Chościak-Popiel blessed the cornerstone. Bishop Wincenty Tymieniecki consecrated the cathedral in 1922.

At that time, three Kowalska sisters worked as domestic servants for various people in Łódź: Genowefa, Helen, and Natalia. The youngest, Natalia Kowalska Grzelak, recalled that period thus:

"Helen and Genowefa worked in houses situated opposite each other on Abramowski Street, while I worked in a house on Nawrot Street. We went to the cathedral on Sundays, and met after Mass to have a chat, if only for a minute.

50

**ST. STANISLAW KOSTKA** Cathedral based on Ulm Minster in Germany. It is the highest building in Łódź (340 feet).

# ŁÓDŹ CATHEDRAL

**THE ŁÓDŹ** diocese was established in 1920 by Pope Benedict XV. Its first bishop was Wincenty Tymieniecki. Previously the area was part of Gniezno dioceses: from 1765 it was part of the Wloclawek diocese, and from 1818 it was part of the Warsaw diocese. After Poland had gained independence in 1918 there was a need for a new administrative division of the Church in the Second Polish Republic. As the dynamically developing Łódź was one of the largest cities in the country, it became an episcopal see.

The Church of St. Stanislaw Kostka, Łódź, became a cathedral in 1922. Helen Kowalska prayed before the main altar of the cathedral in July, 1924. After the outbreak of World War II, Łódź (Litzmannstadt) was incorporated into the Third Reich. In November 1941, the Germans stripped the cathedral of all its valuables, including liturgical vestments, and changed the cathedral into a military storehouse. It was not until 1945 that the damaged cathedral was repaired.

When Genowefa had some free time, she liked to pop out somewhere to have fun. Helen rather looked around for somebody to help; and she always found someone. There was a lonely, sick man in the storage closet under the stairs of the house where she worked. Helen gave him food, washed him, comforted him, and talked to him about God. Finally, she brought a priest so that he could confess and receive Holy Communion. I was there when the priest came. The man was very frail, while Helen was very happy that he had time to be reconciled with God; he died the following day. She always wanted to lead people to God."

It was in Łódź that Helen had an experience that ultimately decided on her entering a convent. It happened in Venice Park (now Juliusz Slowacki Park), which was established at the end of the nineteenth century by a Mr. Reich, the owner of the local mill. The area was known as Venice, as there were ponds connected by canals there. At the beginning of the twentieth century, it was a favorite place for the inhabitants of Łódź; festivals, concerts, balls, and the like were organized there. In July 1924, Helen Kowalska went to a dance in Venice Park.

**HIGH ALTAR**
in Łódź Cathedral, where Helen Kowalska prayed.

53

Her sister Natalia was a witness to the occasion, but she did not then realize what had happened. Years later she recalled that day:

"Genowefa once said that there was a raffle and a dance in Venice Park. She persuaded us to go with her. She even bought Helen a ticket, but the moment Helen got there, she wanted to leave. She wore a pink cretonne skirt with frills at the sides. Her hair was gathered back in a plait, as thick as an arm. She was a very shapely and cheerful girl, and not unattractive.

"When we arrived, someone immediately asked Genowefa for a dance, while we just stood about. Then two young men came up to us, and one of them asked Helen for a dance. She tried to get out of it by saying that she could not dance very well, but he said that he would lead. When they had finished the dance, Helen said that she had to go. I did not know why. I even asked her if she had seen something, but she just said that she would not stay any longer and left. As it turned out, she went to the cathedral, and then left for Warsaw to look for a convent. And after a time she entered the convent."

Helen herself recalled that when she began to dance, she suddenly saw Jesus at her side. He looked as He did during the Passion: exhausted, stripped of His clothing, covered in wounds. He looked at her and said: "How long shall I put up with you and how long will you keep putting Me off?" (*Diary: Divine Mercy in My Soul*, 9). The girl had the impression that the music had stopped and that all had dispersed, and that only she and Christ remained. When the vision vanished, she told her sister that she had to sit down as she had a headache. After a while, however, she slipped out unnoticed, and made her way to the Cathedral of St. Stanislaw Kostka.

The cathedral, not far from Venice Park, was built at the beginning of the twentieth century. When Pope Benedict XV established the diocese of Łódź (1920), the church became a cathedral. Helen knew it very well, as she frequently went to Mass there. That July evening she went into the cathedral and, heedless of the presence of people, fell prostrate, arms outstretched in a cross, before the Blessed Sacrament. She besought God to tell her what to do next. She then heard a voice in her soul: "Go at once to Warsaw; you will enter a convent there" (*Diary*, 10). Like the patron of the cathedral, St. Stanislaw Kostka, who, when he heard the call of his vocation, stopped paying heed to his parents' protests, she too decided to enter a religious order despite the objections of her father and mother.

The next day she began to pack. Her uncle Michal Rapacki tried to stop her. He told her that her departure to Warsaw would cause her parents great distress. But

**A STATUE OF SR. FAUSTINA**, Independence Square, Łódź. In 2005, she became patron of Łódź.

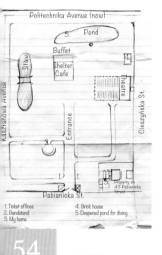

**MAP.** Location of Venice Park (1924).

**JULIUSZ SLOWACKI PARK**. In this Łódź park (formerly Venice Park) there is a chestnut tree close to the site of a dance that Helen Kowalska attended.

**STONE INSCRIPTION** found in a Łódź park commemorates the place where the 19-year-old Helen had a vision (in July 1924).

55

Warszawa.    Most na Wiśle.

# WARSAW **ARCHDIOCESE**

**VIEW OF WARSAW.**
Postcard sent in 1929 from Warsaw to Nałęczów. The bridge, Kierbedź Bridge, was destroyed during World War II.

**THOUGH WARSAW** was the seat of Polish kings to the end of the sixteenth century, it was quite insignificant in the Church heirarchy. It was not until 1798 that it became the diocesan see, and then an archdiocese in 1818. The collegiate church of St. John the Baptist became the episcopal see, wherein four coronations and four royal weddings took place.

Jozef Miaskowski became the first bishop of Warsaw in 1800. His successors included Archbishop Pawel Woronicz (a well-known poet and speaker) and Archbishop Saint Zygmunt Szczęsny Feliński, who was exiled deep in Russia for twenty years.

After Poland had regained its independence, and Warsaw had become the country's capital, its political and religious significance grew. Cardinal Aleksander Kakowski was then head of the archdiocese. At his initiative many churches and chapels were built, and new chaplaincies arose. He died in 1938, nine months before the outbreak of World War II.

Helen was implacable. So her uncle accompanied her to the train station, and she departed for Warsaw.

She arrived at Warsaw Central Station in the evening, not knowing where to go (she did not know anyone in Warsaw). At a loss, she began to pray to our Lady for help. Then an inner voice told her to go to a village near Warsaw and find accommodation for the night. Hence she found hospitality with kind hosts who lived in a village near the capital.

Early the next morning she returned to Warsaw and went to St. James's Church on Grojecka Street, Ochota. When she was praying for help to discern God's will, she heard the words: "Go to that priest and tell him everything; he will tell you what to do next" (*Diary*, 12). He turned out to be the parish priest, Fr. Jakub Dąbrowski. After listening to the girl's story, he decided that she should stay with friends of his until she entered a convent. His friends, Aldona

**THE LIPSZYCS' HOUSE**

in Ostrówek, about 25 miles northeast of Warsaw.

and Samuel Lipszyc, lived in Ostrówek, near Warsaw, where he had previously been a parish priest.

The Lipszycs were a Jewish family that had been baptized in the previous generation. They received the stranger very warmly. She took care of their house and their four little children, while Aldona Lipszyc awaited the birth of her fifth child. Helen went to Warsaw in her free time to look for a convent that would take her. The lady of the house recalled her domestic thus: "Helen came to us with a small bundle; all her possessions were tied up in her headscarf.... She gave the impression of being a bright, healthy, cheerful, and even a happy girl. She had smooth, reddish hair in a big plait, a nice, calm face, somewhat freckled.... She was cheerful, fond of the children, and liked to play with them. I remember that she once organized a 'dressing up' game for them and also dressed herself up and played like a child. I recall her healthy, joyful laughter. She sang a lot, and I associate her with the song she sang most frequently, which I learned from her: 'I am to worship Jesus, hidden in the Blessed Sacrament. I am to give all to Him, His love my life to live. He wholly gives Himself to us, among us He did dwell. To His divine praise, let us devote our lives to Him.'"

Successive journeys to Warsaw ended in failure, as Helen was refused by the convents she had approached. One day she knocked at the convent door of the Congregation of the Sisters of Our Lady of Mercy. Sr. Borgia Tichy recalled: "I remember the time very well. It was in Warsaw, at 3/9 Zytnia Street. One day in 1924, during afternoon recreation, the portress, the late Sr. Klara Himmer, came into the assembly room and announced a 'new vocation' to the mother general, Leonarda Cielecka. The mother general sent the late Mother Malgorzata to the convent door to look into the matter. Mother Malgorzata returned after a short time and loudly related that it was 'no one special. She is modest, a little old, rather frail, a domestic—a cook by trade. Moreover, she is not only without a dowry, but she lacks even the most modest trousseau.' Because Mother Cielecka was not particularly enthusiastic about vocations from the neighborhood, she wanted to reject her right away. Mother Michaela, the superior of the house in Warsaw, present at recreation, asked if she could see the candidate. She did, and gave Helen her consent."

**CHURCH OF ST. CLEMENT**. During her one-year stay with the Lipszyc family, Helen went to Mass at the nearest parish, St. Clement's, in Klembów, over two miles from Ostrówek.

59

**THE LIPSZYC
FAMILY,**
Samuel and Aldona
with their children.

In 1924, Mother Michaela Moraczewska was the local superior of the congregation's Warsaw House on Zytnia Street. She recalled that one day she was told that a young girl was at the door wanting to enter the order:

"So I went down to the parlor and opened the door slightly. The candidate—who sat where she did not notice me—did not make a good impression on me at first sight on account of her somewhat neglected appearance. I thought to myself: No, she is not for us! And I quietly closed the door with the intention of sending a sister to her with a negative answer.

"At that moment, however, I thought that it would be more in accord with love of one's neighbor to ask the girl several superficial questions and then say good-bye. Hence I returned to the parlor and started a conversation with the girl. I then noticed that the candidate made a better impression at close quarters. She had a pleasant smile, an amiable facial expression, a great deal of simplicity, sincerity, and common sense in expressing herself. So I soon changed my mind, and I became eager to accept her. The main difficulty was her poverty, not to mention the dowry, from which the Holy See readily exempted candidates; she had no personal trousseau, and we had no funds for that. However, I suggested that she go into service for a time and save money for the trousseau. She accepted the idea very willingly, and we established that she was to bring her savings to the convent for safekeeping. I left it at that, said good-bye to her, and soon forgot about everything."

Helen herself had reason to recall another situation from the visit most of all: "When Mother Superior, the present Mother General Michaela, came out to meet me, she told me, after a short conversation, to go to the Lord of the house and ask whether He would accept me. I understood at once that I was to ask this of the Lord Jesus. With great joy, I went to the chapel and asked Jesus: 'Lord of this house, do You accept me? This is how one of these sisters told me to put the question to You.'

Immediately I heard this voice: 'I do accept; you are in My Heart.' When I returned from the chapel, Mother Superior asked first of all: 'Well, has the Lord accepted you?' I answered, 'Yes.' 'If the Lord has accepted, [she said] then I also will accept' " (*Diary*, 14).

Helen returned to Ostrówek. She worked there for one year, saving money for her trousseau. Aldona Lipszyc recalled: "I remember that she did not buy anything for herself at all, but saved her wages for her trousseau." She emphasized that Helen's faith, though strong, was also very discreet—she never imposed her piety on anyone. The domestic had become so intimate with the members of the household that after a year she was almost treated as a member of the family. "Though I knew from the start that she would leave us for the convent, we became so attached to her during that year that her departure was a harrowing experience for me", related Aldona.

Mother Michaela Moraczewska forgot about Helen's visit. However, when in Vilnius, she received a letter

**DINING ROOM**
in the Lipszycs' home in Ostrówek near Klembów.

**WOODEN VERANDA**
where Helen Kowalska liked to play with the Lipszycs' children.

# ALDONA **LIPSZYC**

**ALDONA LIPSZYC** was born in 1896, in Tbilisi (now the capital of Georgia), where her father was a military pharmacist.

In 1918 she married Samuel Jozef Lipszyc (an agronomist) in Warsaw, with whom she had seven children. They first lived in Ostrówek near Klembów, then in Zoliborz, Warsaw. In 1938, after the sudden death of her husband, she raised her children single-handed.

During the war she helped to rescue Jews from the Germans despite the fact that she herself suffered privations. Her farm in Ostrówek was close to the railway line to the extermination camp in Treblinka, about a mile through the woods. Many escapees who had jumped off trains chanced on Aldona's farm. She put them up, gave them clothes, bought rail tickets for them and dispatched them to Warsaw. She also sheltered Jews in her home in Warsaw. Furthermore, she provided food for a Jewish family that was hiding in a forest bunker.

After the war Aldona Lipszyc ran, among other things, a day care and a nursery school in Warsaw, and she also helped to organize a puppet theater. She died at the age of 84. Sixteen years later she was awarded the Righteous among the Nations Medal.

**ALDONA LIPSZYC,** pictured here with Sr. Katarzyna (Zofia Steinberg), a Franciscan from the convent in Laski, Warsaw, saved Jews from death during World War II. Her fondness for them arose when she was a pupil at a private Catholic school for girls in Warsaw, where she had several Jewish friends. One of them was sheltered by Aldona after escaping from the ghetto in Warsaw. Sr. Steinberg was a medical doctor of Jewish descent who was often a guest of the Lipszyc family while Helen lived there. She became a Catholic afterwards and became a Franciscan at the Laski convent that took care of blind people.

from Warsaw saying that a young woman had reported to the convent with some money for safekeeping. Moreover, she had referred to the conversation with Mother Michaela, who nevertheless could not remember who the person was. It was only after some thought that she realized who the strange girl was. From that time Helen's savings increased until there was enough for a modest trousseau.

In the summer of 1925, Helen Kowalska took some time to say her farewells to the Lipszyc family, with whom she had become as intimate as with her own family. They tried to persuade her to remain. Aldona in particular, who did not see the sense of convent life, urged Helen to marry and have a family. But the girl remained adamant: she had already made a vow of perpetual chastity to Christ (June 18). However, she promised the Lipszyc family that she would never forget them. And according to the family, Helen kept her promise: the nun had been dead for a year when World War II broke out and the extermination of people of Jewish descent began; but not one of the Lipszyc family perished in the Holocaust.

Aldona Lipszyc displayed extraordinary courage during the Nazi occupation. She not only managed to save all her children, but also helped many Jews who were in danger of death at the hands of the Germans. She hid some of them in her summer home in Ostrówek. Historians know of twenty-two people of Jewish descent who had been helped by the brave widow. She died in 1980. In 1996, the Yad Vashem Institute in Jerusalem posthumously honored her with the title Righteous among the Nations.

**THE LIPSZYCS' HOME** in Ostrówek. Today one can see the kitchen with a ceramic stove from the times of Sr. Faustina as well as the reconstructed room where she lived when she was a servant.

**CARDINAL ROBERT SARAH**, chairman of the pontifical council Cor Unum, blessing Sr. Faustina's house in Ostrówek (September 2011) in the presence of Archbishop Henryk Hoser.

A SISTER OF THE SECOND CHOIR

# Postulancy

**THE CHAPEL**
in the convent
in Żytnia Street
was destroyed
during the Warsaw
Uprising in 1944.
Situated near the
ghetto wall, it had
been a place of
refuge for Jews
fleeing the ghetto.
After the war, it was
the last religious
building to be
reconstructed,
beginning in 1979.
By decision of
Primate Stefan
Wyszyński, taken
in 1980, a parish
church of the
Divine Mercy was
built in place of the
chapel, and on April
23, 2017, during
a Mass celebrated
by Bishop Rafał
Markowski, the
church was
elevated to the rank
of a Divine Mercy
Shrine.

# Postulancy

On August 1, 1925, the eve of the
Feast of Our Lady of the Angels,
Helen crossed the threshold of
the convent enclosure. Now began
her postulancy, a stage that every
candidate to the congregation
had to complete. During this trial
period it became evident whether
a postulant really had a vocation to
the religious life.

The twenty-year-old girl recalled
that she felt exceedingly happy
when the convent door slammed
shut behind her. She had the
impression that she was on the
threshold of paradise, and she gave
thanks to God with all her strength
for finding a convent.

**MOTHER HOUSE** of the Congregation of
the Sisters of Our Lady of Mercy, Zytnia Street,
Warsaw. Helen Kowalska took her savings there
to pay for her trousseau.

**ŻYTNIA STREET, WARSAW.** Parish Church of Divine Mercy, dedicated to St. Faustina, and the Mother House of the Congregation of the Sisters of Our Lady of Mercy.

The convent where Helen commenced her postulancy was the birthplace of the Congregation of the Sisters of Our Lady of Mercy (3/9 Żytnia Street, Warsaw). It was there on November 1, 1862, that St. Zygmunt Szczesny Felinski, the archbishop of Warsaw, consecrated the congregation's first center, the House of Mercy, which was founded by Countess Ewa Potocka, a descendent of the house of Sulkowski, a line of dukes. The congregation's charism was to help girls who had gone astray and fallen women who were in need of a profound moral conversion. Such centers provided spiritual and social help, thanks to which those whom they assisted could return to a normal life in society. Examples of such work were to be found in France. In 1818, Thérèse Rondeau founded a religious order in Laval that looked after prostitutes who desired to change their lives. Countess Potocka went to Laval after her husband's death in 1861. The widowed aristocrat decided to enter the order and took the name Mother Teresa. After eight months she returned to Poland, where she founded the Congregation of the Sisters of Our Lady of Mercy, based on the French model.

The congregation's nuns were divided into two groups, the choirs. The sisters of the first choir (directresses), usually better educated, did educational work with girls, whereas the sisters of the second choir (coadjutresses), mainly from lower social levels, did all the support work—for example, in the kitchen or the garden. All, however, were obliged to be solicitous about the salvation of the souls that had been entrusted to them, even if only

**A BAS-RELIEF** of St. Faustina Kowalska on the wall of the monastery.

69

# CONGREGATION FOUNDER

**MOTHER TERESA, THE FORMER COUNTESS EWA POTOCKA,** (1814–1881) was the founder of the Congregation of the Sisters of Our Lady of Mercy. After the death of her husband, and childless marriage, she decided to devote herself completely to God and to works of mercy. At the suggestion of her spiritual director, Fr. Zygmunt Golian, she set off with two companions for Laval, France, where under the direction of Mother Teresa Rondeau, she completed her novitiate and familiarized herself with educational methods for women and girls who were then described as morally fallen.

After returning to Poland she decided to make use of the experience she had gained in apostolic and charity work. At the invitation of Archbishop Felinski she took over a shelter on Zytnia Street in Warsaw, which was blessed on November 1, 1862. That date is seen as the beginning of the Congregation of the Sisters of Our Lady of Mercy in Poland. Six years later she opened another house in Łagiewniki, Kraków.

In 1878 Mother Potocka came to an understanding with the nuns in Laval to combine the French and Polish convents in order to attain the Holy See's ratification. In time see became head of the vicariate subordinate to the superior general in Laval. Mother Potocka died in Wilanow, Warsaw, at the age of sixty-seven and was interred in the congregation's tomb at the Powązki Cemetery in Warsaw.

through prayer. Helen, on account of her lack of education, was assigned to the second choir and sent to work in the kitchen, where her superior was Sr. Sabina Tronina.

Helen willingly did any kitchen work she was assigned, but she constantly regretted that the congregation devoted so little time to prayer and contemplation. After three weeks she came to the conclusion that she ought to transfer to an order with a stricter rule, where the observance of prayer life was more developed. The idea caused her disquiet. Hence, tormented, she prayed to know the will of God. She then had a vision of Christ. She saw Jesus' face on her cell curtain. The whole of His face was lacerated, and large tears dripped down from His eyes onto her bed. Moved, she asked Christ who had caused Him such pain. He replied: "It is you who will cause Me this pain if you leave this convent. It is to this place that I called you and nowhere else; and I have prepared many graces for you" (*Diary*, 19). She apologized to Jesus, and changed her decision. From then on she was absolutely certain that it was God's will that she should remain in the congregation.

After several weeks, the young postulant was sent with two other sisters to Skolimow, near Warsaw, where the congregation had rented a country house. There was only one sister convalescing there that autumn, and Helen had to look after her. Among other things, she prepared the meals.

While in Skolimow, she once asked Jesus for whom she should pray in particular. She was told that she would find out the next day. The next day she saw her guardian

**THE MOTHER HOUSE** of the Congregation of the Sisters of Our Lady of Mercy is the main center for the devotion to St. Faustina.

**MOTHER MAŁGORZATA GIMBUTT** was Helen Kowalska's novice mistress.

angel, who took her to purgatory. In the blink of an eye she found herself in a misty place that was full of flames. She saw a multitude of suffering souls, but the flames did not harm her. She noticed that the souls prayed unceasingly, but this did not bring them any benefit. She then understood that only someone's prayers from without could help them. She asked them what their greatest torment was. They replied with one voice: their longing for God. Sr. Faustina then understood that she had to pray more for souls in purgatory in order to shorten their suffering and to hasten their being united with God.

She soon returned to Warsaw and recommenced work in the kitchen. She encountered many minor unpleasantries on the part of some of the sisters. One of them was Sr. Marcjanna Oswiecimska, who once got a little cross with Sr. Faustina and ordered her—under strict obedience—to sit on a table while she herself continued to work hard, cleaning work surfaces and scrubbing floors. The sisters who came into the kitchen were astounded that a young postulant was sitting on a table, while an older woman was doing onerous work.

Unfavorable comments were directed at her, that she was lazy, vain, and eccentric. She could not explain anything as Sr. Oswiecimska forbade her to do so. So she sat silently, exposed to cutting remarks, burning with shame. A postulant, Sr. Szymona Nalewajk, who witnessed this situation, recalled that she admired Sr. Faustina for not murmuring, and for the humility with which she bore all the humiliations. Sr. Faustina saw daily unpleasantries and burdens as spiritual exercises that would destroy her pride and egoism.

On January 23, 1926—after several months in Warsaw—Helen left for Kraków to complete her postulancy. When (that same day) she arrived at Łagiewniki, a twenty-nine-year-old sister, Henryka Losinska, a cobbler of the second choir, was dying. Helen had a vision several days later, after Sr. Henryka had died: the sister came to her and bade her to tell the directress of novices, Mother Malgorzata Gimbutt, that the deceased would like her confessor, Fr. Stanislaw Rospond (later a bishop), to offer up one Mass and three ejaculatory prayers for her. Helen was afraid that it was an illusion, so she did not go to see the directress. It was only when Sr. Henryka appeared a second and a third time that she responded to the deceased's request. Fr. Rospond said the Mass, and after three days the late nun appeared again to express her thanks: "May God reward you."

Helen Kowalska spent the last three months of her postulancy in Kraków preparing for a new stage in her religious life. This period starts with the ceremony of the taking of the veil and the reception of a habit and a new name, and it ends with the first profession of vows, which are repeated at least twice before the profession of perpetual vows. The directress of novices, Mother Malgorzata, who, two years earlier, on first impressions, had so negatively assessed Helen as "no one special" prepared the postulants for this ceremony. She did not then know that she was dealing with the most extraordinary postulant in the congregation's history.

**BISHOP STANISLAW ROSPOND** led the ceremony when Sr. Faustina took her religious vows.

**MOTHER MICHAELA MORACZEWSKA** was the first to discern Sr. Faustina's vocation.

73

Warsaw

Kraków

POLAND

# HELEN DIES, FAUSTINA IS BORN

# Novitiate

# CHAPTER 5

# Novitiate

On April 30, 1926, there
was a solemn ceremony, the
taking of the veil, for the
Congregation of the Sisters of
Our Lady of Mercy in Łagiewniki,
Kraków. During the ceremony,
Fr. Stanislaw Rospond said
the following to Sr. Kowalska:
"From today on, you will not be
called by your baptismal name.
You will be called
Sr. Maria Faustina."

The congregation's superior general, Mother Leonarda Cielecka, had chosen the names. Every sister in the congregation was given two names: the first was always Maria (in honour of our Lady, the order's patroness), while the other, her new personal name, was to be henceforth used.

Sr. Klemensa Buczek was a witness at Faustina Kowalska's taking of the veil; she helped her to take off her white gown and veil and to put on her habit. She recalled the event years later: "I had the task of dressing Helen. When the

**ROSARY**. All the nuns in the Congregation of the Sisters of Our Lady of Mercy had rosaries of this style. It was on such beads that Sr. Faustina recited the Divine Mercy Chaplet for the first time.

**SR. KLEMENSA BUCZEK** helped Faustina to put on her habit during the ceremony in which Faustina took the veil.

77

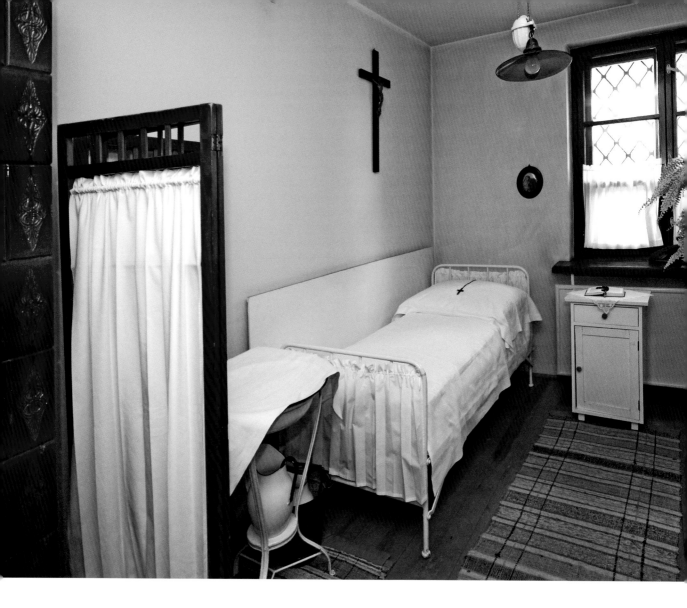

**RECONSTRUCTED CONVENT** cell, Łagiewniki.

candidate received her habit at the altar, I said to her: 'Helen, let us hurry to put on the habit.' Helen fainted. I ran to get some eau de cologne to revive her. . . . Later, I teased her about her being so sorry to leave the world. It was not until after her death that I learned that something else had caused her to faint." When taking the habit, God gave Sr. Faustina to understand how much she would have to suffer, so that she might be fully aware of the road she had chosen in life. She disclosed that it was a harbinger of but one minute of the future.

Sr. Faustina spent the whole of her novitiate—April 30, 1926 to April 30, 1928—in one place, that is, at the convent in Łagiewniki, Kraków, where for the most part she helped in the kitchen, which catered for about one hundred fifty people. Count Aleksander Lubomirski had funded the convent and the House of Mercy in 1891. About one hundred sixty girls lived in the center during the period

**BIBLE AND ROSARY** on a little cupboard by her bed.

**PORTRESS** at the Łagiewniki convent entrance. During Sr. Faustina's time the convent entrance was near the exit gate.

**CONVENT ENTRANCE** of the Congregation of the Sisters of Our Lady of Mercy, Łagiewniki.

**ŁAGIEWNIKI CONVENT,** which the sisters called "Józefów".

between the world wars. It was surrounded by a wall and was inaccessible to outsiders. The novitiate was in the convent, as it is today.

Sr. Faustina's first directress of novices, Mother Małgorzata Gimbutt, was replaced by Mother Józefa Brzoza (June 20, 1926), an experienced nun whose spiritual advice greatly helped the young novice. She told Faustina to be always trusting, simple, and humble. She taught her not to complain, but to be pleased with everything. To be calm when all panicked. To perceive God's blessing in situations that others saw as a curse. A child was her model, one who completely trusted its father, going through life so. Such a childlike attitude, she said, was the key to God's graces.

The young novice took her directress's words to heart and even wrote them in her diary. The accounts of sisters who were in the novitiate with Faustina Kowalska emphasize her winsome simplicity and extraordinary humility. At that time there was a custom of assigning older novices to younger ones as helpers. They were called "angels", and their role was to support the younger novices during their

# ALEKSANDER IGNACY
# LUBOMIRSKI

**THE CONVENT** in Łagiewniki was established thanks to a donation from Prince Aleksander Ignacy Lubomirski (1802–1893). He was a descendent of a great aristocratic line, son of a general in the Russian army and grandson of a magnate in the Polish–Lithuanian Commonwealth. His wife was Julia Radziwill, granddaughter of the chamberlain of Lithuania. Lubomirski was not only the heir to a considerable fortune but also a capable financier who made a huge fortune by investing in the Suez Canal Company. He died childless and was buried in the Père-Lachaise Cemetery in Paris. He was famous as a generous philanthropist. Thanks to a large donation an education center for boys arose on Rakowicka Street in Kraków. Four years later he gave a considerable sum of money to the metropolitan of Kraków, Cardinal Albin Dunajewski. About thirty acres of land were bought and a center for girls was built, along with a chapel and the convent of the Congregation of the Sisters of Our Lady of Mercy. This property was named in honor of St. Joseph, the patron of the whole work, because the sisters ascribed the foundation to his intercession.

**MOTHER MICHAELA MORACZEWSKA** and Mother Serafina Kukulska. Mother Kukulska (1873–1964), as superior of the convent in Walendów, hosted Sr. Faustina in 1933.

**VOTIVE OFFERINGS,** convent chapel, Łagiewniki.

introduction to the routine of religious life. Sr. Krescencja Bogdanik was Faustina's angel. She recalled not only that her charge carried out every instruction scrupulously and without a murmur but that a childlike joy was always evident on her face. In turn, Sr. Ludwina Gadzina—to whom Faustina was an angel—recalled that Faustina always bore every humiliation and unpleasantness, great or small, without complaint or resentment. Faustina explained to Sr. Samuela Wasilewska that one should never complain to people, but to God alone.

Though Faustina was bright and cheerful—so much so that other sisters were drawn to her—she went through a painful period of spiritual darkness at the end of the first year of her novitiate. Yet she did not show how much she was suffering inwardly. Only her mistress and confessor knew of it. A strange aridity crept into this period of her spiritual life. Prayer ceased to bring her consolation and became

**SISTERS** on the first profession day (May 1, 1933). Sr. Faustina (circled) joined them to make her perpetual vows.

83

**SR. KALIKSTA PIEKARCZYK** took her perpetual vows on April 30, 1928, the day Sr. Faustina took her first vows.

burdensome. All her meditations on God came with great difficulty. Unfounded fear began to overcome her. The awareness of her own misery and weakness grew. She referred to books, but instead of becoming enlightened, she became more confused. It seemed to her that her prayers were not pleasing to God, that her receiving sacraments offended Him. She wanted to abstain from Communion, but her confessor firmly forbade this. She did not understand anything he said to her. The simplest truths of the Faith became incomprehensible to her. At a certain moment a terrible thought transfixed her; that she had been abandoned by God. This caused inner torment. Darkness engulfed her soul. She felt as if she were about to die. She did not want to exist, yet did. The temptation of indifference came. She began to ask herself whether a virtuous life made any sense, since it seemed to be disagreeable to God. Doubt arose, and despair immediately after; damnation seemed to await her. A deadly fear almost completely paralyzed her. She then suffered hellish torments, similar to those that damned souls suffer for eternity.

**SR. BORGIA TICHY.** One of the sisters most critical of Sr. Faustina. After many years she admitted that she had judged the mystic unfairly.

**CONGREGATION CONVENT.**
Front entrance (interwar period).

**CONVENT CHAPEL, ŁAGIEWNIKI** (interwar period). Today there is a Merciful Jesus painting behind the altar to the left.

**SR. MARIA JÓZEFA** – Stefania Brzoza was Sr. Faustina's novitiate mistress. She helped Sr. Faustina during her spiritual dark night.

**ST. JOHN OF THE CROSS** was the first to describe the state of a soul in the dark night of the senses. Sr. Faustina and Mother Teresa of Calcutta had such an experience.

**SISTER FAUSTINA'S** wedding band, which she received on May 1, 1933, when she professed her perpetual vows to Christ. The band is engraved with four names: Jesus, Mary, Joseph, and Ignaceus.

Masters of the spiritual life call this state the "dark night of the senses", the phenomenon is best described in the works of St. John of the Cross. The greatest Christian mystics experienced it. Fortunately, the directress of novices, Mother Józefa Brzoza, recognized this state. She assured Sr. Faustina that God had destined her to great sanctity, since He had sent such painful spiritual suffering on one so young. Mother Józefa helped the novice to get through that period of spiritual darkness, which lasted almost eighteen months. Sr. Faustina's faith, hope, and charity were then put to the test. She came out of it cleansed, purged in the fiery furnace of doubt. Plunged into despair, not feeling God's presence, and even feeling rejected by Him, Faustina never ceased to pray to Jesus. In the face of all adversities, she trusted in but His mercy. She assured Him that she would never leave Him, as apart from Him life made no sense.

During this period, Sr. Faustina had a vision of Thérèse of the Child Jesus. St. Thérèse informed her that she would go to heaven and that she would be canonized. Faustina also learned that her parents would go to heaven. She asked if her brothers and sisters would get there too. St. Thérèse did not give her an affirmative reply; she just advised her to pray hard for them.

Sr. Faustina's novitiate concluded with her first religious vows (April 30, 1928). Her parents came for the ceremony, which was presided over by Bishop Stanisław Rospond. As all the guest rooms were occupied by the relatives of other novices, Stanisław and Marianna Kowalska were put up for the night in a shed where garden tools were kept. However, they did not sleep a wink, as they prayed all night for their daughter. Stanisław left Łagiewniki a very happy man. He was deeply moved by what his daughter had said to him during a walk in the convent garden: "You see, Daddy, the One to Whom I made my vows is my Husband and your Son-in-law."

# ST. THÉRÈSE OF LISIEUX

**SR. FAUSTINA** asked many saints to intercede to God for her, but she was particularly attached to the French Carmelite St. Thérèse of the Child Jesus (1873–1897). They had a mystical meeting on the fifth day of Sr. Faustina's novena to St. Thérèse. They both had experience of dark nights of the senses and merciful love.

In her autobiography St. Thérèse described how, when reading St. Paul's First Letter to the Corinthians, she discovered her own particular vocation: "Considering the mystical Body of the Church, I had not recognized myself in any of the members described by St. Paul, or rather, I wanted to recognize myself in all... Charity gave me the key to my vocation. I understood that if the Church has a body composed of different members, the noblest and most necessary of all the members would not be lacking to her. I understood that the Church has a heart, and that this heart burns with Love. I understood that Love alone makes its members act, that if this Love were to be extinguished, the Apostles would no longer preach the Gospel, the Martyrs would refuse to shed their blood... I understood that Love embraces all vocations, that Love is all things, that it embraces all times and all places... in a word, that it is eternal!

"Then in the excess of my delirious joy, I cried out: 'O Jesus, my Love, at last I have found my vocation, my vocation is Love!... Yes, I have found my place in the Church, and it is you, O my God, Who have given me this place... in the heart of the Church, my Mother, I will be Love!.... Thus I shall be all things: thus my dream shall be realized!!!'"

POLAND

# Juniorate

# CHAPTER 6

# Juniorate

Unlike her novitiate, which she spent in one place, the next stage of Sr. Faustina's religious life, that is, her juniorate, was one of constant transfers from one place to another. The juniorate, the time between the first vows—renewed every year—and the perpetual vows, lasted five years.

**A PIECE OF SR. FAUSTINA'S** sweater at the Origins of the Divine Mercy Devotion exhibition (Płock Diocesan Museum).

The new superior general of the congregation, Mother Michaela Moraczewska, had the most to say with regard to the young nun's numerous moves. She had replaced Mother Leonarda Cielecka during the general chapter in October 1928 and was head of the order for the next eighteen years.

"The circumstances were such that it was necessary to move Sr. Faustina frequently to ever different posts, so that she worked in virtually every house of the congregation", explained Mother Michaela. So, as early as October 1928, the newly consecrated nun was transferred to the convent on Zytnia Street, Warsaw, where she helped in the kitchen.

In February 1929, she went to Vilnius for four months to replace Sr. Petronela Basiura. After returning to Warsaw she was assigned work in the congregation's

**KITCHEN IN WALENDÓW.** Sr. Faustina frequently did kitchen work in many of the convents in which she stayed.

**HIGH ALTAR.** This painting of Sr. Faustina and the Merciful Jesus, found in the convent chapel on Hetmanska Street, Warsaw, was displayed in Rome during Faustina's beatification and canonization. In June 1929, Faustina Kowalska was sent to work in the new convent, which the sisters called "Józefinek".

**BARBED METAL CROSS** worn for mortification, under their habits, especially during Lent.

new center on Hetmanska Street. In July she was sent to Kiekrz, near Poznan. Later she returned to Warsaw for six months, but in May 1930, she was delegated to Płock, where she generally worked in the bakery shop and sometimes in the kitchen or bakery, helping the sisters. From there she went for a short time to Biala, a branch of the Płock house. In November 1932, she was in Warsaw for her third probation of five months, the final preparations for her perpetual vows. She went on a retreat in Walendów, where she met Fr. Edmund Elter. Finally, at the end of April 1933, she left for Kraków, where she made her perpetual vows (May 1).

Why did Sr. Faustina change her abode so often? Sr. Ludwina Gadzina asked this question of Mother Józefa Brzoza, who answered that in emergencies it was least difficult to move Faustina to another convent as she never protested but humbly accepted every instruction. Sr. Faustina herself said that she did not murmur about decisions

**STATUE OF SR. FAUSTINA,** Kiekrz, commemorates her stay there .

93

# PŁOCK DIOCESE

**PŁOCK, WHERE SR. FAUSTINA** had
a vision of Merciful Jesus, is a special place in
Poland. The town was one of the first episcopate
sees in Poland, established as early as 1075.
The diocese has had outstanding ordinaries, for
example, Jan Lubrański, Erazm Ciołek, Andrzej
Krzycki, Piotr Gamrat, Henryk Firlej, Wincenty
Teofil Popiel, and Antoni Julian Nowowiejski, who
was tortured to death in a German concentration
camp. The Church of the Assumption is the
bishop's church, consecrated in 1144. Over the
centuries its form has been repeatedly changed.
It was initially Romanesque, then of Gothic,
Renaissance, and Classical style. It houses the
tombs of two Polish rulers: King Wladyslaw
Herman (1043–1102) and King Boleslaw
Krzywousty (1086–1138).

**PŁOCK CATHEDRAL** underwent a thorough
renovation at the beginning of the 20th century.
Wladyslaw Drapiewski's polychromes are of that
period. A Merciful Jesus painting reminds one of Sr.
Faustina having been there.

**THERE ARE** two main attractions in the cathedral:
copies of 12th-century Płock doors (the original doors
were taken to Nowogrod, Russia), and the Royal
Chapel, where two Polish rulers repose.

because she took her vow of obedience to God seriously. Asked by Mother Michaela why she did not indicate which convent house would best suit her, Faustina replied: "I purely want to do the will of God. Wherever Mother sends me, I know that that shall be what God requires of me."

The account of Sr. Paulina Kosinska—who worked with her in the convent's kitchen in Płock—says much of Sr. Faustina's compliance. "The kitchen was narrow, and every now and then somebody passed through, jostling everybody on the way. Apart from that, people constantly rang at the convent door, so it was necessary to go out to them. Yet, throughout all of her time in the kitchen, not once did Sr. Faustina show discontent, even if only by a word or a grimace. She was ever cheerful, ever smiling. Her attitude was not appreciated until she was replaced by another nun, who constantly complained about the working conditions."

Sr. Faustina had a vision during her stay in Warsaw concerning the chastisement that God would cause to fall upon the most beautiful of Polish cities. It would be similar to the one that befell Sodom and Gomorrah. Shocked by the vision,

**BLESSED ANTONI JULIAN NOWOWIEJSKI,** Bishop of Płock from 1908 to 1941, murdered by the Germans in a concentration camp.

DOMINI ET HAEREDES

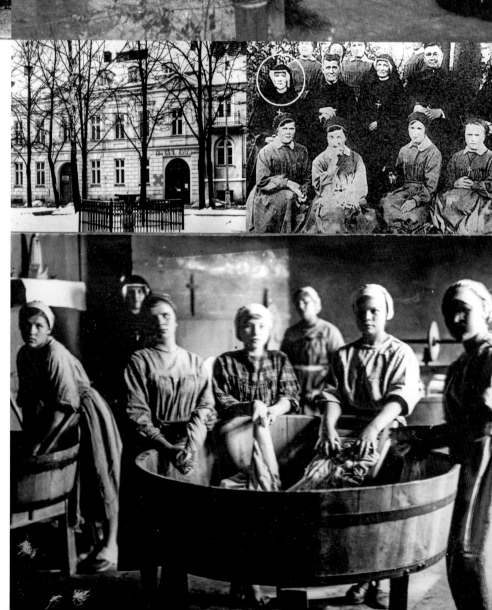

**SR. KSAWERA OLSZAMOWSKA** at the convent in Łagiewniki with a painting of Sr. Faustina Kowalska.

**THREE NUNS** (Mother Franciszka, Sr. Albina, and Sr. Jadwiga). In the background the now non-existent convent in Płock, where Sr. Faustina had a vision of Merciful Jesus (February 22, 1931). Photo from the end of the 19th century.

**CONVENT IN PŁOCK** – a little cross marks the shop where Sr. Faustina worked (1931–1932).

**A GROUP OF NUNS** and their wards in Biala, near Plock. Sr. Faustina is circled.

**SISTERS' CHARGES** at the laundry in the Guardian Angel Center in Płock, in 1928.

she prayed in silence. She then heard Jesus' voice. He told her to unite herself closely with Him during the Eucharist, and to offer His Blood and Wounds to God the Father in expiation for the sins of that city. She was to repeat this without ceasing for a week during every Holy Mass. On the seventh day she saw Jesus again, this time in a bright cloud. She asked Him to look down with kindness upon Poland. When she saw Jesus looking upon Poland kindly, she asked Him to bless the whole country. Jesus did so. He made a big sign of the cross over the country and said that He had blessed Poland for Faustina's sake. The mystic's biographers compare this scene with the biblical narrative of Abraham's discussion with God on the destruction of Sodom. Some commentators think that the said most beautiful of cities was Kraków, which—unlike other cities—was not devastated during World War II.

**TUMSK HILL** and Płock Cathedral where Sr. Faustina attended important Church celebrations during her stay in Płock.

97

**ST. FAUSTINA** Kowalska Museum in the former convent bakery in Płock, where the mystic worked at times. The museum has a reconstruction of her cell.

**CHARGES IN THE SEWING** room at the Guardian Angel Center (Płock), where bed linen was made and then sold.

One day, Faustina went for a stroll with Sr. Samuela Wasilewska. They headed in the direction of Wola and shortly came to an Orthodox church. In those days ecumenical dialogue had not yet been developed; strained relations prevailed between the Orthodox and Catholics. Faustina, even though she was in a Catholic nun's habit, went inside the church, knelt down, and prayed fervently. On coming out she explained to the surprised Sr. Samuela that one ought to worship God everywhere. She also told her that the time would come when Christianity would be united again.

Sr. Faustina also had mystical experiences in Kiekrz, where a new House of Mercy had been opened (March 1928) for underage girls with court sentences from Poznan and its neighborhood. There the nuns had leased a property of between twenty-five and fifty acres. The property included a house—surrounded by a large orchard of four thousand fruit trees—which was right on the edge of Small Lake. Sr. Faustina arrived in Kiekrz on July 7, 1929, to replace Sr. Modesta Rzeczkowska, who was ill. Sr. Faustina made a very good impression there: when she left for Warsaw—after a stay of several weeks—the superior of the house in Kiekrz, Sr. Ksawera Olszamowska, wrote to the mother general, Michaela Moraczewska: "I had the impression that she had a very deep inner life, that it was favored with special graces from God."

**FR. WACŁAW JEZUSEK**, Sr. Faustina's confessor in Płock.

**THE CHAPEL** in the old convent in Płock existed until 1939.

99

**A PICTURE** of Sr. Faustina (convent chapel, Płock).

**THE DIVINE MERCY SHRINE** in Płock. The church tower was built over the site of the cell where Sr. Faustina had a vision of the image of the Merciful Jesus.

Sr. Ksawera was not mistaken. She must have been unusually perceptive as Sr. Faustina did not share her inner experiences with anyone. And she had them in Kiekrz, too, mainly when admiring the beauty of nature. One day, when standing at the edge of the lake admiring the beauty of the created world, she saw Jesus beside her, Who said: "All this I created for you, My spouse; and know that all this beauty is nothing compared to what I have prepared for you in eternity" (*Diary*, 158). She was not aware of the passage of time. She had a free day, set apart for individual meditation. It seemed to her that she had been by the lake for but a short time, whereas she had been there until evening. She discovered the Creator's greatness in the beauty of creation. The order, harmony, and charm of the world that surrounded her convinced her that it all could not have been the work of blind chance.

In May 1930, Sr. Faustina was at the convent in Płock (14/18 Old Market Square) where the sisters ran a center, known as the Guardian Angel, for fallen girls. Bl. Archbishop Antoni Julian Nowowiejski had initially established a center for poor teenage girls on the site. He also set up the habitless Congregation of the Divine Mercy to do educational work in the center. However, in 1899, he linked his work with the

Congregation of the Sisters of Our Lady of Mercy, which was more experienced in such apostolic work. The center was initially run by Mother Kolumba Labanowska. Over a hundred wards lived in the Płock house. Under the supervision of the nuns, they learned trades in laundry work, sewing, embroidery, and farming. The work of the sisters enjoyed such approval that Archbishop Nowowiejski dedicated a book to them—*The History of the Institute of Our Lady of Mercy*. The papal nuncio in Poland, Fr. Achille Ratti, who became Pope Pius XI two years later, visited the convent and center in 1918.

Sr. Faustina also stayed for a short time in the village of Biala, a little over six miles from Płock. The congregation bought a farm there in 1928: one hundred eleven acres of not-very-fertile land, as well as some ruined buildings. Thus was established a branch of the Płock convent and the economic base for the Guardian Angel Center.

Sr. Faustina frequently picked flowers to decorate the chapel. One day, she cut some of the most beautiful roses and, instead of decorating the chapel, decided to decorate the room of the mother superior, who was due to arrive in Biala. On her

**IMAGE OF THE MERCIFUL JESUS** by painter Elżbieta Hoffman-Plewa from Toruń, now in the Divine Mercy Shrine in Płock. The painting was consecrated by Pope John Paul II during his pilgrimage to Poland in 1991. The canvas painting marks the place of a nun's cell where Sr. Faustina had a vision of the image of the Merciful Jesus.

101

**DIVINE MERCY SHRINE,** Płock convent, where Jesus instructed Sr. Faustina to paint an image of Him.

way St. Faustina saw Jesus standing on the porch of the house. He asked her kindly: "My daughter, to whom are you taking these flowers?" (*Diary*, 71). At that moment Faustina understood that she was becoming emotionally attached. She saw that such a tie could well undermine her relationship with Christ. So she threw the flowers down and ran to the chapel to thank God for the grace of coming to know herself.

A vision at the convent in Płock (February 22, 1931) was of key importance in Sr. Faustina's life. In the evening, when in her cell, she saw Jesus clothed in a white garment, His right hand raised in blessing, His left touching His breast, whence a red and pale ray emanated through a slight opening in His garment. Jesus said: "Paint an image according to the pattern you see, with the signature: Jesus, I trust in You. I desire that this image be venerated, first in your chapel, and [then] throughout the world.

I promise that the soul that will venerate this image will not perish. I also promise victory over [its] enemies already here on earth, especially at the hour of death. I Myself will defend it as My own glory" (*Diary* 47-48).

During her next confession, Sr. Faustina told a priest about the instructions she had received from Jesus. But the priest explained that she was to paint the image in her soul. However, when she was leaving the confessional, she heard Jesus say: "My image already is in your soul. I desire that there be a Feast of Mercy. I want this image, which you will paint with a brush, to be solemnly blessed on the first Sunday after Easter; that Sunday is to be the Feast of Mercy. I desire that priests proclaim this great mercy of Mine towards souls of sinners.

**CHURCH IN BIAŁA**
where the mystic attended Mass.

**SR. FAUSTINA** at the convent in Biala near Płock.

**THE CHAPEL IN BIAŁA** in the old convent building, dedicated in 1929.

**SR. FAUSTINA** sometimes baked bread in this oven in Płock.

**THE FLOOR** that the saint walked on in the convent kitchen, Płock.

**BAKING OF BREAD** at the convent in Płock.

Let the sinner not be afraid to approach Me. The flames of mercy are burning Me—clamoring to be spent; I want to pour them out upon these souls"(*Diary*, 49–50).

After this event the mystic went to see the superior of the house in Płock, Sr. Roza Klobukowska, who demanded a sign to confirm the authenticity of the revelations. When, during prayer, Faustina asked for such a sign, she heard that God would give her to know this through the graces that He would grant through the image. So the nun tried to paint Christ as she saw Him in the vision, but she was unable to do it. She asked Sr. Bozenna for help, but in vain.

Meanwhile, news of Faustina's revelations began to spread in whispers around the convent. The atmosphere around her became tense. Some sisters thought that she was a hysteric, others that she was a dreamer, and yet others that she was subject to delusions. They looked at her suspiciously or inquisitively. At times she heard unkind words behind her back.

**BIAŁA, NEAR PŁOCK**. Front row, sitting: Fr. Krogulecki (parish priest), Sr. Alojza, Sr. Tekla, Sr. Faustina, and Fr. Trojanowski (chaplain).

**MOTHER RAFAELA BUCZYŃSKA**, Sr. Faustina's superior during her third probation period in Warsaw (Zytnia Street).

At that time Sr. Faustina did not have a permanent spiritual director. Successive confessors, to whom she had turned for advice, sent her to her superiors, who then sent her to her confessors. As a result Faustina herself ceased to be certain about the origins of her revelations. She began to ignore inner inspirations, but visions of Jesus did not cease.

In November 1932, Sr. Faustina, in a state of complete inner disharmony, left for Warsaw, and then immediately for Walendów for her annual eight-day retreat. The congregation had a 618-acre farm there, with ponds, a mill, farm buildings, and a house. It was donated to the order in 1896 by Count Gustaw Przezdziecki. Several sisters lived there permanently. They kept an eye on the property with the help of farm workers. A convent and a center for girls were built there in 1908, and a church in 1936. The church was still being built when Sr. Faustina arrived for her retreat.

She constantly struggled with her thoughts. One thought told her to fulfil the mission required of her by Jesus, whereas another insisted that she reject it, as revelations were but delusions. She recalled her discussions with her superiors and confessors, who said contrary things. Distressed by the tangle of thoughts, Sr. Faustina decided to reveal her inner life to the retreat leader and to ask for help. The retreat was led by a Jesuit, Fr. Edmund Elter, an experienced spiritual director and a professor of ethics, homiletics, and rhetoric at the Gregorian University in Rome. He was the first priest to confirm her in her spiritual life and the mission entrusted to her. He confirmed that she was on the right path and that the revelations came from God. He also advised her to be faithful to the mission she had received from Jesus. And finally, he advised her to pray for a good spiritual director, one who would be able to discern the stirrings of her soul. After the confession, Sr. Faustina was filled with joy, as—for the first time—a priest, in the Church's name, had confirmed the authenticity of her revelations.

After the retreat in Walendów, Sr. Faustina returned to Warsaw to complete her third probation. That five-month period of preparations for perpetual vows consisted largely of spiritual formation and less demanding work, mainly in a convent storeroom. She also helped some elderly, ill nuns. The work was burdensome at times, bringing humiliation instead of gratitude. It was so when she tidied the room of one of the sisters. Though Sr. Faustina tried to do it as best she could, the elderly nun was always displeased. She constantly followed her about,

**SR. WALERIA WILCZYŃSKA**
was the superior of the convent in Walendow when Sr. Faustina was there.

**CONVENT IN WALENDÓW**
The convent of the Congregation of the Sisters of Our Lady of Mercy was consecrated by Archbishop Stanislaw Gall in September 1934.

106

pointing to the smallest of stains and crumbs on the floor, and complaining that she was slow and careless. Nothing could please her. Sr. Faustina felt exhausted, not so much by the work as by the continual complaints and constant demands. However, she carried out all her instructions without a word. That was not enough for the elderly nun, as she complained to the mother superior. The mystic then understood that one could also be a martyr in little, daily things.

The distrust of the older nuns also hurt Sr. Faustina, particularly the distrust of Mother Janina Bartkiewicz, who sharply cautioned her against false visions. Sr. Faustina was particularly hurt when she told her that Jesus had close contacts with holy people, not with sinners like her. Yet Faustina did not complain to anybody, but offered up her suffering to God for various intentions. And what is more, she was pleased that she could be spiritually united with the suffering Christ, for she recalled St. Paul's words in his Letter to the Colossians: "Now I rejoice in my sufferings for your sake, and in my flesh I complete what is lacking in Christ's afflictions for the sake of his body, that is, the Church" (Col 1:24).

One day, when in Warsaw, Sr. Faustina visited the Congregation of the Franciscan Sisters of the Family of Mary for Adoration—the Franciscans had a neighboring property at the junction of Zytnia Street and Zelazna Street. While praying, she saw Jesus, Who said to her: "Know that if you neglect the matter of the painting of the image and the whole work of mercy, you will have

**THE CONVENT** in Walendów had farmland nearby, which the nuns cultivated.

**SR. RÓŻA KŁOBUKOWSKA** was Sr. Faustina's superior at the convent in Płock.

to answer for a multitude of souls on the day of judgment" (*Diary*, 154). She was horrified by this as she understood that she would have to answer not only for herself at the Final Judgment, but also for others, that she would have to relate to God what she had done in rescuing souls.

On April 18, 1933, after finishing her probation, Sr. Faustina left for Kraków for an eight-day retreat prior to taking her perpetual vows. The retreat leader at Lagiewniki turned out to be an experienced spiritual director, a Jesuit, Fr. Józef Andrasz—the editor-in-chief of the monthly magazine the *Messenger of the Heart of Jesus*, and the national director of the Apostleship of Prayer. He was the second

# FR. EDMUND **ELTER, S.J.**

**FR. EDMUND ELTER** (1887–1955), a Jesuit, was the first religious to discern Sister Faustina's mystical states. He entered the Jesuit Order in 1905. After studying philosophy and theology, he specialized in international law and ethics in Warsaw, Rome, and Paris (1919–1923). Over the next four years he lectured on ethics and the history of philosophy in Nowy Sacz. In 1927 he left for Rome, where he was professor of ethics at the Pontifical Gregorian University. The above photo is of this period (Fr. Elter standing second on the right). For health reasons he returned to Poland in 1932, where he became a valued retreat leader. It was then that he met Sr. Faustina in Walendów.

Fr. Elter became famous as an ethicist and for his academic Thomistic textbook, *Moral Philosophy Compendium*. He was the provincial superior of the Greater Poland Jesuits from 1945 to 1948. From 1948 he worked in Rome, where he died at the age of sixty-eight.

**SR. FAUSTINA**
(on the left)
stayed at this
convent in Biala
(near Płock)
several times
(1930–1932).

**PAPAL NUNCIO
ARCHBISHOP
ACHILLE RATTI**
(the future Pope
Pius XI) visited
Walendów.

priest to recognize the profoundness of her inner life. He gave her three pieces of advice. First, she should not ignore her inner inspirations but should tell her confessor everything. She should follow the inspirations, were she to see that they were of benefit to her or the other sisters, but always in consultation with her spiritual director. Second, he instructed her to reject inspirations not in accord with the Faith, or the spirit of the Church, for they would be of a demonic nature. Third, he advised indifference as to the third kind of inspiration, not concerned with either human souls or their good. She was not to pay attention to such inspirations.

On May 1, 1933, Sr. Faustina solemnly offered up her life to God. The perpetual vows ceremony, in the convent at Lagiewniki, was presided over by Bishop Stanislaw Rospond. The moment the hierarch put the ring on her finger, while saying the nuptial words to Jesus she felt God pervading the very depths of her being. She described this as a moment of loving union, when the Bridegroom dwells in His bride, and she in Him. She knew that she could not be without Him, even for a day. At such a moment, the true value of even the greatest wealth, honor, and delights of this world was revealed. They meant nothing in comparison with but a fraction of a second spent in close proximity to God.

Shortly after her perpetual vows, Sr. Faustina received instructions about her next move. This time she was to go to Vilnius to help in the convent garden. Though she did not have any experience in gardening, she immediately agreed. She left Kraków on May 25, 1933. She had permission from the mother superior

**OUR LADY OF CZĘSTOCHOWA.** Sr. Faustina offered up her religious vows during six hours of prayer before this image.

to stop off in Częstochowa, where she stayed in the congregation house at 9/11 St. Barbara Street. At the convent, situated at the foot of Jasna Gora, the sisters ran (since 1908) a center for girls in need of moral renewal; later they also provided accommodation for pilgrims.

The young nun's main reason for going to Częstochowa, however, was to visit the Marian shrine. Sr. Faustina had always wanted to go there, but the opportunity had never been given to her before. She went to the Chapel of the Miraculous Image at five in the morning, when the image was unveiled to the faithful. She stayed there in deep prayer until eleven, though it seemed to be but a moment to her. The mother superior of the convent in Częstochowa had to send a nun to tell her to come for breakfast and not to miss her train. The mystic said later that our Lady had then told her a lot about supernatural reality. She felt that she was a true Mother to her.

Sr. Faustina visited Poland's spiritual capital only one more time, at the beginning of November 1935, when returning to Vilnius after a retreat in Kraków. We know of but one note concerning the visit, saying that it was on a Saturday and that she prayed before the Jasna Góra image. Faustina's diary contains many references with regard to the fact that she frequently communed not only with Jesus, but also with our Lady. The notes reveal that Mary was repeatedly a great support for the nun. It was so in May 1933, when the mystic was on her way to Vilnius. As yet she did not know that she would spend the next three years of her life in that city.

**CZĘSTOCHOWA** is known as the spiritual capital of Poland, particularly on the grounds of its successful defense of Jasna Gora against the Swedes in 1655.

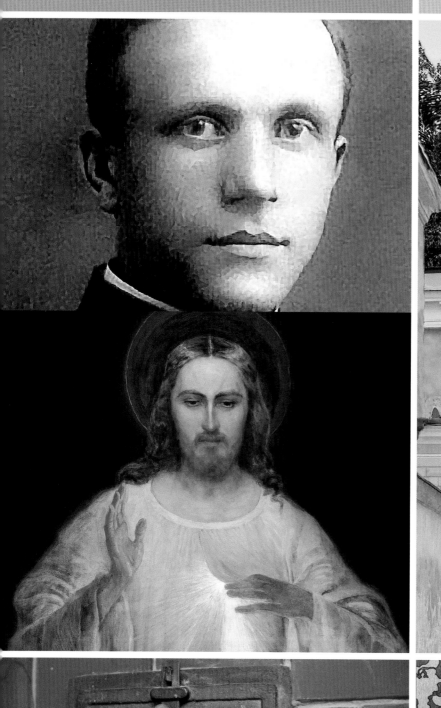

Vilnius

Warsaw

POLAND

# Vilnius

# CHAPTER 7

# Vilnius

Sr. Faustina stayed in Vilnius for almost three years (May 1933 to March 1936). She was assigned work in the garden. Though she had never done such work before, she took on her new responsibility enthusiastically. Just after arriving in Vilnius, she made her way to see the Redemptorists—famous for their well-kept garden—to learn her new trade.

**OSTRA BRAMA**
(Dawn Gate) Staircase. Adam Mickiewicz, Juliusz Slowacki, Jozef Piłsudski, Faustina Kowalska, and Pope John Paul II, among others, went up this staircase to pray before the image of the Mother of Mercy of Ostra Brama.

**OUR LADY OF THE GATE OF DAWN**. This image has been drawing crowds of pilgrims from all over the world to Vilnius for a hundred years.

She soon achieved such results that visitors thought the sisters had an excellent gardener.

The convent, situated on Antakalnis Hill—25 Senatorska Street (today 29 Grybo Street)—initially made a strange impression on Faustina. In Kraków the convent was situated in a solid brick edifice, while in Vilnius it consisted of

**CITY OF CHURCHES.** Vilnius is so known because of its great number of Christian churches, mainly Catholic and Orthodox.

**THE HILL OF THREE CROSSES** overlooks Vilnius – seven Franciscan monks were martyred there in the 14th century when Lithuania was pagan.

a cluster of tiny wooden huts. The sisters had settled there at the beginning of the twentieth century due to the kindness of Duchess Maria Michalowa Radziwillowa. The duchess sent her plenipotentiary, Anna Kulesza, to Vilnius to choose and buy a place in the name of a future foundation. Anna Kulesza prayed for several days to make the right choice. She had a strange dream: she saw herself praying alone before a statue of Jesus in the Church of St. Peter and St. Paul. Then she saw Christ come out of the church, walk along Senatorska Street, stop, and point to the estate of General Bykowski (a Russian). She bought the estate for the congregation (February 16, 1908). The nuns moved in only three months later and opened a center for fallen girls. About ninety girls, known as "penitents",

# DIOCESE OF VILNIUS

## THE DIOCESE OF VILNIUS

was established in 1388 by Pope Urban VI shortly after the baptism of Lithuania. Until 1798 it was within the Metropolitan Archdiocese of Gniezno, then from 1798 to 1925 the Metropolitan Archdiocese of Mohilev. In 1925, after the concordat between the Holy See and the Second Polish Republic, it became an archdiocese. When Sr. Faustina was in Vilnius the ordinary was Archbishop Romuald Jałbrzykowski. Amongst his predecessors we find representatives of, for example, the following family lines: Radziwiłł, Sapieha, Pac, and Tyszkiewicz. The Cathedral of St. Stanisław and St. Władysław in Vilnius is the metropolitan church. Its present form is from the end of the eighteenth century, when it was restructured in the classical style. Its vaults house royal tombs, for example, those of Elżbieta Habsburżanka's and Barbara Radziwiłł'. King Władysław's heart can be found in the crypt.

**MOTHER IRENA KRZYŻANOWSKA**, Sr. Faustina's superior in Vilnius, and later in Kraków.

**MEMENTOS OF FR. SOPOĆKO** in the former convent building in Antakalnis, Vilnius.

lived there during the interwar period. The house was maintained largely by proceeds from baking bread, from laundering linen for the military hospital, and from the farm of a few acres as well as from the garden.

Mother Irena Krzyżanowska was the superior of the convent in Vilnius. She was a great support for Faustina and was actively involved in spreading the Divine Mercy devotion. A yet greater help turned out to be Fr. Michal Sopoćko, a lecturer on the theology faculty at Stefan Batory University, a spiritual father at the Vilnius Archdiocesan Seminary, and a confessor in many congregations, including the convent on Antakalnis Hill. He was the priest for whom Sr. Faustina had been praying so insistently for a long time. She had actually seen him in a vision before her arrival in Vilnius and recognized him immediately when he came to the convent on Senatorska Street for the first time. She had no doubts when she heard the following words in her soul: "This is My faithful servant; he will help you to fulfil My will here on earth" (*Diary*, 263).

Initially, Fr. Sopoćko distrusted Sr. Faustina. He recalled years later: "I met Sr. Faustina in the summer (July or August) of 1933. She was one of my penitents at the Congregation of the Sisters of Our Lady of Mercy in Vilnius, where I was an ordinary confessor. She attracted my attention by her extraordinarily subtle conscience and close union with God; usually there was no matter to be absolved, and she had never offended God by a mortal sin. At the very outset she told me that she had known me for a long time because of a vision, that I was to be the director of her conscience, and that I had to realize God's plans, which she was to communicate to me. I made light of what she said and put her to a test that occasioned Sr. Faustina, with her superior's permission, to look for another confessor. After a time, she returned to me and declared that she would bear anything and not depart from me." The thing that surprised the priest most about Sr. Faustina was the fact that she knew of his intention of resigning from his position as the congregation's confessor, though he had not confided this to anyone. Sr. Faustina dissuaded him. Fr. Sopoćko agreed to become her spiritual director. But earlier, he had subjected her to a humiliating test. He sent her to a psychiatrist to see if she was sound of mind. Dr. Helena Maciejewska's opinion was very favorable. The examination evoked a serious argument, with the mystic's opponents maintaining that she was mentally ill.

**NUNS IN THE CONVENT GARDEN**
on Antakalnis Hill. Sr. Faustina is first from the right, somewhat on her own. The statue of St. Joseph, in the background, is now at the Church of St. Peter and St. Paul in Vilnius.

On July 13, 1934, when Sr. Faustina was in the convent garden, she heard her guardian angel tell her to pray for the dying. After a prayer for that intention, which she said with the gardeners, the nun heard another voice in her soul—a woman's. It was the voice of Filomena Andrejko: "Pray for me until I tell you to stop. I am dying." At that time there was a sister with that name in the convent on Zytnia Street, Warsaw. She was dying that very day. It was 3:00 P.M. when Faustina heard Sr. Filomena's request; she was in the twelfth hour of her death throes. The mystic immediately began to pray to the Most Sacred Heart of Jesus. At 5:00 P.M., Sr. Faustina once again heard a female voice in her soul, which simply said: "Thank you." The nun stopped praying. The following day news reached Vilnius that Sr. Filomena Andrejko had died the day before at 4:45 P.M.

Sr. Faustina kept repeating to her confessor that God had placed him in her path and that He wanted the Merciful Jesus image to be venerated all over the world. Fr. Sopoćko recalled: "Driven by my curiosity as to what the picture would

**STEFAN BATORY UNIVERSITY, VILNIUS,** where Fr. Michał Sopoćko lectured in theology.

**FR. MICHAL SOPOĆKO**
(1888–1975) was Sr. Faustina's permanent confessor and spiritual director during her stay in Vilnius. His stole, among other mementos of him, can be found in a former convent building on Antakalnis Hill.

be like, rather than by a belief in the authenticity of Sr. Faustina's visions, I decided to set about having the picture painted. I came to an understanding with an artist, Eugeniusz Kazimirowski, who lived in the house I lived in. He undertook to paint the image for a certain sum. I also obtained permission from Sr. Faustina's superior to allow her to visit the artist twice a week to describe the image that he was to paint."

Eugeniusz Kazimirowski was a well-known Vilnius artist. He learned to paint in various studios in Kraków, and also in Lwow, Munich, Paris, and Rome, where he completed his studies at St. Luke's Academy in 1900. In 1914, he settled in Vilnius and became a lecturer at the Bialystok Teacher Training College. He also worked as a scene designer, painting mainly landscapes and portraits. It so happened that in the 1930s Kazimirowski lived and had his studio in the priests' quarters on the ground floor of the convent (Visitation Sisters) next to

**VILNIUS PANORAMA**. Historical capital of Lithuania, Vilnius was part of Poland during the interwar period.

the Church of the Sacred Heart. Fr. Sopoćko lived in the same building (2 Rossa Street—today 6 Rasu Street), on the first floor. He persuaded his neighbor to paint the image that Kazimirowski did not imagine would be the work that would immortalize him.

He worked on the painting from January to June 1934; Fr. Sopoćko posed for him. The superior of the congregation's convent in Vilnius, Mother Irena Krzyżanowska, recalled: "In order not to draw our sisters' attention to Sr. Faustina's inner experiences, I went to morning Mass with her every Saturday at Ostra Brama [Dawn Gate]. After Mass, we stopped by at the artist's studio, and Sr. Faustina gave him precise information regarding the image he was painting. The artist tried hard to conform to all of Sr. Faustina's instructions." Doubts as to certain details arose during the work. Sr. Faustina questioned Jesus about them. He gave her appropriate explanations during several visions in 1934. As to the meaning of the rays, Christ said: "The two rays denote Blood and Water. The pale ray stands for the Water which makes souls righteous. The red ray stands for the Blood which is the life of our souls... These two rays issued forth from the very depths of My tender mercy when My agonized Heart was opened by a lance on the Cross" (*Diary*, 299).

**BAKSZTA STREET, VILNIUS**, where Fr. Michał Sopoćko lived before entering the seminary.

**SACRED HEART CHURCH**. During Communist times this Vilnius church (Visitation Sisters) was used as a prison.

**EUGENIUSZ KAZIMIROWSKI**

(1873–1939). Though he painted many pictures, Eugeniusz Kazimirowski is known for only one image: the Merciful Jesus. Here he is among his pupils.

**THE ONLY MERCIFUL JESUS** image that Sr. Faustina saw. It arose under her direct supervision.

The finished work did not please Sr. Faustina. When she saw it, she had difficulty concealing her disappointment. The image was not in the least as beautiful as in her vision. However, the saddened nun did not say anything to the painter. She said farewell to Mother Krzyżanowska, who went off to take care of some matters in the town while she returned to the convent. She went to the chapel and burst into tears. She was depressed that the painting did not reflect the Savior's beauty, and wondered whether it was at all possible to paint it. Then she heard Christ say: "Not in the beauty of the color, nor of the brush lies the greatness of this image, but in My grace" (*Diary*, 313).

When the painting was finished, Fr. Sopoćko put it in a dark corridor at the Bernadine Sisters' convent, near St. Michael's Church, where he was the rector. He recalled: "The painting contained new elements, so I could not hang it up in the church without the archbishop's permission. But I was ashamed to ask and even more ashamed to speak of its origins." Sr. Faustina did not give up, however, and she told her confessor that Jesus demanded that His image be displayed for public veneration. At that time (1935) the Triduum that ended the Jubilee of the Redemption of the World—the nineteenth centenary of the death and Resurrection of Christ—was to be celebrated at Ostra Brama. Ostra Brama, with its miraculous Virgin Mary, Mother of Mercy image, was Vilnius' main pilgrimage center and the most prominent place of this Christian devotion in the Vilnius region.

Sr. Faustina's confessor was wondering how Jesus' demand could be fulfilled when, all of a sudden, the parish priest of Ostra Brama, Canon Stanislaw Zawadzki, asked him to give a homily during the Triduum. Fr. Sopoćko agreed, but on condition that the Merciful Jesus image would be placed in the Ostra Brama cloister window. And so it was. In the priest's opinion: "It looked impressive, and it drew everyone's attention more than the Mother of Mercy image." On the first day of the Triduum, Fr. Sopoćko gave a fiery homily about God's mercy, emphasizing that it demanded public veneration. He frequently pointed to Kazimirowski's painting during the homily.

St. Faustina was present at that Mass. She then had another vision. When Fr. Sopoćko began to talk about God's Mercy, the image suddenly came to life, and the rays from Jesus pierced the hearts of the people gathered there. She noticed that not all were pierced to the same degree; some more, some less. Her next vision occurred when she was returning to the convent. A great multitude of demons barred her way, furious with her, and threatening her with torments, as she had snatched away the effects of many years of their work. When she asked where they had come from, they replied: From

**KAZIMIROWSKI'S STUDIO.** Kazimirowski painted his version of the Merciful Jesus in the former quarters for priests at the convent of the Visitation Sisters. Today it is the Chapel of the Sisters of the Merciful Jesus.

125

human hearts. Before falling asleep that night, Sr. Faustina had yet another vision. She saw the image of the Merciful Jesus moving above Vilnius, fettered by nets, cutting all of them. After freeing the inhabitants, Christ made a sign of the cross and vanished.

On May 12, 1935, Marshal Jozef Piłsudski died. That day Sr. Faustina had a vision. She saw a certain soul being separated from its body amid terrible torments. In her diary, she did not mention whose soul it was, but that it was a person that was known worldwide. The vision had nothing in it of heavenly raptures. The mystic saw the souls of little children, similar to decaying corpses and terrible monsters, emerging from a swamp-like abyss loudly accusing the dying person. Apart from the monstrosities, a woman also emerged holding an apron full of tears, and she too was accusing the dying person. Sr. Faustina trembled all over, seeing that incredible scene. She understood how terrible the hour of judgment might be for a sinner. For at that hour all one's deeds would be revealed, and each of them would be witnesses at the Last Judgment. She saw them speak against the dying person. However, she thought that that soul would not be damned, but would have to atone for its deeds, suffering hellish torments, though with one difference: that its torments at some point would come to and end.

**A CELL**
(of Sr. Faustina's time) divided by partitions, at the Lithuanian Divine Mercy Center, in the only remaining convent building on Antakalnis Hill.

126

The next day, the nun told Fr. Sopoćko that she had seen Marshal Piłsudski dying and that he would avoid damnation thanks solely to the intercession of the Mother of Mercy. That was significant, as Piłsudski was not a religious man. Questions about the Faith did not concern him much, but he greatly venerated and respected Our Lady of Ostra Brama.

Sr. Faustina also had revelations about people who zealously did God's will on earth. Those who united their suffering with Christ's suffering on the Cross occupied a special place. She wrote that such souls were pure and innocent, who offered themselves up to God. They thus kept the world in existence and—as St. Paul wrote in his Letter to the Colossians—they completed what was lacking in Christ's afflictions for the sake of His body, that is, the Church. In another vision, Jesus Himself said of them that "the Heavenly Father looks upon them with special pleasure. They will be a marvel to Angels and men. Their number is very small. They are a defense for the world before the justice of the Heavenly Father and a means of obtaining mercy for the world. The love and sacrifice of these souls sustain the world in existence" (*Diary*, 367).

Sr. Faustina also had visions concerning Poland's future, about which she told Fr. Sopoćko. She foretold that very hard times would shortly come upon the country and that Poles would be taken away to the east and to the west. That happened several years later,

**TINY HUTS**.
"A few tiny huts, scattered about, make up the convent", was how Sr. Faustina described the convent on Antakalnis Hill, Vilnius. Only one hut has survived: the one in which the mystic lived.

127

**THE CATHEDRAL** of St. Stanislaw (bishop) and St. Wladyslaw.

**METROPOLITAN OF VILNIUS**, Archbishop Romuald Jałbrzykowski (1876–1955), sometimes heard Sr. Faustina's confessions, particularly when Fr. Michal Sopoćko was not in Vilnius. He did not conceal his skepticism with regard to the nun's revelations.

when World War II broke out and Nazi Germany and the Soviet Union invaded Poland. Sr. Faustina also said that one of Poland's most beautiful cities would be destroyed—like Sodom—for the sins that were committed there. When her confessor asked her about the sins for which it was to be punished, she replied that it was for killing unborn children. After the war, Fr. Sopoćko understood that it concerned Warsaw, which was turned into ruins during the Uprising.

At that time Faustina frequently prayed for Poland. At a certain moment, during prayer for her country before the Blessed Sacrament, a pain gripped her soul. She then—interceding to our Lady and all the saints—began to beseech Christ to bless Poland. She begged Christ not to look upon the sins of her countrymen but on the tears of children, the misery of little girls and boys suffering from cold and hunger. She besought Him, for the sake of those innocent beings, to grant the grace that she so desired for her country. She then saw Jesus, Who had tears in His eyes. Moved by her prayer, Christ said: "You see, My daughter, what great compassion I have for them. Know that it is they who uphold the world" (*Diary*, 286).

Soon, it turned out that Jesus had a new task for the Polish mystic. First, she heard (May 1935) His words in her soul: "You will prepare the world for My final

coming" (*Diary*, 429). Later (June 9, Pentecost) she received another message: "By your entreaties, you and your companions shall obtain mercy for yourselves and for the world" (*Diary*, 435). She was not certain that she had understood the Lord Jesus correctly. She wondered whether He wanted her to found a new congregation. Both Romuald Jałbrzykowski, archbishop of Vilnius, and Fr. Sopoćko advised her not to make any rash decisions and to wait patiently. Her uncertainty as to how she was to do God's will was a source of spiritual suffering for her.

Sr. Faustina desired to unite her will completely with God's will. She strove to fulfil in her life that which she said daily in the Our Father: "Thy will be done." She wrote in her diary (February 4, 1935): "From today on, my own will does not exist." And then she knelt down, and with a flourish, she crossed out what she had written, as if wanting to seal her submission to God's will. At that moment she heard a voice within her: "From today on, do not fear God's judgment for you will not be judged" (*Diary*, 374).

Faustina knew that God wanted a new congregation to be founded, one that would preach and entreat His will for the world. Jesus Himself had told her directly: "I desire that there be such a congregation" (*Diary*, 437). But she did not know whether she was to found it herself or to realize the mission in her present congregation. On the one hand, she felt incapable of forming a new congregation, and on the other, she could not imagine reconciling the new mission of preaching God's

**CHURCH OF ST. PETER AND ST. PAUL.** Sr. Faustina sometimes visited on Antakalnis Hill, Vilnius.

**STATUE OF ST. JOSEPH** from the chapel of the Congregation of the Sisters of Our Lady of Mercy, Antakalnis Hill, Vilnius. It is now in the Church of St. Peter and St. Paul.

129

**ST. MICHAL'S, VILNIUS.**
Fr. Sopoćko was its rector from June 1934 to November 1938.

130

mercy with the order's charism—that is, of looking after fallen girls. Invoked in her prayers, St. Ignatius of Loyola, founder of the Jesuits, told her that the rule could be applied in her congregation. But that did not dispel Faustina's doubts. Jesus told her that she should not make any decisions without the consent of her confessors. But they were not able to discern how the nun was to proceed. She herself had several visions of the location of the new convent, and she even drew up a rule for the proposed congregation. She wrote that in the new congregation there would be no distinction between the sisters, no mothers, no reverends, no venerables. All would be equal, irrespective of descent. However, she did not set up a new religious order.

On September 13, after Archbishop Jałbrzykowski had heard her confession, Sr. Faustina had a vision of an angel who had come to punish the world. She fervently began to pray for a postponement of the punishment, the words coming of their own accord. Suddenly she saw that the prayer was disarming the angel. The next day Jesus appeared to her and taught her to recite the prayer on the rosary: "First of all, you will say one OUR FATHER and [one] HAIL MARY and the I BELIEVE IN GOD. Then on the OUR FATHER beads you will say the following words: 'Eternal Father, I offer You the Body and Blood, Soul and Divinity of Your dearly beloved Son, Our Lord Jesus Christ, in atonement for our sins and those of the whole world.' On the HAIL MARY beads you will say the following words: 'For the sake of His sorrowful Passion have mercy on us and on the whole world.' In conclusion, three times you

**JÓZEF PIŁSUDSKI,** head of state.

**JÓZEF PIŁSUDSKI,** salutes Polish soldiers in front of Vilnius Cathedral.

131

**WARSAW DESTROYED.** Sr. Faustina's vision concerning the destruction of one of the most beautiful cities in Poland was fulfilled during World War II.

will recite these words: 'Holy God, Holy Mighty One, Holy Immortal One, have mercy on us and on the whole world' " (*Diary*, 476).

The prayer that Jesus had dictated to Faustina (September 14, 1935) is known as the Divine Mercy Chaplet. In subsequent revelations Christ told the mystic of the great graces that were connected with the prayer if it was trustfully said. Through the chaplet one can entreat anything that is in accord with God's will, though particular promises concern the dying, as one chaplet, said beside a dying person, is sufficient to obtain for them the grace of a happy and peaceful death, without fear and dread. Faustina entered Jesus' words on this subject in her diary: "At the hour of their death, I defend as My own glory every soul that will say this chaplet; or when others say it for a dying person, the pardon is the same. When (205) this chaplet is said by the bedside of a dying person, God's anger is

placated and unfathomable mercy envelops the soul" (*Diary*, 811). At some other time, our Savior told her: "Even if there were a sinner most hardened, if he were to recite this chaplet only once, he would receive grace from My infinite mercy" (*Diary*, 687).

In Vilnius, Jesus again demanded the establishment of the Divine Mercy Feast on the first Sunday after Easter: "On that day the very depths of My tender mercy are open. I pour out a whole ocean of graces upon those souls who approach the Fount of My Mercy. The soul that will go to Confession and receive Holy Communion shall obtain complete forgiveness of sins and punishment. On that day all the divine floodgates through which graces flow are opened. Let no soul fear to draw near to Me, even though its sins be as scarlet" (*Diary*, 699). At another time Christ complained to Faustina: "My Heart is sorrowful because even chosen souls do not understand the greatness of My mercy. Their relationship [with Me] is, in certain ways, imbued with mistrust. Oh, how much that wounds My Heart! Remember My Passion, and if you do not believe My words, at least believe My wounds" (*Diary*, 379).

**THE MYSTIC'S** prediction that Poles would shortly be transported to the east and west materialized soon after her death.

**SEAL CERTIFYING** that Fr. Sopoćko had crossed the Polish-Soviet border on August 6, 1947 .

A SOUL THAT ENCOUNTERS GOD

# Diary

# Diary

Though Sr. Faustina's life
abounded in many mystical
visions and revelations, her
stay in Vilnius was marked
by the mundane daily routine
of a convent enclosure. The
monotonous rhythm of convent
life meant that the days were
much alike, filled with the
same repetitive occupations:
prayer, work, and rest.

However, Sr. Faustina was not bored. She discovered many treasures in a life that, to an outsider, might well have seemed grey and monotonous. Boredom and dullness vanished when she looked at things through the eyes of faith. Then no two hours were alike. Morning graces were not granted again in the afternoon. Time passed, but was never the same. Each moment, a different experience, confirmed the spiritual truth that God never repeats Himself.

The superior of the convent in Vilnius, Mother Irena Krzyzanowska, emphasized that although Faustina had a very rich inner life, she was extraordinarily

**SR. FAUSTINA KOWALSKA**, the author of the most widely read work of 20th-century Christian mysticism.

137

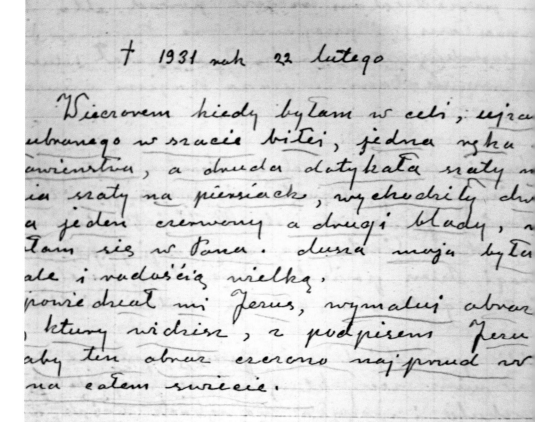

**A DIARY FRAGMENT**
where Sr. Faustina describes Jesus instructing her to paint an image of Him.

**SR. FAUSTINA**
kept her diary over a period of four years at the request of her confessor and spiritual director, Fr. Michał Sopoćko, who was the first person to read it.

humble outwardly, and she never made any sister feel that she herself was somehow exalted or privileged because of her relationship with Jesus. The mystic concealed her spiritual experiences from people, not sharing them with anyone. She did not seek people's admiration or recognition, but the favor of God alone. She compared herself to a little violet hidden in the grass, which, trodden on, forgetful of itself, gives off a pleasant fragrance.

In observing the modest gardener, busying herself daily with vegetable patches and flowerbeds, an outsider would have found it difficult to imagine that he had one of the greatest mystics in Church history before them. Yet, as Sr. Elzbieta Siepak, author of numerous works on St. Faustina Kowalska, wrote: "Under the cover of a grey and daily routine was hidden an extremely rich and colorful spiritual life, reaching the very summits of mysticism. Sr. Faustina, taught by Jesus,

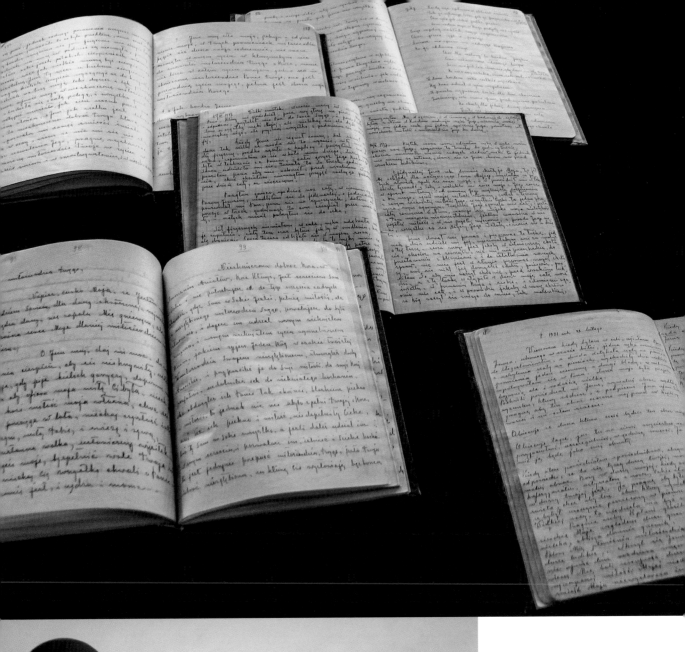

**BLOTTING PAD**
and ink.
Sr. Faustina used
these when
writing her diary.

139

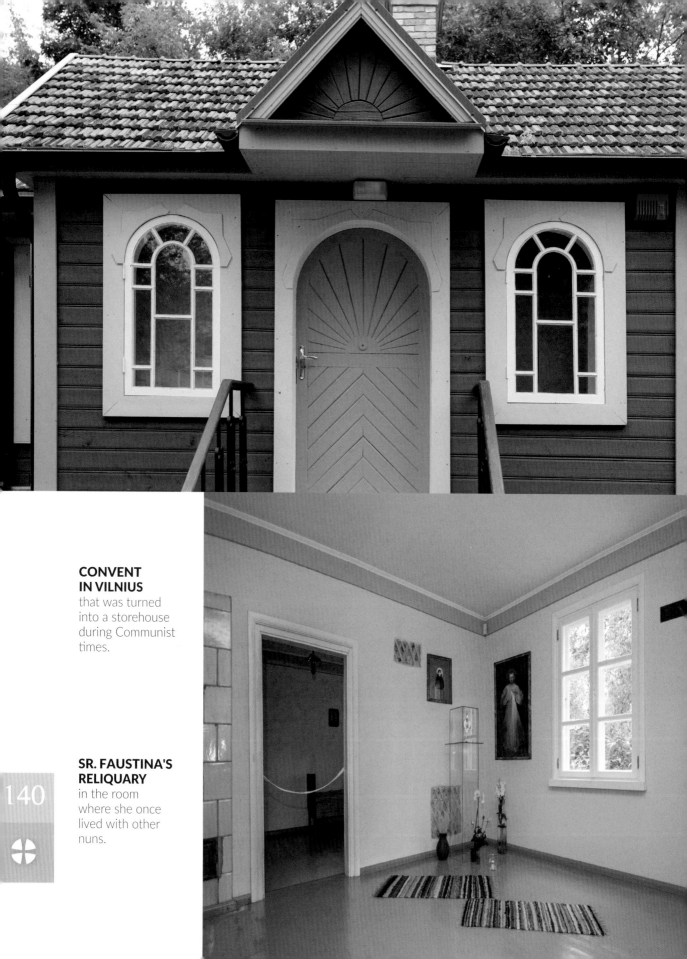

**CONVENT IN VILNIUS**
that was turned into a storehouse during Communist times.

**SR. FAUSTINA'S RELIQUARY**
in the room where she once lived with other nuns.

quickly discovered that the essence of human life on earth was to be united with God in love and that the greatness of man did not depend on exterior things—social rank, education, function, or even great works—but the extent to which one was united with God in love. This was the fundamental aim of her life, to which she was consistently able to subordinate all the affairs and events of daily life." The mystic wrote of her own soul, that neither revelations nor raptures nor gifts made it perfect. Only an intimate inner union with God could do that. She emphasized that sanctity was only possible when a person's will was perfectly united with the will of God.

The best testimony to her rich spiritual life is her diary, which consists of six handwritten notebooks that she kept for a period of four years. Fr. Sopoćko told her (1934) to keep notes, as he had noticed that Sr. Faustina's long confessions annoyed the sisters who had to wait in line. So he told the mystic only to accuse herself of her sins in confession and to write down all her spiritual experiences in a notebook, which she was to give him to read. At first, she thought that the task was beyond her, for she was aware that no words could express her experiences. However, she accepted that she had to be obedient to the will of God, passed on to

**ST. MICHAL'S, VILNIUS** was the first church to have the Merciful Jesus image permanently displayed (from April 4, 1938).

141

her by her spiritual director. So she began to write in her free time, secretly, without crossing out or correcting anything, just as her confessor had told her to do.

In the summer of 1934, Fr. Sopoćko went on a pilgrimage to the Holy Land. He wrote: "I was absent for several weeks, and Sr. Faustina did not confide her experiences to other confessors. On my return I learned that she had burned her diary in the following circumstances. Apparently an angel had appeared to her and told her to throw it into the fire, saying: 'You are writing nonsense and only exposing yourself and others to great tribulations. What have you got from this mercy? Why are you wasting time on writing about illusions? Burn it all, and you will be calmer and happier!'—and similar things. Sr. Faustina did not have anyone to advise her, so when the vision recurred she did what the supposed angel had told her to do. She realized later that she had done the wrong thing. She told me about everything and complied with my instruction to rewrite everything." For a penance, Fr. Sopoćko told her to reconstruct the destroyed manuscript. An effect of this is the diary's lack of chronological order, as Sr. Faustina interwove descriptions of current experiences with reconstructed notes.

**THIS STOVE** was used by Sr. Faustina; perhaps she burned the first version of her diary in it.

**SR. FAUSTINA'S DIARY** was made up of six notebooks, kept from 1934 to 1938, and another little notebook entitled *My Preparations for Holy Communion.*

*Od dziś nieistnieje wemnie wola własna*

*w chwili kiedy ukleklam, aby przekazalić wolę w...
...mi Pan korat, uslyszalam glos w duszy Twej, od dziś nie lękaj s...
Bożych, albowiem sądzenia nie będzien*

When reading Sr. Faustina's diary, Fr. Sopoćko, a discerning theologian, frequently stopped, amazed by the depth and pertinence of the formulations from the pen of a simple nun, one who had not even finished secondary school. He saw this as the best proof of the supernatural character of her revelations. After all, Faustina could not have thought up what God had said about Himself: "I am the Lord in My essence and am immune to orders or needs. If I call creatures into being—that is the abyss of My mercy" (*Diary*, 85).

Years later, he wrote of his most extraordinary penitent: "In coming to know Sr. Faustina better, I noted that the gifts of the Holy Spirit usually worked within her in a covert way, but also overtly at certain, quite frequent moments, partially imparting an intuition that quickly encompassed her soul, rousing impulses of love to noble, heroic acts of self-sacrifice and self-denial. The gifts

**CROSSED-OUT ENTRY IN FAUSTINA'S DIARY** dated February 4, 1934: "From today on, my own will does not exist."

# FR. MICHAŁ SOPOĆKO'S **DIARY**

**SR. FAUSTINA** was not the only one to keep personal notes on the spiritual life. Her confessor Fr. Michał Sopoćko intermittently kept a diary from the first years of his priesthood until his death. In this, the most personal of his works, he wrote much on Sr. Faustina and on the many years of effort to spread devotion to Divine Mercy.

This work, of an autobiographical and recollective nature, was not widely known for many years. It was first published in 2010 – thirty-five years after his death – through the efforts of Fr. Henryk Ciereszki, Fr. Sopoćko's biographer, and later an auxilliary bishop of Bialystok. As Archbishop Edward Ozorowski has noticed, the diary "gives one direct access to the writer's soul", from which there emerges "a living person: habits, weaknesses, character traits, but simultaneously a strong faith and Gospel zeal."

of knowledge, understanding, and wisdom were manifest most often, thanks to which Sr. Faustina clearly saw the nothingness of earthly things and the importance of suffering and humiliation. She came to know God's attributes directly, but most of all His infinite mercy."

In her diary Sr. Faustina wrote of the stirrings of her soul, and also of her relationship with the supernatural world: meetings with Jesus, Mary, saints, angels, or souls in purgatory. Though she began to take notes, with her spiritual director's instructions in mind, in time the purpose of the notes began to change. Jesus Himself explained this to her when she once saw Him leaning over her when she was writing. Christ asked: "My daughter, what are you writing?" (*Diary*, 1693). Sr. Faustina replied that she was writing about Him, of His presence in the Blessed Sacrament, of His inconceivable love and mercy toward people. Then

145

**THE PRIMATE OF POLAND**, Cardinal August Hlond, was very kindly disposed towards devotion to Divine Mercy. It was at his request that Fr. Michał Sopoćko wrote his first, profounder theological work on this subject.

Christ said to her: "Secretary of My most profound mystery, know that yours is an exclusive intimacy with Me. Your task is to write down everything that I make known to you about My mercy, for the benefit of those who, by (67) reading these things will be comforted in their souls and will have the courage to approach Me. I therefore want you to devote all your free moments to writing" (*Diary*, 1693).

Deeply moved by the immeasurable vastness of God's mercy, Sr. Faustina asked that she might, like His saints, extol and reflect one of His virtues. Of all God's attributes, she chose mercy. Like a hallmark, she wanted it to be impressed upon her heart and soul, both in this life and the next. She wrote that love is the measure of all our deeds. Only love gives value to what we do. It can change little, inconspicuous things into great things in the eyes of God. The purer one's love, the greater its disinterestedness and readiness to make sacrifices for others.

Jesus asked Faustina Kowalska for an act of pure mercy: "I desire that you make an offering of yourself for sinners and especially for those souls who have lost hope in God's mercy" (*Diary*, 308). On Holy Thursday (March 29, 1934) she wrote down an "Act of Oblation", which she had already made during her third probation period:

"Before heaven and earth, before all the choirs of Angels, before the Most Holy Virgin Mary, before all the Powers of heaven, I declare to the One Triune God that today, in union with Jesus Christ, Redeemer of souls, I make a voluntary offering of myself for the conversion of sinners, especially for those souls who have lost hope in God's mercy. This offering consists in my accepting, with total subjection to God's will, all the sufferings, fears and terrors with which sinners are filled. In return, I give them all the consolations which my soul receives from my communion with God. In a word, I offer everything for them: Holy Masses, Holy Communions, penances, mortifications, prayers. I do not fear the blows, blows of divine justice, because I am united with Jesus. O my God, in this way I want to make amends to You for the souls that do not trust in Your goodness. I hope against all hope in the ocean of Your mercy. My Lord and my God, my portion—my portion forever, I do not base this act of oblation on my own strength, but on the strength that flows from the merits of Jesus Christ. I will daily repeat this act of self-oblation by pronouncing the following prayer which You Yourself have taught me, Jesus: 'O Blood and Water which gushed forth from the Heart of Jesus as a Fount of Mercy for us, I trust in You!'

[Signed] S. M. Faustina of the Blessed Sacrament, Holy Thursday, during Holy Mass, March 29, 1934" (*Diary*, 309).

The congregation had a custom where sisters drew lots on New Year's Day for a patron who was to look after them throughout the coming year—on January 1, 1935, Sr. Faustina pulled out a card with the words "Most Blessed Eucharist" (*Diary*, 360).

Sr. Faustina did not have to wait long for the effects of the act of oblation. She began to experience the states of sinners, whose suffering she had taken on herself. Her soul became arid, restless, and full of torments; distrust and despair stole into her heart, curses and blasphemies filled her mind. The nun steadfastly endured that state, knowing that she was thus helping hardened sinners. In addition there were humiliations; for example, she sometimes had to eat dinner while kneeling on the floor (she received this penance whenever she accused herself of an infidelity or a fall). But she humbly carried out the superior's orders.

**BERNARDINE CONVENT,** Vilnius, where Fr. Sopoćko was the nuns' chaplain.

147

**EXHIBITION IN ŁAGIEWNIKI**, dedicated to Sr. Faustina, where the *Diary* manuscript was first exhibited as were publications of it in many languages.

One day Sr. Faustina told Fr. Sopoćko of the great difficulties he was to experience in connection with his stay at the Church of St. Michael. Those difficulties increased until they culminated in January 1936, when the priest decided to ask her to pray for him. Years later he recalled: "To my great surprise, that very same day all my difficulties vanished, like a soap bubble. Sr. Faustina informed me that she had taken my suffering on herself and that—on that day—she had suffered as never before in her life. When she was in the chapel asking the Lord Jesus for help, she heard: 'You yourself undertook to suffer for him. Are you cringing now? I allowed but a part of his suffering to touch you.' At that point she told me—very precisely— what the cause of my difficulties was, which was apparently communicated to her supernaturally. The precision was very striking, the more so in that she herself could not have known of the details in any way. There were several similar occurrences."

Sr. Faustina wrote in her diary that, if angels were to be capable of being jealous of us, then they would envy our suffering. For the one who suffers can unite his suffering with Christ's Passion on the Cross and thereby participate in the work of the world's redemption. But angels could yet more envy people the Eucharist, that is, the reception of Holy Communion, a real fusion of one's own body with Christ's Body. When, after a Mass, some sisters told Sr. Faustina that she was carrying herself royally, she replied that after Communion she really felt like a queen, as royal Blood flowed within her. She acknowledged that she drew all her strength to carry out her mission from the Eucharist, in which there was a most personal and intimate meeting with God. Toward the end of her life, she

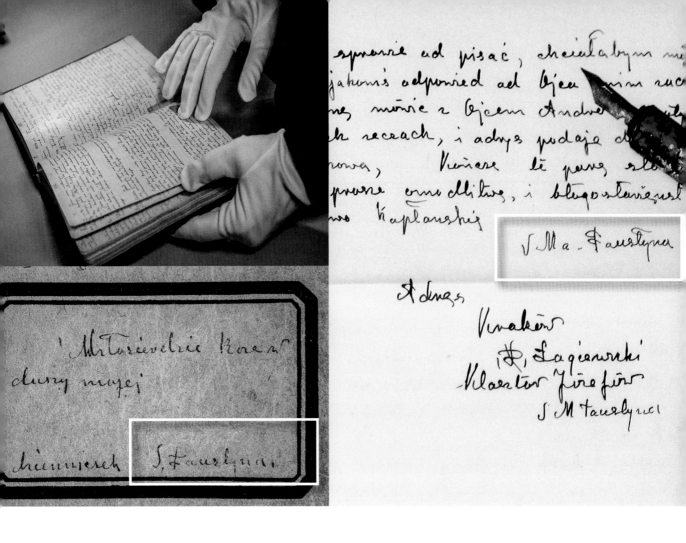

actually wrote that all that was good in her was due to Holy Communion, which she received as often as possible, and which had completely transformed her inner self.

Sr. Faustina often tangibly felt Christ's real presence in the Eucharist. She experienced that which theologians call a Eucharistic ecstasy, that is, a mystical union with God in the Blessed Sacrament. After receiving Communion, she repeatedly felt Jesus' distinct presence in her soul for quite some time. This did not hamper her in her daily duties, even in dealing with matters that required special care and attention. She wrote in her diary that Jesus accompanied her everywhere, that she went to work and recreation with Him, rejoiced with Him, and suffered with Him. His company meant that she did not feel alone, abandoned. She noticed that not solely a spiritual union, but also a physical one, was accomplished in the Eucharist.

Fr. Michal Sopoćko repeatedly asked himself this question: "What am I to make of Sr. Faustina and her revelations?" He even tried to draw up a profile of her, taking into account various aspects of her personality:

**SR. FAUSTINA'S** letter to Fr. Sopoćko, written in Łagiewniki and sent to Vilnius.

**THE DIVINE MERCY CHAPLET** that was first published by Fr. Sopoćko in a booklet entitled *Christ, King of Mercy* (Kraków, 1937).

**SR. FAUSTINA** often asked her superiors to allow her to wear a hair shirt or a penitent's belt.

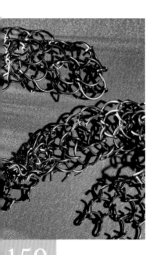

150

"Regarding her natural disposition, she was completely stable, without a sign of psychoneurosis or hysteria. Naturalness and simplicity characterized her relations both with the sisters in the congregation and with strangers. There was no artificiality or theatricality in her, no affectation or any desire to draw attention to herself. On the contrary, she strived not to stand out in anything and spoke about her inner experiences to no one, apart from her confessor and her superiors. Her emotionality was normal, kept on a tight rein by her will, not easily manifesting itself in changeable moods and emotions. She was not subject to depressions, or annoyance in setbacks, which she bore calmly, subjecting herself to God's will.

"Intellectually, she was prudent, marked by common sense about things, even though she had virtually no education: she was barely able to read and write without making mistakes. She gave her companions pertinent advice when they turned to her, and I myself tried her several times by suggesting certain doubts, which she rightly resolved. She had a colorful imagination, but not an overactive one....

"Morally, she was completely sincere, without the least exaggeration or sign of falsehood. She always spoke the truth, though at times it caused her distress. ...

"As to supernatural virtues, she was making evident progress. Indeed, from the beginning, I saw in her the consolidated and tried virtues of purity, humility, zeal, obedience, poverty, as well as love of God and neighbor, but one could easily note their gradual growth, particularly towards the end of a life of increasing love for God, which she revealed in her poems.

"As for Sr. Faustina's revelations, there is nothing that would oppose the faith or morals or that concern the debatable opinions of theologians. On the contrary, all aims at a better understanding and love of God."

News that Sr. Faustina's mother—Marianna—was dying reached Vilnius in February 1935. The nun received permission from her superiors to go to Glogowiec. It was her first and only visit to her home village since entering the congregation. The mystic prayed for her dying mother throughout the journey. On arriving, she heard that the doctor had no hope of her getting well. But her mother recovered during Faustina's several days in Glogowiec. She outlived her daughter by almost thirty years. The nun also visited the little church in Swinice Warckie, where she had been baptized and received her First Communion and where, during prayer, she heard Jesus: "My chosen one, I will give you even greater graces that you may be the witness of My infinite mercy throughout all eternity" (*Diary*, 400).

At that time Sr. Faustina was seriously ill. When she had collapsed in the convent garden (August 12, 1934) and a doctor was called, some of the nuns did

not really believe that she was ill. But the doctor declared that Faustina's condition was very serious, and Fr. Sopoćko gave her Extreme Unction. The mystic recovered from the collapse, but she remained very weak. Medical examinations revealed that she had tuberculosis, and it was at a very advanced stage. The Mother General Michaela Moraczewska decided to relieve Faustina of all her onerous duties and to move her from Vilnius to a place where she would have better medical care.

During the last night before her departure from Vilnius, an older sister, Antonina Grejwul, almost seventy, of Latvian descent, approached Sr. Faustina. "After confession I was restless and doubtful as to whether the Lord Jesus had forgiven me. Crying, I asked Sr. Faustina to pray for me", she recalled. Sr. Antonina had been "suffering inwardly" for several years, as it seemed to her "that all her confessions had been bad ones". She fervently asked the younger sister to ask Jesus whether He had forgiven her. The mystic kept her word and heard a voice in her soul during prayer: "Tell her that her disbelief wounds My heart more than the sins she committed" (*Diary*, 628). When Sr. Antonina learned of this, "she wept like a child."

On March 21, 1936, Sr. Faustina finally left the city that was so closely connected with her mission.

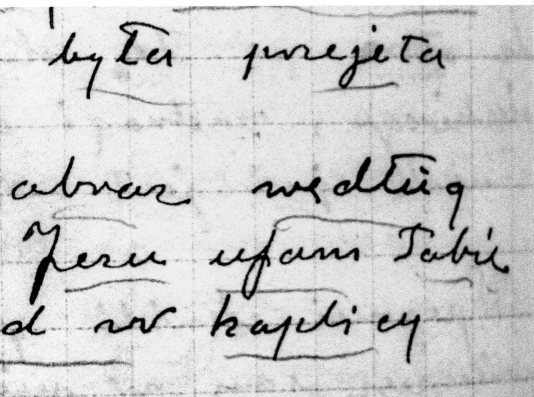

**A LITTLE PICTURE OF JESUS**. Sr. Faustina gave it to a nun from her own congregation – Sr. Antonina Grejwul.

**JESUS, I TRUST IN YOU**. These words often appeared in Sr. Faustina's writings like a refrain.

151

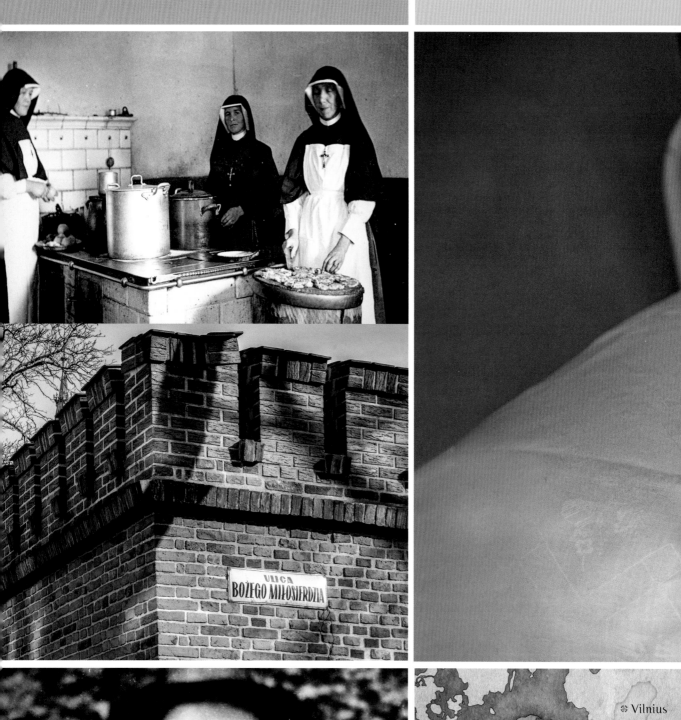

ULICA
BOŻEGO MIŁOSIERDZIA

Vilnius

POLAND

Derdy    Warsaw
         Walendów

Kraków

# Illness

# CHAPTER 9

# Illness

She recalled in her diary (March 21, 1936) that a bright angel accompanied her on the journey. He was constantly with her on the train. She also saw an angel standing on every church that they passed by—they, however, emanated a paler light than her companion, who was invisible to other people. She noticed that the spirits guarding the churches bowed to the spirit that was protecting her.

**TRAIN JOURNEY.** Sr. Faustina saw angels on church roofs during her train journey from Vilnius to Warsaw.

This angel vanished when she knocked on the convent door. Sr. Faustina stayed but four days in the capital. During that time she talked to the superior general, Mother Michaela Moraczewska, about founding a new religious order. The superior said that that type of work required a lot of prudence in spiritual discernment and recommended that her subordinate remain in the congregation

155

and continue to listen intently to God's inspirations. On March 25, Faustina left for the convent in Walendów, near Warsaw, where she had already been (November, 1932).

Sr. Faustina spent several weeks in Walendów. As a sister of the second choir she did simple physical work there. Other sisters recalled that she did all her duties without taking off her habit. One day, when she was cleaning the refectory, one of the sisters asked her why she had not changed into overalls or into some other working clothes. She replied that she had not entered the order to then take off her habit. Hence some of the sisters referred to Faustina as a "woman of fashion", and the like. But in reality she was characterized by a great love for the religious attire, a sign of absolute dedication to her vocation. She once said to a future nun, Sr. Romana, who was still discerning her vocation: "Were people to know what a convent was, they would climb over the walls to get in."

**CONVENT IN WALENDÓW.** Sr. Faustina spent several weeks there in 1936.

**THE NUNS**
run an orphanage and a kindergardten in Walendów.

157

It was in Walendów that Sr. Faustina met Sr. Beata Piekut, only two years younger than the mystic, who had been delegated there from Warsaw for just one month. Sr. Beata was certain that she would be back in the capital by Easter (April 12, 1936), but Sr. Faustina corrected her. Sr. Piekut recalls: "I remember that it was on March 25, a bright, sunny day. I was gazing through the window, conjecturing about the coming Easter. Then Faustina came up to me and asked: 'Why is Sister so sad?' I told her of my longing for Warsaw, where I was to have stayed longer. And to that, she said: 'But why? After all, Sister will not leave here in a hurry.' 'So, am I to die here?' I angrily snapped back. 'No, but Sister will stay here somewhat longer than Sister had planned. Whereas I, in contrast to Sister, shall not be here long . . . ,' I heard in reply. 'I suppose Sister is playing at being some sort of prophet'—I tried to break off the dialogue. 'It is not possible that I am to stay in Walendów any longer, though I was delegated only for a month, while Sister wants to leave us in a hurry despite the fact that Sister came here for good?!' 'Perhaps it would be better for Sister to leave, but the Lord Jesus will reward Sister,' she said calmly. That was too much for me. I am not hiding

**SIDE DOOR,**
convent chapel,
Walendów.

**GARDEN
PATH,**
Walendów. The
sisters erected
a cross on this
path.

the fact that she made me angry, but, at the same time, what she had said interested me greatly. Her prophecy intrigued me. How could she know what was to happen, since the mother general had not made any further decisions regarding me? It turned out that she was right. On Good Friday, I received a note from the mother general, which said that she was very sorry that she could not recall me from Walendów and that she would explain why after Easter." In the end Sr. Beata Piekut remained in Walendów for the next ten years.

During Holy Week of 1936—while in Walendów—Sr. Faustina wrote a letter to Fr. Sopoćko in Vilnius. She confided her spiritual experiences to him: "As Father knows, I am still communing interiorly with the Lord Jesus. Jesus is not sparing me His light; He is granting me a more profound knowledge of Him. I feel a strange inner power urging me to act, which occasions an indescribable

**SR. BEATA PIEKUT** met Faustina Kowalska in Walendów (1936). She was the vice-postulator for Sr. Faustina's beatification process.

**RUNNING THEIR FARM** demanded a lot of work from the sisters. They had a car, which was a sensation in those days.

Zamierzam wydać obrazek Miłosierdzia Bożego, jeżeli uzyskam aprob
tę Arcypasterza. Przypominam, że Siostra mówiła mi o nowennie czy te
Koronce, a może o innej modlitwie, jaką nauczył Siostrę Pan Jezus.Ch
bym ją umieścić na odwrotnej stronie obrazka, by w taki sposób wzbud
u większej ilości ludzi ufność w Miłosierdzie Boże i pobudzić ogół d
szczególniejszej czci Pana Boga w tym Jego najwyższym przymiocie. Pr
bym tedy, by Siostra była łaskawa przesłać mi odpis tej nowenny czy
ki albo modlitwy i to możliwie wkrótce.

Jakkolwiek ufam mocno, że Siostra wyzdrowieje, o co się modlę, al
wszelki wypadek proszę w jakikolwiek sposób zapewnić i zabezpieczyć
pamiętnik od zniszczenia. Chciałbym go mieć, jeżeli jest taka wola B
a może go kto inny otrzyma. W każdym razie proszę dokładnie podkreśl
wszystko to, co według Siostry było wyraźnie pochodzenia Bożego, szc
że to, co się odnosi do owego święta i do zgromadzenia. Jeżeli te r
są istotnie pochodzenia Bożego, mamy wielki obowiązek je szanować i
nie wszystko wypełniać.

Na prośbę Siostry o swojem zdrowiu donoszę, że do cierpień ducho
przyłączyły się i fizyczne, które czasami przykuwają mię do łóżka. T
czuję się lepiej i przystępuję do pracy normalnej. Cierpienia fizycz
duchowe bardzo są nam potrzebne, dlatego winniśmy je pokornie i z wd
nością przyjmować, za nie dziękować Miłosierdziu Bożemu oraz prosić

agony to arise in my soul. But I would not change the agony for all the world, for God's love caused it.

"I feel as if but one thing links me with the world; that is, my desire for all souls to know God and His great mercy!

"I would like to mention that I experienced Palm Sunday in a strange way. Jesus gave me an insight into the feelings of His divine and merciful Heart. I saw many things when the Lord Jesus rode into Jerusalem.

"On the same day, I saw the congregation very clearly, its exterior and interior development. Many things are not a secret to me. I am waiting patiently for the hour, which is close, to set to work. . . .

"One more thing, Father. I clearly see that there will be not only a male and female congregation, but also a large association of lay people, to whom all can belong and recount God's mercy through deeds, in showing mercy to one another."

When in Walendów, Sr. Faustina not only experienced Palm Sunday in an unusual and intense way, but also the whole of the Paschal Triduum. On Good Friday, she had a vision of Christ on the Cross. At three o'clock, she saw the dying Jesus, when He said, "I thirst." At that moment she saw two rays emanate

**SR. BORGIA TICHY**, Sr. Faustina's superior in Vilnius.

**CONVENT OF THE CONGREGATION** of the Sisters of Our Lady of Mercy in Derdy.

161

# FR. JÓZEF **ANDRASZ, S.J.**

**APART FROM** Fr. Sopoćko, Fr. Jozef Andrasz, S. J., (1891–1963) had the most influence on Sr. Faustina. He felt that he had a religious vocation very early in his life. He entered the Jesuit Order at the age of fifteen. After being ordained in 1919 he worked as a writer and editor at the Jesuit publishing house in Kraków. He then initiated a multi-volume series, Interior Life Library, wherein he translated many works into Polish. He also wrote several books, one of which, *Together with a Priest*, saw twenty editions.

From 1932 he was the permanent confessor at the Congregation of the Sisters of Our Lady of Mercy in Łagiewniki, Kraków. During the last few years of Sr. Faustina's life he was her spiritual director. After the mystic's death he was involved in realizing her message about the devotion to Divine Mercy. Adolf Hyla's painting of the Merciful Jesus arose under his supervision, which is still venerated in Łagiewniki. He died in Kraków at the age of seventy-two.

from His side—red and pale—such as in the picture. During Easter she also experienced a mystical union with Christ. No words could express what she felt when she was so closely united with God.

Sr. Faustina was next sent to Derdy, only a little more than a half mile from Walendów. The order had a house there, situated in a forest. On May 10, 1936, the mystic wrote about it in a letter to Fr. Sopoćko: "Our little house in Derdy is indeed like a house from a fairy tale. It is surrounded by a forest, and there are no buildings nearby—peace and quiet. Everything helps the spirit to concentrate. Only the birds of the forest break the silence, praising their God through their twittering. I see God in everything that surrounds me." The property in Derdy was donated to the Congregation of the Sisters of Our Lady of Mercy in 1881 by Countess Maria Tyzenhauz-Przedziecka. The nuns initially set up a rest center there for the sisters and girls from the house in Warsaw. In time, however,

**THE CHURCH TOWER**
in Walendów stands high over the flat Mazovian landscape.

163

**THE KITCHEN IN DERDY.** Sr. Faustina's main task in Derdy was to prepare meals for several sisters and over 30 wards.

a separate House of Mercy arose, where several dozen girls lived, though it was formally a branch of the convent house in Walendów.

In Derdy, Sr. Faustina was entrusted with the duty of cooking meals for several sisters and more than thirty wards. Because of her tuberculosis, the superiors decided not to burden her with onerous work. That is why she saw her stay at that convent as a rest. In a letter to Fr. Sopoćko, she wrote: "I have such a trivial duty that it seems to be a rest rather than a duty. I look after the kitchen and the larder, and I have not the least difficulty with this duty. I prepare dinners for seven sisters and thirty-six schoolchildren. I have a lot of time for everything, and I have been ordered to sleep for two hours in the afternoons. I do some of my spiritual exercises such as the Rosary in the forest; at the same time, I deeply inhale fresh air." The superior of the convent in Walendów at that time, Mother Serafina Kukulska, remembers Faustina's stay very well. She recalled that the mystic "had a girl to help her in the kitchen, a neophyte of a very disagreeable

**CONVENT IN DERDY**. Chronologically the Derdy convent was the congregation's third house in Poland; it was built after the Warsaw and Kraków convents. This corridor leads to the convent chapel.

165

disposition with whom no one, anywhere, wanted to work. It was precisely that same girl, who worked with Faustina, who changed beyond recognition. Such was Sr. Faustina's quiet but godly influence on that sinful soul."

It seemed that Walendów and Derdy would be beneficial for Faustina's health. But that was not the case; her tuberculosis got worse. Her superiors decided to move her to the convent in Łagiewniki, where the conditions were better. So she left Derdy (May 11, 1936) and made her way to Kraków. In Łagiewniki, she began work in the greenhouse and then in the garden. She had such huge crops, several times larger than those of the other nuns, that it caused a sensation in the whole convent. Sr. Klemensa Buczek recalled that she could pick eighty tomatoes from one of Faustina's plants, and over three hundred pounds of strawberries were picked daily from her relatively small strawberry patch.

At that time the issue of God's mercy gave Fr. Sopoćko no peace. Years later, he recalled: "In the middle of April 1936, Sr. Faustina, at the order of the superior general, departed for Walendów, and then for Kraków, while I seriously thought over the notion of Divine Mercy; I began to seek confirmation that it was God's greatest attribute—as Sr. Faustina had said—in the works of the Church Fathers, for I could not find anything on the subject in the works of later theo-

**CONVENT KITCHEN**
in Derdy. This kitchen has changed in appearance since the time Sr. Faustina worked here.

166

✤

logians. It was with great joy that I came across similar expressions in the works of St. Fulgentius and St. Ildefonsus, but especially in the works of St. Thomas Aquinas and St. Augustine, who—commenting on the Psalms—wrote at length on Divine Mercy and saw it as God's greatest attribute. From then on I did not have any serious doubts as to the supernatural nature of Sr. Faustina's revelations. From time to time I began to write articles on the subject in theological periodicals, substantiating, rationally and liturgically, the need for a feast of Divine Mercy on the first Sunday after Easter."

As far as understanding the truths of the Faith was concerned, the professor of theology acknowledged how much he owed to Sr. Faustina, the uneducated nun from the second choir: "There are truths of Holy Faith that one sort of knows, and often recalls but neither understands them well nor lives them. It was so in my case as to the truth about God's mercy. I had thought about that truth so many times in meditations, particularly on retreats, spoken so many times about it in homilies, and repeated it in liturgical prayers, but I never went into its essence, nor into its significance for the spiritual life; I particularly did not understand, and, for the time being, could not agree, that Mercy was the supreme attribute of the Creator, the Redeemer, the Sanctifier. So it was necessary for a simple and saintly soul, closely united with

**A LITTLE PICTURE**
of the Holy Family of Nazareth, which Sr. Faustina gave Sr. Jolanta on the occasion of her perpetual vows (April 30, 1927).

167

**SIX NOTEBOOKS**
that make up the Diary.

**THE TITLE PAGE**
of one of the notebooks of the Diary.

**PRAYER BOOK,**
rosary, and Diary kept by Sr. Faustina.

God, to, as I believe, at God's inspiration, tell me about it, and motivate me to study the subject, to research and meditate on it." In another place, he wrote: "The intuition of a simple nun, barely familiar with the catechism, was, in such subtle matters, so pertinent, and so in accord with the psychology of contemporary society, that it cannot be explained but by supernatural action and enlightenment. Many a theologian, after years of study, would not be able to resolve such difficulties even remotely as well and as easily as Sr. Faustina."

At that time the Jesuit Fr. Jozef Andrasz, whom the mystic had known from Kraków, even before her perpetual vows, became her new spiritual director and confessor. She highly valued his ministry, calling him a "spiritual leader". or a "luminous pillar", who lit up her path to a close union with God. Jesus called him

a "friend of His Heart, His substitute, a veil" behind which He was hidden. He declared to the nun that that He Himself had chosen him, so that she might not go astray in her spiritual quest.

When in Kraków, Sr. Faustina kept in contact with Fr. Sopoćko by mail. At that time he was still trying to spread the Divine Mercy devotion in Vilnius. He particularly sought to establish the Divine Mercy Feast in the Church. To that end he wrote and published (1936) a treatise entitled *God's Mercy*, which he sent to the Polish bishops gathered at a synod in Czestochowa. But his efforts had little effect, for it was a time when the Holy See had banned the establishment of new feasts. Fr. Sopoćko tried again during the Marian Congress in Vilnius (July 1937). He suggested that a resolution be sent to the Vatican requesting the establishment of a Divine Mercy Feast, but the Archbishop of Vilnius, Romuald Jalbrzykowski, did not agree to it. Fr. Sopoćko also tried to interest the papal nuncio, Archbishop Francesco Cortes, who happened to be in Vilnius, but his appeal did not meet with understanding. That same year, Sr. Faustina's confessor published the treatise *On the Idea of Divine Mercy in the Liturgy*, which substantiated that the devotion was not at all new, as one could find many references to it in liturgical books.

The decision of the Vilnius chancery, which refused him an imprimatur for chaplets, novenas, and litanies on Divine Mercy, was a painful blow to Fr.

**SACRED HEART OF JESUS CHURCH.** Sr. Faustina took part in the Sacred Heart of Jesus procession at this Kraków church (June 1936).

**DEDICATION** of a memorial plaque on the building of the former Cebulski printing house in Kraków (where the first booklet of Sr. Faustina's prayers was printed) by Archbishop Marek Jędraszewski on September 28, 2017.

*Jezu, ufam Tobie!*
**CHRYSTUS—KRÓL MIŁOSIERDZIA!**

Koronka do Miłosierdzia Bożego
*(do prywatnego odmawiania na różańcu)*
Na początku: Ojcze .. Zdrowaś... Wierzę. .

*Na dużych paciorkach:* Ojcze przedwieczny, ofiaruję Ci ciało i Krew, Duszę i Bóstwo Najmilszego Syna Twojego a Pana naszego Jezusa Chrystusa na ubłaganie za grzechy nasze i świata całego.

*Na małych paciorkach:* Dla Jego bolesnej męki miej miłosierdzie dla nas i świata całego. *(10 razy)*

*Na zakończenie:* Święty Boże, Święty mocny, Święty Nieśmiertelny, zmiłuj się nad nami! *(3 razy)*

L. 671/37.
Za pozwoleniem Władzy Duchowne

Wydał: J. Cebulski — Kraków, Szewska 22

**CONVENT DOOR** of the Congregation of the Sisters of Our Lady of Mercy in Łagiewniki.

**BLACK HABIT** worn by the sisters of the Congregation of the Sisters of Our Lady of Mercy.

**BLOTTING-PAD** in the Sr. Faustina Museum, Łagiewniki.

Sopoćko. But the priest was not discouraged. He requested permission from the Kraków chancery, which he received, for a little book of prayers based on Sr. Faustina's revelations, first published in 1937. It was entitled *Christ, King of Mercy*, and it was published by Jozef Cebulski, whose publishing house was at 22 Szewska Street, Kraków. The mystic and her superior, Mother Irena Krzyzanowska, visited the publishing house on September 27, 1937. She wrote of the visit in her diary. She mentions that she had been in the printing house, and that she saw a Divine Mercy prayer booklet, as well as a reproduction of the Merciful Jesus image. She did not hide her delight in seeing, for the first time, that her mission was now in the open, and that a mass circulation would reach many.

Returning from Cebulski's printing house, they decided to go to Holy Mass at Poland's most famous Gothic church, that is, the eighteenth-century St. Mary's Basilica. During the Eucharist, God gave Sr. Faustina to know what a great work had just started. She saw a great multitude of souls, souls who would be saved thanks to the Divine Mercy devotion. At the same time, she felt unworthy of being called to such a momentous task by God Himself, a task concerning the whole of humanity. She began a conversation with Him, thanking Him for inviting her to such an extraordinary work, and also for allowing her to see its

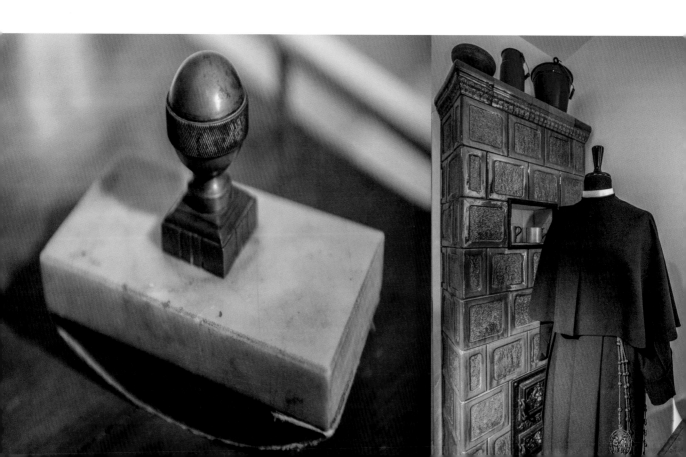

future fruits. So she immersed herself in a prayer of thanksgiving, contemplating God's generosity and His fidelity to His promises.

In the period between the world wars, the Congregation of the Sisters of Our Lady of Mercy was of a contemplative-active character. The nuns spent most of their time in convents, going out very rarely, mainly to see to urgent matters. It is for that reason that we have very little information as to Sr. Faustina's stays outside convent walls. But there were situations when nuns went out together—for example, to participate in solemn processions and devotions. The Jesuits at the Sacred Heart of Jesus Church (26 Kopernik Street, Kraków) organized an annual Sacred Heart of Jesus procession. In her diary, Sr. Faustina wrote of taking part in such a ceremony (June 19, 1936). Participating in the procession, she suddenly saw two rays emanate from the Blessed Sacrament, as in her vision in Plock, and like the rays in the Merciful Jesus image.

The issue that takes up considerable space in Sr. Faustina's diary is Christ's instructions concerning the new congregation that she was to found. This issue

**INTERIOR OF THE FORMER CONVENT** infirmary where Sr. Faustina died (October 5, 1938) ), and the boards from the coffin of St Faustina.

171

**BASILICA INTERIOR.**
Sr. Faustina prayed at the Basilica of the Assumption of the Blessed Virgin in Kraków (September, 1937).

is the main source of the young nun's doubts, anxieties, and suffering. For a long time she could not reconcile two two types of revelation from Jesus she had received. In the first type, Jesus expressed His desire for a new congregation, which would proclaim and entreat God's mercy for the world. In the second type, He said that His will was that Faustina should remain in her mother congregation. Sr. Faustina grappled with this problem over the last four years of her life, and neither Fr. Sopoćko nor Fr. Andrasz were able to help her in this. She felt as if she was on a cross, stretched out between heaven and earth, torn between the vow of obedience, and the inspirations from her revelations. She but wanted to do God's will, but she was unable to discern it with certainty. Hence she experienced an interior struggle, the source of much spiritual suffering.

On May 4, 1937, during a discussion with the superior general, Sr. Faustina decided to ask for consent to leave the congregation. Mother Michaela Moraczewska described the occasion: "Before setting out on a visit to the Kraków house [1937], I asked my Councilors whether it would be advisable to permit Sr. Faustina to leave the congregation were she to remain anxious. My advisers thought that it would be. We would be sorry to lose such a good and eager sister, but we were afraid of going against the Will of God. I found her to be calm, but when she came for a discussion she at once renewed her request. With our decision in mind, I consented straightaway. I noticed that this surprised her. She asked if I would take care of all the necessary formalities. To my reply that I would not know how to justify her desire to leave the congregation just because of the revelations, she asked if she could go and see Fr. Andrasz, who, as it turned out, was temporarily absent. Of course, I consented, and we parted."

Shortly after the discussion, Mother Michaela went away for several days to the order's house in Rabka. On returning to Łagiewniki she was surprised to find Sr. Faustina still doing her duties, as if nothing had happened, and nothing pointed to her leaving the order. The superior invited the nun for a conversation and asked her what had happened. "To which she replied, sincerely, and in all simplicity, that the moment I had allowed her to act freely, she felt as if she were in a black chasm, completely alone, abandoned, unable to take a step, so that she gave up the idea of leaving the congregation. We talked a little more about the subject, sincerely, and from that time on the matter has not been raised between us. Today, it seems to me that that sudden darkness in her soul was the sign we had been waiting for from God." Everything points to the fact that Sr. Faustina

**SISTERS AT HARVEST TIME.** Nuns who normally had other daily duties also helped in the fields when it was necessary, for example, during haymaking.

saw this in the same way, as from that time on she did not make any effort to leave her order.

That did not mean that the subject of a new congregation ceased to appear in her diary. On June 27, 1937, she noted that God gave her to discern His will as to the Divine Mercy apostolate. She saw that it would have three aspects. First, consecrated souls, separated from the world, were to pray for Divine Mercy for the whole of humanity, and for blessings for priests. Second, people who were to link prayers with acts of mercy, particularly the protection of children's souls from evil. Third, people who were to be immersed in the world, not bound by any vows, but who would lead a life of prayer and do acts of mercy.

As Sr. Elzbieta Siepak wrote: "It is only within the context of the work so understood, which is one, but of three 'aspects,' that one can explain the divergence of Sr. Faustina's visions concerning the localization of the future congregation. Once, it was to be a small church, with a convent of twelve cells

**CONVENT GREENHOUSES** and garden in Kraków. St. Faustina worked there from 1936 to 1937.

near it (*Diary*, 563); another time, the walls of a building without doors or windows (*Diary*, 559); next, a small chapel in which Fr. Sopoćko was giving Holy Communion to six sisters (*Diary*, 613); and then a convent that looked after children of five to eleven years of age, protecting them from evil (*Diary*, 765). Yet another time, she saw a convent where everything was poor and very scanty, but there was a great spirit there (*Diary*, 892). In the last vision connected with this subject, Sr. Faustina, looking at the convent of the new congregation, saw a large and spacious building: 'The persons living in this convent were still wearing lay clothes, but a thoroughly religious spirit reigned there, . . .' (*Diary*, 1154). That last vision directly preceded a complete description of the structure of this one work of mercy: contemplative congregations, people from various institutions of consecrated life, and others, who, through prayer and deed, participate in Jesus' work of mercy."

**SISTERS WITH THEIR CHARGES** outside the convent in Łagiewniki during recreation time.

175

POLAND

Kraków

Rabka

# Dying to Oneself

# CHAPTER 10

# Dying to Oneself

Sr. Faustinas desire to be totally united with her beloved God was fulfilled in a way that even the greatest Christian mystics did not experience. The modest nun was granted a spiritual union with the Holy Trinity, which she described in her diary.

**STAINED-GLASS WINDOW**
in the hospital chapel, Prądnik, Kraków.

God pervaded the whole of her being, and enlightened her mind as to His Essence. At the same time, He allowed her to participate in His inner life, so that she could, as if from within, commune with the Holy Trinity. She saw the Three Divine Persons, though it was evident to her that They are of One Essence; none greater or lesser, more beautiful or more perfect, but All are One. Their bond—Love. It was precisely through love that Sr. Faustina could come to know God, be united with Him. She wrote that whoever communicates with One of the Three Persons, simultaneously communicates with All Three. The saints in heaven experience this most fully. Sr. Faustina saw the Most Holy Trinity as the Creator of all

**PHOTOGRAPHS OF SR. FAUSTINA**
from the last years of her life show ever-more-sunken cheeks—a sign of advancing tuberculosis.

179

**VISION OF SAINTS**

Sr. Faustina not only saw Jesus and Mary in visions, but she also saw certain saints. During one of those visions she saw Polish saints—Stanislaw Kostka, Andrzej Bobola, and Prince Kazimierz—interceding for Poland before the throne of God.

creation, Who kept the world in existence, as the Source of all life and happiness. She then experienced delights so great that she could not express them.

But that was not the end of her mystical experiences. After that experience she heard Christ say: "I want you to be My spouse" (*Diary*, 912). She submitted to God's will: first there was a mystical betrothal, and next the nuptials, during which she felt such an immense freedom of spirit, of which she had no idea before. Masters of the spiritual life think that the state in which Sr. Faustina had found herself could only be compared to a union with God, such that the saints experience in heaven.

Sr. Faustina wrote of wanting to be a saint many times. She often confided to Jesus that she wanted to love Him with a love so great that nobody had hitherto shown Him. That aspiration to sanctity was not an expression of egoism, but a profound understanding of the ultimate purpose of a person's life. She frequently spoke to other nuns about it, infecting them with a similar desire. One day Sr. Chryzostoma Korczak said that hair would first grow on her own hands before Faustina became a saint. Sr. Faustina burst out laughing and said: "I shall love Sister yet more for it."

Some of Sr. Faustina's supernatural visions concerned her terrestrial home—Poland. She once saw three saints before the throne of God: Stanislaw Kostka, Andrzej Bobola, and Prince Kazimierz, who were interceding for Poland. A large book from before the throne

was given to her to read. She noticed that it was not written in ink, but in blood. She could decipher but one word—Jesus.

Sr. Faustina wrote that she frequently prayed for Poland, for she saw God's great anger at Poland's ingratitude. She then defended her countrymen, reminding Him of His promises of mercy, throwing herself into its abyss and immersing her country in it. This prayer was very exhausting. She wrote: "My country, how much you cost me! There is no day in which I do not pray for you" (*Diary*, 1188).

During another vision she saw God's anger weighing heavily over Poland. She saw such great misdeeds committed by her countrymen and women, that the only just punishment would be the everlasting destruction of the country. Even the most terrible of punishments seemed to her to be a great mercy in comparison to the guilt of Poles. Horrified by this, she saw that only chosen souls kept the world in existence.

Faustina prayed not only for Poland, but also for Russia, where atheistic Communism was raging. She was distressed by the fate of persecuted Christians in the Soviet Union. She offered all the prayers she had said on December 16, 1936, as well as all her suffering that day, for Russia. After Holy Communion, Jesus said to her: "I cannot suffer that country any longer. Do not tie My hands, My daughter" (*Diary*, 818). She then understood that if it had not been for the prayers of particular souls, faithful to God, the Russian nation would have been wiped off the face of the earth.

**MURAL OF GOD** the Father in the chapel at Łagiewniki. During one of her mystical ecstacies, Sr. Faustina felt that her will was united with His will.

**THE NUMBER OF VICTIMS** of Communism in the 20th century is estimated at about 100 million. When Sr. Faustina began to write her diary, the Great Famine in Ukraine, under Soviet rule, was ending – an artificially created disaster that claimed several million victims.

Meanwhile the tuberculosis, diagnosed much too late, worsened and wreaked ever greater havoc in Sr. Faustina's body. She felt worse and worse, but some sisters still did not believe that she was ill; they suspected that she was pretending. In time, however, she became so ill that it was evident to the people around her. Sr. Faustina felt ever worse, coughing frequently, and with every cough she felt as if her lungs were disintegrating. She had the impression that she was decomposing from within, slowly changing into a corpse. Her state of health became so serious that, on December 9, 1936, the mystic found herself in the hospital at Prądnik (today the John Paul II Hospital). She lay in isolation wards (Nissen huts I and III) next to the Chapel of the Sacred Heart of Jesus, in which she frequently prayed. Free of convent duties, she had a lot of time to write her diary. It was in the hospital that she wrote about many of her mystical experiences.

At that time it was Jesus Himself Who encouraged Sr. Faustina to keep a diary. He asked her to be His secretary. She was to proclaim and announce His great mercy to everyone, especially to sinners. "Souls perish in spite of my bitter Passion. I am giving them the last hope of salvation; that is, the Feast of My Mercy. If they will not adore My mercy, they will perish for all eternity. Secretary of My mercy, write, tell souls about this great mercy of Mine, because the awful day, the day of My justice, is near" (*Diary*, 965). At another time, the Savior told her: "In the Old Covenant I sent prophets wielding thunderbolts to My people. Today I am sending you with My mercy to the people of the whole world. I do not want to punish aching mankind, but I desire to heal it, pressing it to My Merciful Heart" (*Diary*, 1588). The Lord, Who is love and mercy itself, does not want anyone to die in sin and to suffer the pains of eternal damnation, eternal separation from Him. Out of His great love and mercy for all people, He is calling on us sinners to take advantage of this extraordinary gift of His mercy and take hold of His generous promise. By believing in Him and in His promise of mercy, by turning to Him with trust and confessing our sins, and by receiving Him in Holy Communion on this, the last day of the Easter Octave, the Lord promises to grant complete forgiveness of sins and punishment. Turning to Jesus in trust and accepting His mercy is the last hope of mankind's salvation. Jesus also informed Sr. Faustina that there were "three ways of exercising mercy toward your neighbor: the first—by deed, the second—by word, the third—by prayer. In these three degrees is contained the fullness of mercy, . . . even the strongest (163) faith is of no avail without works" (*Diary*, 742).

On Shrove Tuesday (February 9, 1937), Sr. Faustina was given to know of the great multitude of sins, and of the chastisements connected with them, that the

# IX MILLION PERISH IN SOVIET FAMINE

## Peasants' Crops Seized, They and Their Animals Starve

arnyard fowl, two peasant women garner of grain spilled in sowing. They must do eep alive in a land of plenty—the Ukraine —where 6,000,000 children, women and men have died of starvation. The women were permitted, as a great privilege, to pick the kernels.

Russia's beautiful thoroughbred horses, known the world over, are used now in the agricultural districts. The animals, needed on every farm, are dying off by the million of starvation. Ten million died in a few years. Here one horse is dead another is too weak to stand. Peasants begging food to save their livestock were driven off by armed soldiers.

## orter Risks Life Get Photographs howing Starvation

ATION stalks through the Ukraine section of So-ussia, leaving a ghastly trail of death and agony. kraine is the most fertile grain-producing district

cts contained in the series of articles, of which first, were obtained by Thomas Walker, an Amer-paperman, now resident in London, at the peril

Mr. Walker entered Russia last Spring he smug-camera.

e the photographs shown with these articles were nder the most adverse and dangerous possible cir-s, the evidence they present is more grim and an words.

### By THOMAS WALKER,

rnalist and Traveler and Student of Russian Af-s. Who for Several Years Has Toured the Union of Soviet Republics.

E recently toured the Ukraine district of Soviet Rus-here 6,000,000 peasants have perished from starva-in the past eighteen months, due to the excessive of their crops by the Bolshevik government.

Winter, Red Army soldiers, under orders from Mos-so much of the season's crops from the peasants that unable to feed themselves and their livestock through

hs accompanying this articles were taken and brought out of Rus-pockets. Fortunately, I rched. I threw away a mera before coming to the border, so as not to arouse the suspicions of the Russian customs officials regarding photographs. The Soviet travel regulations distinctly state that all camera films are to be developed within U. S. R. R., and pictures detrimental to the Bolshevik cause are destroyed and the owner of the films is arrested.

### Meets Immigrants.

#### (Run Model Farm)

Starting from Moscow late in the Spring of 1934 on what was advertised by the Intourist Travel Bureau as a complete tour of the Ukraine, we first went to a large Collective Farm near Tambov. Honesty compels me to state that this was indeed a model farm.

Conversation with the workers on this farm established the fact that practically all of these people were immigrant Communists from either America, England or Germany, who had even brought their farming implements with them, at their own expense, from abroad.

At the railway station at Veron gh I asked the glib-tongued In

In his article describing the enforced famine in the Ukraine, Thomas Walker tells of finding this little Russian peasant boy standing beside his dying father and weeping bitterly. The father had been shot for approaching too closely to forbidden territory while the two were picking up grains of wheat spilled on the ground. Now the boy must wander alone, almost certainly to die of starvation.

Death from starvation in a Soviet hay cart! Although he worked on a community farm where food was plentiful, this peasant could not get enough to eat to keep life in his body. Weary from his forced labor, he crawled into this hay cart to find rest. His eyes closed—and never opened again.

(All Pictures Copyright, 1935, by American Newspapers, Inc.)

the railway station—why were they all in rags, and why did they have such agonizing looks on their faces. To which he replied:

"They were sleeping in the rail-way station because they were all workers from a factory near mea, which also accounts for their old clothing, being on holi-day and having sat up all night so as not to miss the train, nat-urally they looked tired."

The look of agony and intense misery on all the faces of these mea. Questioning a few of these peasants convinced me that we tourists are being shown only the rosy side of a very horrible con-dition.

I decided to leave the tour as planned by Intourist and start on

traveling only with a small bag of Russian make so as not to attract attention. I arrived there early in the morning. I set out to walk the six kilometers to the Collective Farm.

Two of the peasants were mar-ried and had children, who per-ished by starvation during the year 1932-33. I left them as they start-

### Peasants, Horses Starve

#### (Death on Highway)

About halfway out I came upon a party of three peasants and three horses in varying stages of starvation (see photograph). One peasant had died the night previ-ous. One horse had just died and another laid down that was too weak to get on its legs again.

These peasants stated that they had been at the Collective Farm several days previous and had begged the officials for some wheat straw to feed the horses and to be allowed to fill their wa-ter barrels. Both requests were refused, and they were ordered away from the farm at the point of revolvers.

### Search for Grain.

#### ('A Great Privilege')

The collective farm near Belgor-od is a concentration camp of forced labor, and in these drastic times in this section it is deemed a privilege to be a prisoner on this farm. Supervision on this farm is by Red Army soldiers, who carry loaded rifles and shoot to kill

of the GPU, and requisitioned prac-tically all of the harvest.

In this connection it may be in-teresting to state that over ten mil-lion horses have perished in Soviet Russia since 1929. Most of these animals had belonged to independ-ent peasants.

Recently, however, trials have been held in Moscow and Smo-lensk, attempting to fix the blame on the managers of certain Bol-shevik stock farms for the starva-tion of thousands of Russia's prime horses.

harvesting and storage of grain.

As a great privilege, pea were permitted to pick up grains of wheat that fell on ground in the process of sowing.

### Food Hunter Shot

#### (Red Bullets Fly)

Walking around this farm came upon two peasant women were picking up grains of wh after the menace of harvest under the most dirty conditi imaginable. (See photograph.) They were distinctly forbid t ke any wheat that was outs of certain limits.

A father and son had been bu picking up these grains of wh when apparently the father cam too close to the prohibited terri-tory to suit a Red soldier and w promptly shot in the back by guard without warning and left to die where he fell. (See pho-graph). The son was in tea when photographed.

Both father and son were em-ployed on this farm at the

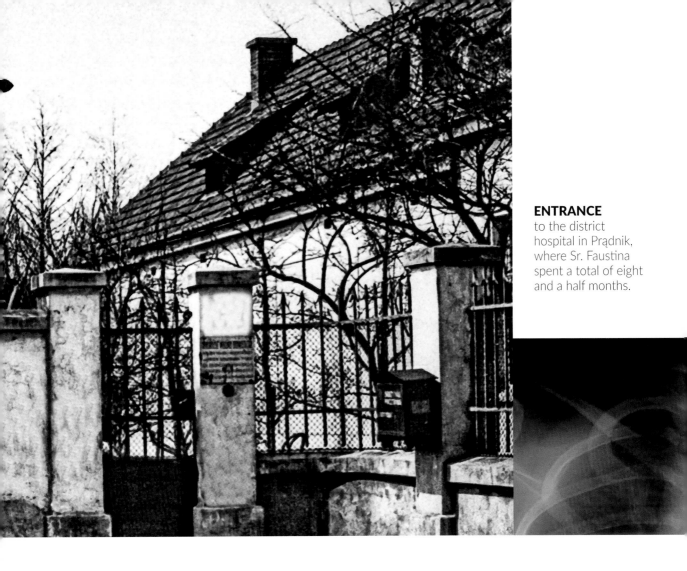

last two days of carnival, the season of merrymaking before Lent, had brought. In but one moment God showed her all the world's misdeeds, committed on but one of those days. When she saw this, she fainted through fright. Though she knew the depths of God's mercy, she was amazed that He still allowed humanity to exist. Then God showed her the chosen souls, thanks to whose prayers the world still existed. After that vision, Sr. Faustina received Holy Communion for two days as an act of reparation for the world's sins and then renewed her act of oblation for the sake of sinners. A time of spiritual suffering began, but she recognized that many souls would thus turn to God. As a matter of fact, she had earlier repeatedly prayed to take the suffering on herself. On October 3, 1936, while saying the Rosary, she suddenly saw a ciborium with the Blessed Sacrament, uncovered and quite full of hosts. She heard a voice from the ciborium: "These hosts have been received by souls converted through your prayer and suffering" (*Diary*, 709). She then felt God's presence, just as child would have.

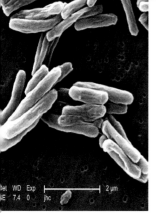

Fr. Sopoćko recalled that Sr. Faustina had the gift of sensing the sins of other people. When she was with people who were in a state of sin, she experienced intense pain in the same places where Christ had wounds: her temples, side, feet, and hands. After an increase in these pains—according to Fr. Sopoćko—she could even tell the sorts of sins that had been committed. She wrote that she had frequently felt the Lord Jesus' Passion in her body. Christ showed her various scenes from His own life. One day, she wrote that she was a witness to the Passion—she saw Jesus crowned in thorns, tormented by His executioners. She also had several visions of the Upper Room and Christ's Eucharistic feast with the apostles. She was most moved when, before the Consecration, Jesus raised His eyes to heaven and conversed with His Father. She emphasized that we would not know of the importance of this moment until eternity. Though God permitted the nun such intimacy with Him in her frequent mystical states, she was never self-righteous or self-satisfied. On the contrary, she was always aware that she was unworthy of such great graces. One day, after Holy Communion, she heard Jesus say: "You see what you are of yourself, but do not be frightened at this. If I were to reveal to you the whole misery that you are, you would die of terror" (*Diary*, 718). But Christ added that the nun's great trust and humility compelled Him to shower graces upon her ceaselessly.

God gave the humble mystic to know not only of man's ultimate end, which is eternal happiness with Him in heaven, but also of the place man could find himself for eternity if he were to reject God's invitation. One of Sr. Faustina's most moving visions concerns eternal damnation. She wrote of being led by an angel to the abyss of hell, a place of misery where the damned suffer various torments: the first of which was the loss of God; the second, perpetual pangs of conscience; the third, the impossibility of changing their fate; the fourth, a spiritual fire, but one not destructive of their souls; the fifth, a continual darkness, together with a horrible, suffocating smell; the sixth, the constant company of Satan; the seventh, a terrible despair, with hatred of God, vile imprecations, curses and blasphemies. In her vision, though darkness reigned all around, the damned and the demons saw each other, their own evil, and the evil of others. The mystic noticed that there were, apart from those which all the damned suffered together, particular torments for specific souls, dependent on the sins that they had committed. She called them torments of the senses, difficult even to describe.

Sr. Faustina's vision confirms the changeless Church teaching on the existence of hell and eternal damnation, as expressed in Holy Scripture, the works of the Church Fathers, and the Magisterium. It is precisely because of the real threat of perdition

**LEYLAND BUS**
Holy Spirit
Square, Kraków,
1937.

**FLORIAŃSKA
STREET**,
Kraków. View
from Market
Square.

**MICHAEL THE ARCHANGEL.** A statue in the convent at Plock when Sr. Faustina stayed there. Such statues of the leader of the heavenly hosts were to be found in all the houses of the congregation.

that the call to conversion, and to seek help in God's mercy, sounds so dramatic. "I, Sr. Faustina, by the order of God, have visited the abysses of hell so that I might tell souls about it and testify to its existence. I cannot speak about it now; but I have received a command from God to leave it in writing. The devils were full of hatred for me, but they had to obey me at the command of God. What I have written is but a pale shadow of the things I saw. But I noticed one thing: that most of the souls there are those who disbelieved that there is a hell" (*Diary*, 741).

During her stay in the hospital, Sr. Faustina not only filled her notebooks on the subject of mercy, but she also had the opportunity to show mercy actively. God constantly revealed to her who particularly needed help at the moment of death. As early as her third day in the hospital, the nun, carrying out Jesus' command, recited the Chaplet of Divine Mercy at the bedside of a certain woman who was in the throes of death. Just before dying, the woman opened her eyes, and on her face there was an expression of blissful peace. Faustina felt the power of mercy envelop the dying soul, and she heard: "At the hour of their death, I defend as My own glory every soul that will say this chaplet; or when others say it for a dying person, the pardon is the same. When (205) this chaplet is said by the bedside of a dying person, God's anger is placated, unfathomable mercy envelops the soul, and the very depths of My tender mercy are moved for the sake of the sorrowful Passion of My Son" (*Diary*, 811).

She always endeavored to be with patients at the hour of death, reciting the chaplet in order to obtain mercy for the them. She personally saw God's mercy sometimes touch sinners at the last moment in a wondrous and mysterious way. It seemed that there was no hope of salvation for them, yet souls touched by God's unexpected grace suddenly turned to Him with such fervor that they instantly received remission of their sins and punishments. Sr. Faustina also saw this in cases of those who were unconscious, not showing any outer sign of repentance or contrition. However, she also saw people—which filled her with horror—who voluntarily and consciously rejected God's mercy, scorning it. Even at the moment of death, God gives a soul the grace to see ultimate things clearly, and have the possibility of returning to Him. Yet there were people so obdurate that they consciously chose hell. Thus all the prayers said on their behalf, even the endeavors of God Himself, were of no avail.

Faustina never ceased to pray for the dying. "She did this with the conviction that she was rendering the sick a service and pleasing the Lord Jesus", recalled Mother Irena Krzyżanowska years later. "Having gotten to know of it, I forbade her to do it, having in mind her poor state of health. She immediately stopped going to the bedsides of the ill and just continued to pray for them." At that time Sr. Faustina was so

THE LAST
JUDGMENT
(Hans Memling)
National
Museum,
Gdańsk.

# VISION **OF HELL**

**SR. FAUSTINA** was not the only twentieth-century mystic to have a vision of hell. On July 13, 1917, three little Portugese shepherds had a similar vision: Lúcia dos Santos, and Jacinta and Francisco Marto. Their vision has gone down in history as the first Fatima secret. Sr. Lúcia described the vision thus:

"Our Lady showed us a great sea of fire which seemed to be under the earth. Plunged in this fire were demons and souls in human form, like transparent burning embers, all blackened or burnished bronze, floating about in the conflagration, now raised into the air by the flames that issued from within themselves together with great clouds of smoke, now falling back on every side like sparks in a huge fire, without weight or equilibrium, and amid shrieks and groans of pain and despair, which horrified us and made us tremble with fear. The demons could be distinguished by their terrifying and repulsive likeness to frightful and unknown animals, all black and transparent. . . We then looked up at Our Lady, who said to us so kindly and so sadly: 'You have seen hell where the souls of poor sinners go.'"

The Fatima vision – like Sr. Faustina's visions – was not intended to frighten people, but to show them the real threat of eternal damnation, and first and foremost how God wants to save souls.

**PAINTING OF SR. FAUSTINA** (based on a photograph) at the convent in Łagiewniki.

weak that she sometimes could not even hear Holy Mass. But she persistently prayed for many of those who were dying, and not only in the hospital, but also—thanks to the gift of bilocation—in many places far from Kraków. For example, she knew exactly when sisters from her congregation or members of her own family were dying.

Apart from the gift of bilocation, Sr. Faustina also had the gift of levitation. Sr. Kajetana Bartkowiak's account bears testimony to it: "One day I went to Prądnik to visit her. I knocked on her door. She had always responded: 'Come in, please.' But that time, I knocked and knocked, but no one answered. I thought that she must be in the room, as she was ill. So I opened the door and went in. I saw her above the bed, gazing into the distance, as if seeing something, and so completely other—transformed. I stood beside a little cupboard, on which there was a miniature altar. And I was seized with fear. But after a while she roused herself and said: 'Oh, Sister, you have come. Good. Do take a seat, please.'"

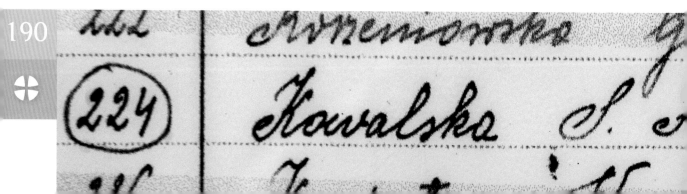

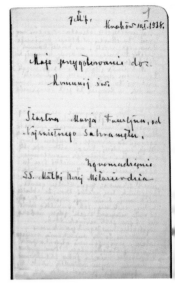

Fr. Sopoćko confirmed the information about the mystic's levitations. He recalled; "I once saw Sr. Faustina in an ecstasy. It was on September 2, 1938, when I paid her a visit at the hospital in Prądnik while on my way to Vilnius. Having bidden her farewell, and having gone about a hundred yards, I remembered that I had brought her about fifty copies of prayers (a novena, litany, and chaplet) on God's mercy that she had written, and that had been published in Kraków. I immediately returned to give them to her. When I opened the door to her room, I saw her in a sitting position, almost raised above her bed, absorbed in prayer. Her eyes were fixed on some invisible object, her pupils somewhat dilated. At first she paid no attention to me. I did not want to interrupt her, and so I intended to withdraw. Shortly, however, she came to herself, noticed me, and apologized for not having heard me knock or enter. I gave her the prayers and said farewell, and she said: 'Until we meet again in heaven!' "

The ill nun experienced many extraordinary graces at the hospital in Prądnik. She wrote of one in her diary. Once she was suffering greatly, as she had not been to confession for three weeks. She lay on her bed crying. Then Fr. Andrasz came into her room and proposed that he hear her confession. Glad, she willingly made her confession. She told him of all the stirrings of her soul, and he gave her the Litany of the Holy Name of Jesus for penance. When she wanted to tell him that she had a certain difficulty in saying the prayer, he stood up and gave her absolution. At that moment such a great light began to radiate from his figure that Sr. Faustina realized it was not Fr. Andrasz, but Jesus Himself in bright garments. After a moment He vanished and the mystic remained alone. At first she was worried, but shortly a sort of peace entered her soul. She noticed that Jesus had heard her confession like all her confessors.

After almost four months of treatment, Sr. Faustina had regained enough strength to be discharged from the hospital (March 27, 1937). She returned to the convent in Łagiewniki, but her health suddenly worsened. Her superiors decided to send her to Rabka, a health resort famous for treating many tuberculosis sufferers. The congregation had a house there (12 Slowacki Street), which was called "Loreto". It was both a rest center and a place where children were looked after. Faustina arrived there on July 29,

**PAGE**
from Sister Faustina's Diary: *My preparation for Holy Communion.*

**HOSPITAL REGISTER.**
The entry in the hospital register shows when Sr. Faustina was there for the last time. She was received on April 20 and discharged on September 17, 1938.

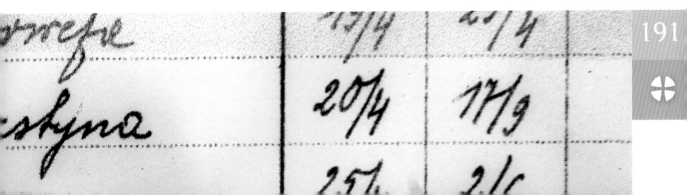

**ŁAGIEWNIKI CONVENT**
where Sr. Faustina spent the greater part of her religious life (almost six years).

but she stayed only a few days. It turned out that the severe mountain climate was bad for her health. She did not feel well, and she was frequently unable to get out of bed. Hence she had to return to Kraków (August 10). In her diary, she wrote of a certain event that had occurred in Rabka. St. Joseph, one of the most venerated saints in the congregation, whose statues are to be found in every convent, had appeared to her. He instructed Faustina to recite daily the Our Father, the Hail Mary, and the Creed, as well as a prayer to him. He also promised to help her to spread the devotion to the Divine Mercy.

After her return from Rabka she did not go back to work in the garden, as it was beyond her strength; however, she began duties at the convent gate. The homeless, the poor, and beggars frequently knocked at the gate for her. She did not send anyone away empty-handed and always strove to do as much as she could for those who came. One rainy day, a young, frozen, down-and-out person appeared at the door and asked for something to eat. Sr. Faustina hurried to the kitchen, but there was nothing for the poor. She did not give up, however, and after a while she found some soup. She heated it up, crumbled some bread into it, and took it to the beggar. When taking the empty mug from him, she suddenly discerned that the beggar was Christ Himself, Who then vanished. When she returned to her cell, reflecting on what had happened, she heard an inner voice: "My daughter, the blessings of the poor who bless Me as they leave this gate have reached

My ears. And your compassion, within the bounds of obedience, has pleased Me, and this is why I came down from My throne—to taste the fruits of your mercy" (*Diary*, 1312).

During a vision (Łagiewniki, October 1937) Jesus communicated the following formula to her for venerating God's mercy: "At three o'clock, implore My mercy, especially for sinners; and, if only for a brief moment, immerse yourself in My Passion, particularly in My abandonment at the moment of agony. This is the hour of great mercy for the whole world. I will allow you to enter into My mortal sorrow. In this hour, I will refuse nothing to the soul that makes a request of Me in virtue of My Passion " (*Diary*, 1320). Later, Christ once again repeated that the hour of His death is a time of special graces: "I remind you, My daughter, that as often as you hear the clock strike the third hour, immerse yourself completely in My mercy, adoring and glorifying it; invoke its omnipotence for the whole world, and particularly for poor sinners; for at that moment mercy was opened wide for every (145) soul. In this hour you can obtain everything for yourself and for others for the asking; it was the hour of grace for the whole world—mercy triumphed over justice.

"My daughter, try your best to make the Stations of the Cross at this hour, provided that your duties permit it; and if you are not able to make the Stations of the Cross, then at least step into the chapel for a moment and adore, in the Blessed Sacrament, My Heart, which is full of mercy; and should you be unable to step into the chapel, immerse yourself in prayer there where you happen to be, if only for a very brief instant. I claim veneration for My mercy from every creature, but above all from you, since it is to you that I have given the most profound understanding of this mystery" (*Diary*, 1572).

It is known that Sr. Faustina also stopped by St. Joseph's, a neo-Gothic church in Podgorze, Kraków. On December 27, 1936, she was returning from the convent to the hospital in Prądnik by horse and carriage with a certain woman taking a child to be baptized. The carriage stopped in front of the church. Her companion laid the baby in Sr. Faustina's arms. She took it tenderly and offered it to God, praying that it might some day bring Him great glory. She then felt certain that the Lord would grant it extraordinary graces. The child had been left at the convent entrance in Łagiewniki a few nights earlier. The sisters took care of the child and found a foster family for it. A neighbor, a woman, not only took it in but also gave the child her surname. Sr. Faustina dropped the woman and child off at the church, where the child was baptized by Fr. Tadeusz Siepak.

The beginning of 1938 once again saw a worsening of Sr. Faustina's health. Hence her superiors decided to send her back to the hospital in Prądnik after Easter. This time she was there for five months (April 20 to September 17, 1938). The nun knew that her death was close at hand; God had revealed to her that she would die on October 5. During that time she filled many pages of her diary with her own

**THE NAME IGNACEUS** engraved on Sr. Faustina's wedding band in honor of St Ignatius Loyola.

**ST. IGNATIUS LOYOLA.** Painting of the congregation's patron in the convent hall, Łagiewniki.

**FROM 1931 THE CENTER** in Rabka was a place of rest for sisters and wards. Sometimes it was also a place where children were looked after.

**ST. THÉRÈSE** of the Child Jesus Church, Rabka-Zdrój.

prayers. Her intimate relationship with Christ continued; before Pentecost, He personally led a three-day retreat for her. The mystic wrote of three of Jesus' conferences: on spiritual struggle, on sacrifice and prayer, and on mercy. When it turned out that Sr. Faustina could not receive the Eucharist, an angel from heaven—a seraph—appeared and gave her Holy Communion for thirteen days.

Her second stay in the hospital was a time of preparation for her passage to eternity. All the people who came into contact with her at that time emphasized that she was radiant with joy, despite her illness. Mother Serafina Kukulska recalled: "I often visited her, and I always found her in a cheerful disposition, even joyful, at times as if radiant, but she never let me in on the secret of her happiness. She felt very happy in Prądnik, and she never complained about her suffering. The doctor, the sisters, and the sick were all very good to her." Another nun, Sr. Dawida Cedro, from the Congregation of the Sisters of the Most Sacred Heart of Jesus, remembered Faustina thus: "She did not demand anything for herself. As to food, she was highly disciplined; when other ill people complained, everything to her was always good, even splendid. She bore suffering with a smile, and one should mention that she suffered a lot, for she had tuberculosis of the lungs, bowels, and throat. Dr. Adam Silberg, a neophyte, even said that it was a great thing to smile when in such pain and suffering."

Lying in her hospital bed, offering up her suffering to God, Sr. Faustina wrote that when she was praying for Poland she heard Jesus say: "I bear a special love for Poland, and if she will be obedient to My will, I will exalt her in might and holiness. From her will come forth the spark that will prepare the world for My final coming" (*Diary*, 1732). A prayer for Poland was one of the most frequent prayers she said. She once wrote: "My beloved native land, Poland, if you only you knew how many sacrifices and prayers I offer to God for you! But be watchful and give glory to God, Who lifts you up and singles you out in a special way. But know how to be grateful" (*Diary*, 1038).

In June 1938 Sr. Faustina's condition was so serious that she could no longer keep her diary. In August she decided to say farewell to her religious community. She then wrote her last letter, which was to the superior general of the congregation, Mother Michaela Moraczewska:

"My most dear Mother, it seems to me that this is our last contact on earth; I feel very weak, and I am writing with a trembling hand, suffering as much as I can bear. Jesus does not try us beyond our strength; if the suffering is great, so too is God's grace. I have com-

**LORETO**.
The congregation's house in Rabka was known as Loreto.

**THIS CIBORIUM**
was used at Loreto while Sr. Faustina was there.

**RABKA.**
Our Lady's grotto in a wood on convent grounds.

195

**HOSPITAL CHAPEL**
at Prądnik.
Sr. Faustina often prayed there.
A plaque on the wall recalls this.

**ON THE DESK** –
Sr. Faustina's farewell letter (August 1938) to her superior.

196

pletely abandoned myself to God and His holy will. An ever greater longing for God has seized me. Death does not frighten me. My soul abounds in great peace. I still do all my spiritual exercises. I also get up for Holy Mass, but not for all of it, as I begin to feel unwell. But when I can, I take advantage of the graces that Jesus left for us in the Church.

"Most dear Mother, I thank you from the depths of my heart, overcome with immense gratitude for all the good that I experienced in the congregation from the first moment until now. Mother, thank you particularly for your heartfelt sympathy and your instructions at difficult times, times that seemed to be unbearable. May God reward you handsomely!

"And now, in a spirit of monastic humility, I humbly beg your pardon, most dear Mother, for not observing the regulations exactly, for the bad example I gave the sisters, for the lack of zeal throughout my religious life, for all the tribulation and suffering that I might have caused you, Mother, though unwittingly. My dear Mother's goodness was a great support for me at difficult times.

"In spirit, I kneel at my most dear Mother's feet and humbly beg for forgiveness for all my transgressions, and I ask for a blessing at the hour of my death. I trust in the power of Mother's prayer, and the prayers of my beloved sisters; I feel that some sort of power is helping me.

"I apologize for my bad handwriting, but my hand is trembling and becoming numb. Good-bye, most dear Mother; we shall see each other at the foot of God's throne in heaven. But now, may God's mercy be glorified in us and through us.

"I kiss your hands, most dear Mother, with most profound reverence, and beg for prayers.

"The greatest misery and nothingness
Sr. Faustina."

On August 24, there was such a sudden decline in Sr. Faustina's health that the sisters were convinced that death was near. The next day she received extreme unction, after which she felt better. Shortly afterwards, Fr. Michal Sopoćko visited her several times. He recalled: "At the isolation hospital in Prądnik, I found Sr. Faustina already prepared for death. I visited her during the week and among other things, we talked about the congregation she wanted to found. But she, dying, stressed that it was a delusion, as also were, perhaps, all the other things she had talked about. Sr. Faustina promised to talk to the Lord Jesus about the subject during prayer. The next day I said Holy Mass for her, during which I thought that just as she was unable to paint the image, and only indicated what it was to be like, so too she was unable to found a new congregation, but only gave general pointers; her urgency, however, denoted the necessity for a new congregation in the coming times. When I next went to the hospital and asked if she had anything to say about the matter, she told me that she did not need to say anything, as the Lord Jesus had already enlightened me during Mass. Then she added that I was largely to try to get the first Sunday after Easter to be the Feast of Divine Mercy and that I was not to occupy myself too much with the new congregation; that after certain signs I would know what was to be done in the matter, and by whom it was to be done. She also said that a pure intention was lacking in the homily I gave that day on the radio (which was really so), and that I was mainly to strive for it in the whole matter. She said that she saw me receiving the vows of the first six candidates to the congregation, at night, and in a small wooden chapel. She told me that she would soon die,

**AN ILLUSTRATED BOOKLET**
of the Stations of the Cross, which Sr. Faustina, shortly before her death in 1938, gave Sr. Kajetana Bartkowiak. It was used while praying the Stations of the Cross, for example, during an illness.

**LAST DAYS.**
During her last days on earth Sr. Faustina was surrounded by white things— white walls, white screens, white towels, and white bedding.

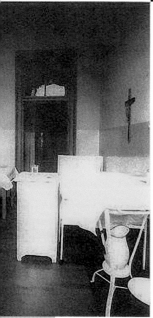

and that she had said and written everything that she had to. Earlier she had described a small church and the congregation's first house and told me that she grieved over the fate of Poland, which she loved very much, and for which she frequently prayed. Following the advice of St. John of the Cross, I virtually always treated that which Sr. Faustina related to me with indifference and did not ask for details. I did not ask about Poland's fate either, about which she so grieved. She herself did not tell me about it, but sighing, she covered her face from the horror of the image that she then probably saw. Virtually everything that she had foretold in the matter of the new congregation was most precisely fulfilled."

On September 17, 1938, Sr. Faustina Kowalska returned to the convent in a hopeless condition to die among her religious sisters. During farewells, Dr. Adam Silberg, a Jew who had converted to Catholicism, asked her for the little picture of St. Thérèse of the Child Jesus that was always on the little cupboard by her bed. A nurse protested. She thought the little picture needed to be disinfected. But Dr. Silberg replied: "Saints do not pass on infections." After the outbreak of World War II, there was no certain information about the fate of that director of the hospital in Prądnik. The hospital archives do not even have a photograph of him.

Five days later (September 22) sensing that death was close, Faustina apologized to all the sisters in the congregation for all her mistakes, weaknesses, and transgres-

sions. When one of the nuns asked her if she was afraid, she replied: "I am not afraid of death; I am longing for it." During her last talks with the superior of the house, Mother Irena Krzyżanowska, she said that she would bring the congregation yet more consolations after her death, as God desired to canonize her, and that through her intercession He desired to spread the devotion to Divine Mercy throughout the world. "I sensed a lot of gravity in her, and I had the strange feeling that Sr. Faustina accepted that assurance as a gift of mercy from God, and without a trace of pride", recalled her superior. The sick nun then gave Mother Irena six notebooks—her diary—to pass on to the superior general, Mother Michaela Moraczewska. On September 26, Fr. Sopoćko came from Czestochowa specially to say farewell to the dying nun. But she did not have the strength to talk to him. She just whispered to him: "I am sorry, Father, I am having a conversation with my Heavenly Father. I have said everything I had to say."

On October 5, 1938, Faustina joyfully told the sisters: "The Lord Jesus will take me away today!" Feeling great physical pain, she asked for a pain-killing injection, but after a while she decided against it, explaining that she wanted to offer up the pain to Christ. Fr. Józef Andrasz arrived at the convent in the afternoon and gave her absolution and extreme unction. At six o'clock, Fr. Teodor Czaputa and the nuns said a prayer for her at her bedside, and then they all dispersed. Only Sr.

**CONVENT CELL**
window, Łagiewniki. Sr. Faustina Kowalska departed from this world in the cell above the commemoration plaque.

199

**A PICTURE**
of St. Thérèse
of Lisieux
stood on
a little
cupboard by
Sr. Faustina's
hospital bed
during her
last stay at
Prądnik.

**MARIANNA
KOWALSKA**
at her
daughter's
graveside.
Sr. Faustina's
body was
interred in the
convent tomb
from 1938 to
1966.

Liguoria Poznańska remained in the cell. She was to inform Mother Irena and the sister—Amelia Socha—when the death throes began.

A young nun, Sr. Eufemia Traczyńska—doing her juniorate in Łagiewniki—unexpectedly became a witness to Faustina's death. She had heard from Sr. Amelia that Faustina would be a saint. She very much wanted to see how a saint departed to heaven; hence she tried to be present at Sr. Faustina's death. But she did not get permission to keep vigil at Sr. Faustina's bedside, as she was too young. So, during prayer, she asked the souls in purgatory to wake her when Sr. Faustina was about to die. She later recalled: "I went to bed at the usual time, and I immediately fell asleep. All of a sudden, somebody roused me: 'If Sister wants to be at Sr. Faustina's death, then Sister should get up.' I immediately understood that it was a mistake. The sister who was to have woken Sr. Amelia had mixed up the cells and had come to mine. I immediately roused Sr. Amelia, put on my gaberdine and bonnet, and ran quickly to the infirmary. Sr. Amelia followed me. This was about eleven o'clock at night. When we got there, Sr. Faustina slightly opened her eyes, gave a little smile, bowed her head. . .I looked at Sr. Amelia, but I did not say anything. We continued to pray. . . The Candlemas candle was burning all the time. After a while, Mother Superior, Irena, came, while the sister on duty was no doubt still waking somebody. Together with Mother Superior, we continued to pray for quite some time." Sr. Faustina Kowalska died in the odor of sanctity at a quarter to eleven, the evening of October 5, 1938.

The sisters made the following entry in the congregation's Book of the Deceased: "The late Sr. Faustina attained complete union with God through love, perceiving God's will in every event, in all the directives of her superiors. She left the best possible reminiscences at the sanatorium through her delicacy and gratitude for everything. So it was in 'Józefów,' for despite her intense suffering she asked the sisters not to tire themselves by keeping watch over her; it was only over the last few nights that they did so. To the question 'Are you suffering a lot?' She replied: 'Yes, a lot, but it is good for me.' Despite being very thirsty, she did not drink the water that was offered to her, but was content with wetting her tongue. Though her body was utterly exhausted and consumed by fever, she was strong in spirit to the very end. Her eyes fixed on heaven on the eve of her death, smiling, she asked the sister-nurse to sing, who obligingly sang: 'Hail, Fount …', which pleased the patient very much. She would not allow

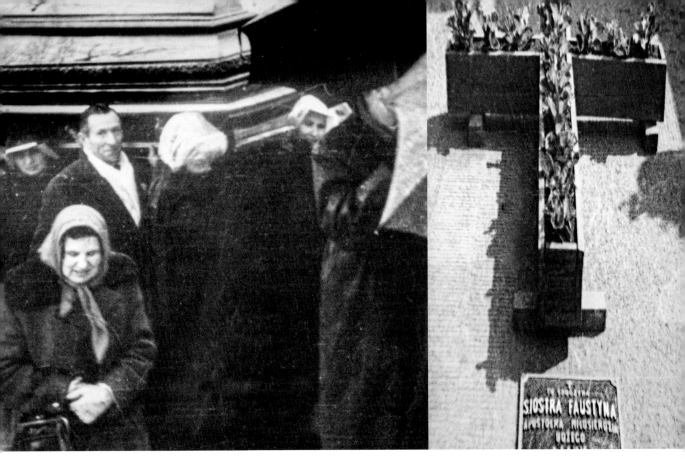

sisters who visited her to come too close in order not to be infected by her, saying: 'Be more careful about yourself Sister.' She raised our spirits to the very end by her faithful observance of the rules, while she humbly apologized to everyone for any transgressions. She requested that none of her family visit her on account of the travel costs. Not at all fearful before her death, she passed away peacefully and quietly in the Lord at 11:00 P.M."

At dawn on October 6, Sr. Faustina's body was moved to the crypt under the chapel, where it lay until the funeral. The nuns recalled that the deceased looked better then than she did during the last weeks of her life, when she was ravaged by illness. Not only the sisters went to pray at the crypt, but also the wards from the workshop, as well as the farm workers. One of the nuns related that "there was no sense of dejection, but an inner joy" in the whole house. It came from the conviction that Sr. Faustina was with Jesus.

The funeral was on October 7, the Feast of Our Lady of the Rosary, and the Requiem Mass was celebrated by a Jesuit, Fr. Wladyslaw Wojton. The sisters carried the coffin—on their own shoulders—to the tomb in the cemetery at the far end of the garden. Nobody from Faustina's family was at the funeral. Her family and closest friends were not informed of her death, as she did not want those poor people to incur the costs of the journey. When she was laid to rest in the convent tomb, her mission on earth came to an end, but a completely new stage had just begun.

**SR. FAUSTINA'S REMAINS.**
On November 25, 1966, Sr. Faustina's remains were transferred from the cemetery near the convent in Łagiewniki to the convent chapel.

**APOSTLE OF DIVINE MERCY.**
Epithet on Sr. Faustina Kowalska's grave.

201

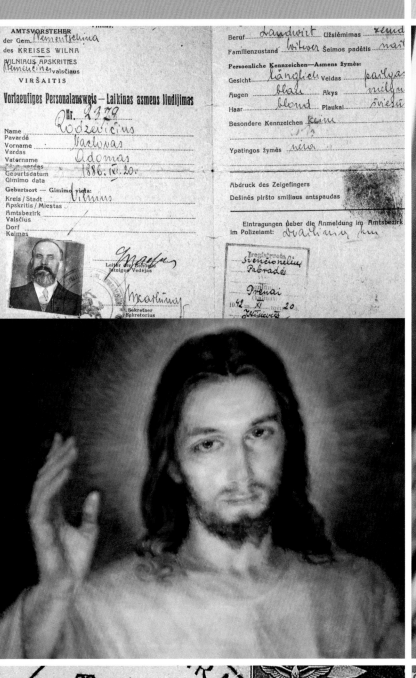

# War

men:
Jahr: rok:   Zeit: czas:
durch: przez:
an: do:   durch: przez:   dzień

Zofie [Stszanow...]

92_

Brat Ruchna
p. Medron

---

...hn Michael heute im Konzentrationsla...

Auschwitz f.g. verstorben. Nächres du...
den Kommandeur der Sicherheits Poli-
und S.D. im Distrikt Krakau

Der Kommandant

---

## ПОЧТОВАЯ КАРТОЧКА
## CARTE POSTALE

Куда  г.  Львов
Наименование места, где находится почта, и области или края, а для станций — наименование железной д...

Район, село или деревня.

ул.  Романовича 3 - ul. Romanow...
Улица, № дома и квартиры.

Кому  др. П. Каспшицкий
Подробное наименование адресата.

Dr.  T. Kasprzycki

г. Старобельск, почт. ящ.

Адрес

CHAPTER 11

# War

S. Faustyna

Jezu ufam Tobie!

Sr. Faustina said that her death would not mean the end her mission, but just the beginning. In the Gospel, Jesus said that "unless a grain of wheat falls into the earth and dies, it remains alone; but if it dies, it bears much fruit" (Jn 12:24).

**PICTURES OF THE MERCIFUL JESUS AND SR. FAUSTINA** were reproduced during the war in tens of thousands by a photographer from Vilnius, Michał Nowicki; they were ordered by Fr. Michał Sopoćko.

**DURING THE WAR** Polish mothers received information about the deaths of their sons in German or Russsian.

It was just so with the mission of this simple sister, who died at the same age as Christ. After her departure no one spoke of the mission she had received from Jesus of spreading the devotion to Divine Mercy. One year after her death World War II—the bloodiest conflict in world history—broke out; the mystic had foretold this several times. Poland was one of the first victims of the war. She lost her independence, divided between two totalitarian states: Nazi Germany and Stalinist Russia. A time of violence, cruelty, suffering, and hate ensued. That exceptionally difficult period, however, favored the spread of the message about the Divine Mercy, for people sought remedies for doubt, hate, despair, and the feeling that life was meaningless.

**DURING WORLD WAR II** about 6 million Polish citizens were killed (of which 50 percent were of Jewish descent and 50 percent were Polish). The Germans prepared special places of death for their victims, for example, Ponary (photo at the top of the page), and Auschwitz (photo on the right of the page).

While Sr. Faustina was alive, only Fr. Jozef Andrasz, Fr. Michał Sopoćko, and some of the congregation's superiors knew of her message. Events during the war occasioned the nun's confessor to speak publicly of the deceased sister's mission and to spread the devotion in forms that she had advocated. In 1940 the superior general, Mother Michaela Moraczewska, decided to do the same thing. Sr. Beata Piekut recalled: "Mother General assembled all the sisters and officially informed us that it had all apparently—I emphasize, apparently—taken place. In conclusion, she said: 'This is to be known to you, sisters, but do not tell anyone about it.' Meanwhile, that same day, but a little earlier, a surprising thing happened to me. While I was walking along a street in Warsaw, a woman asked me to teach her the Divine Mercy Chaplet. I was in a great hurry, so I asked her to walk with me while

## CRUCIFIX IN LICHEN
Riddled with bullets by Berta Bauer, a member of the Hitler Youth. This Nazi thus wanted to show her pupils her hatred of Christianity.

## THE ULMA FAMILY
from Markowa near Rzeszów, murdered by the Germans on March 24, 1944, for hiding Jews. The family was declared blessed by the Church in 2023.

**THE GERMANS** eliminated the Polish state and formed a governor-generalship with Kraków as its capital. It was completely under German control.

207

I prayed aloud. But as I began, she interrupted me and told me that it was not that chaplet. I was amazed, as I did not know of any other Divine Mercy chaplet. I told her that. And she replied reproachfully: 'You sisters are so jealous about the devotion . . .' I did not know what to say. It was not until evening, after a meeting with the Mother General, that I understood what the woman meant."

During the turmoil of the war, the Divine Mercy devotion developed largely in the four cities that were connected with Sr. Faustina: Kraków, Vilnius, Warsaw, and Płock. It is difficult to separate Sr. Faustina from the mission Christ gave her to fulfil. Hence her renown for sanctity grew together with the development of the devotion—and precisely in the forms that the mystic had communicated to the world. Numerous pilgrims began to come to her graveside at the

**DIVINE MERCY**
prayers and pictures of Merciful Jesus printed in 1940 at the initiative of the Congregation of the Sisters of Our Lady of Mercy with the approval of the Church authorities.

nościach nie poddawali się rozpaczy lecz zawsze ufnie zgadzali się z wolą Twoją, która jest samym Miłosierdziem. Przez Pana naszego Jezusa, Chrystusa — Króla Miłosierdzia, który z Tobą i Duchem Świętym okazuje nam miłosierdzie na wieki wieków. Amen.

**Koronka do Miłosierdzia Bożego.**
(Do prywatnego odmawiania na różańcu)
Na początku: Ojcze... Zdrowaś... Wierzę...

nościach nie poddawali się rozpaczy lecz zawsze ufnie zgadzali się z wolą Twoją, która jest samym Miłosierdziem. Przez Pana naszego Jezusa, Chrystusa — Króla Miłosierdzia, który z Tobą i Duchem Świętym okazuje nam miłosierdzie na wieki wieków. Amen.

**Koronka do Miłosierdzia Bożego.**
(Do prywatnego odmawiania na różańcu)

convent cemetery in Łagiewniki. They obtained graces through the intercession of this extraordinary nun who had died in the odor of sanctity. Sr. Elzbieta Siepak related that images and medals of the Merciful Jesus enjoyed great popularity in Kraków at that time, while many of those who visited the convent chapel gladly recited the chaplet. Nuns from Łagiewniki frequently enclosed chaplets and pictures of the Merciful Jesus in food parcels that were sent to prisons and concentration camps.

Fr. Franciszek Cegielka, who had been a prisoner in Dachau concentration camp, recalled that he wrote the chaplet on a scrap of a German newspaper. One day, when he was lying on a plank bed with a high fever, Fr. Ogrodowski came and told him that he would certainly get better if he propagated the chaplet. Fr. Cegielka asked him how he had obtained his chaplet. Fr. Ogrodowski told him that he had obtained it from some newcomers to the camp. Fr. Cegielka recited the chaplet while he was in bed in the sick room; he recited it with Fr. Dominik Sierszulski, who was in a bed next to him. The Divine Mercy Chaplet—particularly well known among Polish priests in Dachau—gave him and the vast majority of Polish prisoners strength and hope.

Fr. Jozef Andrasz played a great part in spreading the devotion to the Divine Mercy; he had been Sr. Faustina's confessor in Kraków, and he lived at the convent in Łagiewniki from 1942 to 1945. He actually saw it as his most important mission in life, and he remained faithful to it until his death in 1963. It was precisely under the direction of Fr. Andrasz that another image of the Merciful Jesus was painted (in Łagiewniki) according to Sr. Faustina's vision. The artist was Adolf Hyła, who came to the convent and offered to paint a picture for the chapel as a votive offering for his family's having survived the war. It was then that Fr. Andrasz gave him a little picture of a reproduction of Kazimirowski's painting and an excerpt from Sr. Faustina's diary about her vision. The painting—which was completed between November 1942 and March 1943—was displayed in the convent chapel in Łagiewniki (March 7, 1943). The sisters, however, thought that there was really no room for it at the main altar, where it was displayed for devotions to Divine Mercy, so they commissioned Hyła to paint another image that would be suitable for the church's side altar. Thus Hyła's second painting was consecrated in the chapel at Łagiewniki (April 16, 1944); it is the world's best-known image of the Merciful Jesus. Hyła had originally depicted Christ against the background of a meadow, but in 1954 he repainted the background in a dark color and added a floor under the Savior's feet. This image quickly became

**FR. MICHAŁ SOPOĆKO**, under a false identity, avoided the Gestapo for 30 months.

**THE BERNARDINE CHURCH** in Vilnius where a German patrol sought Fr. Sopoćko.

# MARTYROLOGY OF THE CHURCH

**OF THE PROFESSIONS** in Polish society, it was the clergy that suffered the greatest losses at the hands of the Nazis. According to historians the Germans killed about 2800 of the Polish religious (the Soviets killed about 200); 846 Polish priests died in Dachau concentration camp alone. Shortly after the war, the primate of Poland, Stefan Wyszyński, wrote in his notes: " I recall Fr. Bogdański, lecturing to us, class seven seminarians, on the theology of the liturgy. It was a time of great changes in the world, where two powers were grappling with each other: love and hate. Hate was winning. Fr. Bogdański was aware of the situation wherein he was forming future priests. He told us: 'The time will come when they will drive nails into your tonsures.' . . . Of the 16 who were to be ordained in 1924, only two of us now remain. God called 13 to Dachau. Only four returned, the rest died as martyrs in the camp. Of those that returned three were 'guinea pigs.' They suffered terrible transplant experiments. Moreover, two from our course also experienced communist prisons. I think our professor's forecast of 1919 was more than fully fulfilled."

**PRIMATE STEFAN WYSZYŃSKI**
was wanted by the Germans and had to go into hiding..

**BLESSED MICHAŁ KOZAL**, bishop of Włocławek. The Nazis tortured him to death in the concentration camp in Dachau in 1943.

**ST. MAXIMILIAN KOLBE**
murdered by the Germans in 1941 in the concentration camp at Auschwitz.

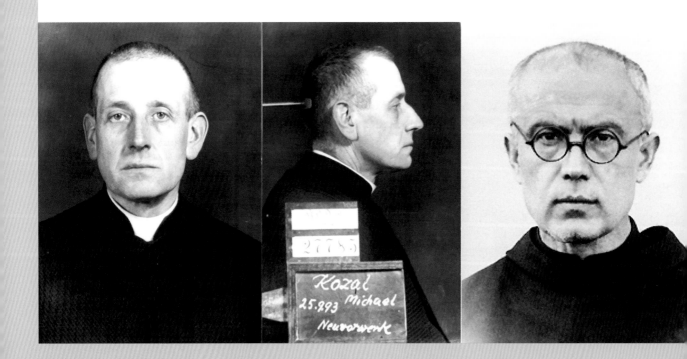

famous for the numerous miracles associated with it, and copies and reproductions are to be found in countless places all over the world. Jesus' wish was thus fulfilled: "I desire that this image be venerated, first in your chapel, and [then] throughout the world" (*Diary*, 47). Hyła's first painting can be seen in the congregation's chapel in Wroclaw; Mother Irena Krzyżanowska took it there in 1946.

The propagation of the Merciful Jesus image was not Fr. Andrasz's only achievement. In 1943 he initiated a solemn devotion to the Divine Mercy on the third Sunday of each month at the convent chapel in Łagiewniki. The faithful thronged to the devotion from all over Kraków, seeking spiritual support and hope during those difficult times. A young laborer, Karol Wojtyla, who then worked in the nearby Solvay chemical factory and secretly studied theology at

**ADOLF HYŁA**
(1897–1965).
Hyła was Jacek
Malczewski's
pupil. Mainly
famous for
his religious
paintings,
Hyła repeated
the Merciful
Jesus motif in
many of his
paintings.

211

the seminary in Kraków, was among those who frequently went to pray there. Owing to Fr. Andrasz, the Divine Mercy Feast was first solemnly celebrated at Łagiewniki (April 16, 1944). He proclaimed the necessity of its being celebrated throughout the Church. Moreover, he noticed that many new feasts (such as those of Corpus Christi, the Most Sacred Heart of Jesus, and Christ the King, as well as Marian feasts) were the result of private revelations. He thought that the Divine Mercy Feast might be established on the same basis, although he advised patience, for he knew it would be a long and laborious process.

Apart from Kraków, Vilnius also saw an intense development of the devotion during World War II. The inhabitants' recollections of the 1935 Easter celebrations, when the image of the Merciful Jesus was first publicly displayed, favored this. But Fr. Michał Sopoćko's efforts turned out to be decisive; he undoubtedly deserves to be known as an apostle of Divine Mercy.

In 1939 Fr. Sopoćko had a considerable number of Merciful Jesus images and novenas brought from Kraków to Vilnius. After Soviet soldiers had entered the city, he began to distribute the images and novenas. He tirelessly propagated not only private devotion to the image, but also the prayers Sr. Faustina had received during her visions. When the novenas had run out, Fr. Sopoćko duplicated the prayers himself and distributed them to those who were interested. But the demand was so great that he had to ask the Vilnius chancery for permission to reprint the Kraków editions. He received permission, and at the beginning of 1940, a huge number of images with prayers appeared in circulation. Little reproductions of the image, the size of a human fingernail—which Fr. Sopoćko had ordered from Michał Nowicki, a photographer in Vilnius—also became popular. These were hard photographic prints that could be sewn into uniform epaulettes, caps, or belts. They were possessed by Poles held in the prison in Lukiszki, those murdered in Ponary (a place of mass executions), those taken to Siberia in four great deportations, and those who managed to leave the Soviet Union with General Anders' army and eventually reached the West. It is not insignificant that Eugeniusz Kazimirowski's original painting was on display in the Church of St. Michael (Vilnius) throughout World War II.

From the time of the war and occupation, the inhabitants of Vilnius remembered Fr. Sopoćko as an exceptionally zealous priest. He strove to raise people's spirits by telling them of God's mercy. He organized clandestine meetings at his home. Jadwiga Osińska, a young classics graduate from the Stefan Batory University in Vilnius, participated in the meetings. In the summer of 1940 she

**FR. JÓZEF ANDRASZ** became a great promoter of the Divine Mercy message after Sr. Faustina's death.

212

✚

declared that she wanted to become a nun, but that she could not find a suitable congregation. She asked the priest for help and added that she had several female friends who were thinking along the same lines. The priest sent her on vacation to the convent of the habitless Sisters of the Angels in Pryciuny so that she might discern her vocation. On returning, the girl stated that she wanted to devote her life to "worshipping God in His infinite mercy". Such was the beginning of the congregation that had been foretold by Sr. Faustina.

On October 15, 1940, Jadwiga Osińska made her private vows and, in honor of the Apostle of Divine Mercy, took Faustina as her religious name. Izabela Naborowska joined her a year later and took the name Benigna. By January 1942 four more had joined them: Ludmila Roszko, Zofia Komorowska, Adela Alibekow, and Jadwiga Malkiewiczowna. They called themselves "Faustinians". Fr. Sopoćko gave them their religious names, wrote the regulations for them, and established their prayer routine. Everything was done secretly, for such things were banned by the occupying forces.

In March 1942, the Germans began to arrest Vilnius's religious. Fr. Sopoćko had to leave the city, as he was being sought by the Gestapo for helping Jews. He

made his way to the convent of the Ursulines in Czarny Bór, where he worked as a carpenter, concealing his true identity for eighteen months. He kept in contact with his charges by mail. He wrote that God wanted to place them among "sinners, atheists, the indifferent, the schismatics, the abandoned, pagans, the ill, prisoners, the homeless, orphans, as well as the despairing." As Czarny Bór was not quite two and a half miles from Vilnius, the Faustinians visited him for spiritual advice.

On April 11, 1942, on the eve of the Feast of Divine Mercy, the sisters made temporary religious vows and took the name Congregation of the Sisters of the Merciful Jesus Christ the Redeemer. Because they had to conceal their vocation from the occupying forces, they continued to live with their families, but they led a convent routine. In a letter from Czarny Bór, Fr. Sopoćko informed them that he had been praying daily for five years—during every Mass—for the establishment of the congregation. He returned to Vilnius in August 1944 and received the private, perpetual vows of the first six Faustinians at the chapel of the Carmelite Sisters on November 16. He described that day in his memoirs: "After the retreat, six young ladies from various parts of the city arrived at the Carmelite Sisters' convent on a pre-arranged day. It was very early in the morning, dark, and during the curfew. In an atmosphere reminiscent of the catacombs, they heard Mass and, at five in the morning, they made their private vows. The hospitable Carmelites had prepared a modest meal, during which an inexpressibly joyful mood prevailed among those who had just been espoused to Christ. Oh, how happy they were despite various shortages, how rich despite the poverty that was everywhere, how brave and trustful despite the dangers lying in wait at every turn."

None of the six sisters knew of Sr. Faustina's diary—kept in Kraków—in which there is a description of six sisters of the future congregation receiving Holy

Communion from Fr. Sopoćko. The mystic saw them gathered in a modest chapel without decorations or prie-dieux.

The third city that saw the devotion spread during the Nazi occupation was Warsaw. In 1941, an image of the Merciful Jesus appeared in the congregation's chapel (Zytnia Street). It had been painted by Lucyna Zabielska as a votive offering. A year later, Stanislaw Batowski's painting was also to be found in the chapel. This painting was burned during the Warsaw Uprising in 1944, but Mother Michaela Moraczewska, who liked Batowski's painting a lot, had earlier commissioned him to paint another image of the Merciful Jesus. This was painted in 1943 and can be found in the little Church of Divine Mercy, on Smolensk Street, Kraków.

Yet another image of the Merciful Jesus was painted in Warsaw during the German occupation, but it was not exhibited until after the war. The painting, by Zdzislaw Eichler, was to have been for the newly built Church of the Immaculate Heart of Mary (Szembeka Square), but when the parish priest, Fr. Jan Sztuka, saw the painting, he became frightened and refused to take it. The Germans regarded the image of the Merciful Jesus as an expression of Polish nationalism, as the two rays that emerged from Christ's Heart were the

**SR. IRENA KARDIS** - Congregation of the Sisters of the Angels - participated in illegal courses for catechists organized by Fr. Sopoćko in Vilnius.

**CARMELITE CONVENT,** 29 Poplawska Street, Vilnius, where Fr. Sopoćko received (1944) the simple vows of the first six candidates for the future Congregation of the Sisters of Merciful Jesus.

215

**FR. JOZEF JARZĘBOWSKI, M.I.C.** was the first Divine Mercy apostle in the United States.

# FR. JOZEF **JARZĘBOWSKI, M.I.C.**

**FR. JOZEF JARZĘBOWSKI, M.I.C.** (1897–1964) a Marian Father, was one of those that did most in popularizing the devotion to Divine Mercy. In 1939, he met Fr. Sopoćko in Vilnius, who told him about Sr. Faustina and her mission. In danger of being arrested by the Soviets he vowed – before a painting of Merciful Jesus in St. Michael's – that if he managed to flee the country he would become an apostle of Divine Mercy.

He succeeded. He reached North America in 1941, having crossed the whole of Siberia and the Pacific Ocean. He had with him Fr. Sopoćko's writings on Divine Mercy, which he published in the United States. It was thanks to him that the Marian Fathers in North America became involved in propagating the mission that Sr. Faustina had initiated. In 1950, Fr. Jarzebowski settled in Great Britain, where he established the Divine Mercy College at Fawley Court (Henley-on-Thames) – a school that formed almost 3,000 pupils –a library, and a museum.

When dying he wrote these last words in his diary: " In a word, life is beautiful; beautiful, because God is good, beautiful, because there is suffering for God, beautiful, because there are souls that love Him more, more generously than I do, but there are souls to beat one's breast with, to call on His abounding Mercy. "

**STANISLAW BATOWSKI'S** Merciful Jesus. Batowski's first painting was burned when the congregation's chapel on Zytnia Street was destroyed by fire during the Warsaw Uprising.

**MERCIFUL JESUS** painted during the war by Zdzisław Eichler. Today it is in the Church of the Transfiguration, 13 Miodowa Street, Warsaw.

same colors as the Polish national flag—red and white. In addition, the artist had a burning city as a background and a white lamb in a stream of blood at the Savior's feet. The parish priest was afraid that the Germans might send priests and parishioners to a concentration camp in reaction to such a "patriotic provocation". So a Capuchin, Fr. Benwenut Kwiatkowski, hid the painting at the convent of the Westiarki Sisters of Jesus. Today it can be seen at the Capuchin friary (13 Miodowa Street, Warsaw); King Jan Sobieski III's heart can also be found there in a sarcophagus.

In 1941 the devotion also spread in the United States. This was mainly due to a Polish Marian priest, Fr. Jozef Jarzebowski, who narrowly escaped with his life from the Soviet Union. He considered that he owed his escape to God's mercy. Hence, after arriving in America, he began to spread Sr. Faustina's message. He had with him the Vilnius memorandum about the devotion, which was written by Fr. Sopoćko. At his initiative, the Felician Sisters in the United States soon published a booklet—*Father of Mercy*—containing a novena, a litany, and a chaplet to God's mercy; they also issued a little image of the Merciful Jesus as well as Fr. Jarzebowski's introduction to the booklet. The edition sold out quickly. The demand for a new edition of the booklet was so great that the Marian community in America decided in 1944 to establish the Divine Mercy apostolate in Stockbridge, Massachusetts. The apostolate propagated Sr. Faustina's message by publishing articles, booklets, and brochures in Polish and English. The rectors of Polish Catholic missions in other countries also propagated the devotion.

# Germination

# CHAPTER 12

# Germination

The next stage in the history of the propagation of the devotion to Divine Mercy came after World War II. Poland emerged from that conflict not only in frightful ruins (with six million citizens having been murdered), but also enslaved by a Communist system that was imposed on her.

**STAINED-GLASS WINDOW,** Myslibórz, that depicts the Crucifixion of Jesus, which Sr. Faustina saw in a vision concerning the future congregation.

In 1945, as a result of border changes, Vilnius was incorporated into the Soviet Union. There followed a mass resettlement of Poles from the Vilnius region to Poland. Archbishop Romuald Jalbrzykowski and all those connected with the chancery and the seminary had to leave Vilnius. The Faustinians desired to live in a convent, wear habits, and lead a community life, but that was not possible under Soviet rule. Hence three of them left Vilnius in 1945, and the other three joined them a year later. The sisters met in Poznan, where they renewed their religious vows and decided what to do next. They resolved to bring the Divine Mercy apostolate to realization just as

Sr. Faustina had foretold when she wrote of the vocation's three aspects. So there would be the congregation, a lay institute, and a way for all to live out the devotion.

In the summer of 1945, two of the sisters, Faustina Osinska and Benigna Naborowska, approached the apostolic administrator of Gorzow, Fr. Edmund Nowicki, for permission to settle in his diocese and open a religious house. The administrator gladly agreed and assigned them to a parish in Myślibórz. The nuns arrived there on August 25, 1947. They saw the date as a providential sign, for it was the anniversary of the day Faustina Kowalska was born. Another sign was the fact that the little church was built in the year she was born—1905. From the moment of its existence, the church, funded by Polish workers, was the center of Catholicism in the Protestant region of Myslibórz. It was to be a center for radiating the devotion to Divine Mercy. Fr. Sopoćko visited the place for the first time in 1947. He wrote in his memoirs: "I made my way to Myslibórz. . . . I first went to the church, and to my great surprise I noticed in the altar nave a somewhat damaged stained-glass window that depicted the Lord Jesus on the Cross. I contemplated it with joy and amazement, as Sr. Faustina had spoken of such a church and such a stained-glass window." So the mystic's confessor confirmed that it was the church she saw in her visions concerning a new congregation.

Polish bishops had approached Pope Pius XII as early as 1946 with a request to establish the Divine Mercy Feast. A year later the Holy Father officially directed

**MYŚLIBÓRZ PARISH**
church.
St. John the
Baptist's.

**CHURCH OF THE HOLY CROSS,**
Myślibórz.
Sisters of
the new
congregation
took it over in
1947.

**MOTHER HOUSE**
Congregation
of the Sisters
of Merciful
Jesus in
Myślibórz.

223

**SISTERS FROM MYŚLIBÓRZ** with Fr. Władysław Wantuchowski (Jesuit).

**SISTERS OF MERCIFUL JESUS** in Myśliborz. Mother Superior Benigna seated.

**PORTRAIT OF FR**. **JÓZEF ANDRASZ** (in the convent in Łagiewniki). He was Sr. Faustina's confessor and a great propagator of the devotion to Divine Mercy.

the matter to the Congregation for Sacred Rites and Ceremonies. About the same time, Fr. Sopoćko, summoned by Archbishop Jalbrzykowski personally, arrived in Poland from Vilnius with the last transport of displaced persons; he was to stay for good. He settled in Bialystok and was a lecturer at the Bialystok Major Seminary. At the same time he never ceased striving to establish a feast day in honor of God's mercy. He found a great ally in August Cardinal Hlond, the Polish primate, who even gave him funds (1947) for the publication of his Latin treatise entitled *On Divine Mercy and the Establishment of Its Feast*. The primate also sent a theologian to the Vatican to promote the idea of introducing a new feast day in the liturgical calendar. Largely because of Fr. Sopoćko's endeavors, professors from university and seminary theology faculties, who were assembled at a theological conference in Kraków (1948), sent a resolution to Rome requesting the establishment of the Divine Mercy Feast. That same year Fr. Sopoćko wrote that there were already one hundred fifty votive offerings hanging beside the images of the Merciful Jesus in Vilnius and in other cities, which bore testimony to the numerous graces granted to the devotees of Divine Mercy.

The devotion also spread in Sr. Faustina's home area during the postwar years. This was connected with Fr. Franciszek Jablonski, the Swinice Warckie parish priest who had been in Dachau concentration camp during the war and had vowed that if he survived, he would a build a church in honor of God's mercy as an act of thanksgiving. He kept his word, and in 1950 he laid the foundation stone of the church in Dzierzawy, over six miles from Swinice Warckie. The church, dedicated to the Divine Mercy, was consecrated eight years later, and an Adolf Hyła Merciful Jesus image—specially commissioned by Fr. Jablonski—was hung in the chancel.

About that time Sr. Faustina's other confessor was also continuing his mission of propagating the message about God's mercy. In 1947 Fr. Jozef Andrasz published a booklet, entitled *Divine Mercy, We Trust in You!*, which popularized the devotion in the forms that were advocated by Sr. Faustina. The whole first edition sold out very quickly. The second edition was to appear in 1948, but the Communist censors in Kraków banned the propagation of the booklet. Fortunately, the text found its way abroad. The Marian Fathers in the United States decided to publish the little work

**FRAGMENTS**
of Fr. Józef Andrasz's manuscript on the Divine Mercy.

**FR. JÓZEF ANDRASZ'S**
booklet, *Divine Mercy, We Trust in You!*

WRZESIEŃ.—Serce Jezusa, ucz nas obrony praw Kościoła.

Serce Jezusa, ulituj się nad Indianami Ameryki Łacińskiej.

PAŹDZIERNIK.—Serce Jezusa, mnóż dzieła miłosierdzia dla upośledzonych i biedaków.

Serce Jezusa, błogosław tym, co troszczą się o chorych na Misjach.

LISTOPAD.—Serce Jezusa, ochronę roztocz nad Miejscami Świętymi.

Serce Jezusa, w opiece miej wolność i wzrost szkół katolickich.

GRUDZIEŃ.—Serce Jezusa, przez Eucharystię odnów rodziny.

Serce Jezusa, daj, by Kościół na Filipinach spełnił swe względem Dalekiego Wschodu zadania.

•

POSŁANIEC SERCA JEZUSA

4105 N. Avers Ave.   Chicago 18, Illinois

Za specjalnym upoważnieniem Władzy Kościelnej.

**PAPAL INTENTIONS** for 1950, with the image of Merciful Jesus, published in Polish in Chicago.

**SR. JADWIGA OSIŃSKA,** the first superior of the Congregation of the Sisters of Merciful Jesus (died 1955).

in English. Thanks to them, the English edition found many readers in Canada, Australia, New Zealand, Asia, and Africa. Later the booklet was translated into Spanish and Portuguese and, with the imprimaturs of local bishops, sold in great numbers in all the South American countries. German and Italian translations followed, and the little work reached Western Europe.

In 1955 Fr. Andrasz learned that the Faustinians in Myslibórz had been officially approved. The order was initially called the Congregation of the Sisters of the Merciful Jesus Christ the Redeemer, but in 1973 the name was shortened to the Congregation of the Sisters of the Merciful Jesus. In consequence of the approval, Fr. Andrasz sent large parts of Sr. Faustina's diary to Myslibórz. Until that time the Faustinians did not know it at all, as it had never been published, and the manuscript was to be found at the convent in Łagiewniki. It was only then that the sisters could read of how their spiritual patron saw the charism of the new congregation. She wrote down what she had heard from Jesus on the subject: "Your purpose and that of your companions is to unite yourselves with Me as closely as possible; through love You will reconcile earth with heaven, you will soften the just anger of God, and you will plead for mercy for the world. I place in your care two pearls very precious to My Heart: these are the souls of priests and religious. You will pray particularly for them; their power will come from your diminishment" (*Diary*, 531).

Just after the approval, the new congregation was touched by a painful experience. The superior general, Sr. Faustina Osinska, died unexpectedly at a hospital in

Jésus j'ai confiance en vous [1]

Sang et Eau sortis du Sacré-Cœur de Jésus, comme Source de la Miséricorde pour nous, j'ai confiance en vous.

Sœur FAUSTINE

Apôtre de la miséricorde Divine

Née le 25 août 1905, au village de Olocowice-Polog. Décédée après de grandes souffrances le 5 décembre 1938, à Łagiewniki près de Cracovie.

Les personnes qui obtiendront des grâces par l'intercession de Sœur Faustine, sont priées d'en avertir le Postulateur de la cause Révérend Père SUWALA S. A. C. Società dell' Apostolato Cattolico, 57 Via Pettinari, ROMA-ITALIA, et, en France M. l'Abbé Aloys MISIAK, Pallottin Institution Saint-Stanislas OSNY (Seine-et-Oise).

Imprimi Potest 25 février 1952
Ceslaus Wedzioch
Superior Regionis misericordiae Dei
S. Ap. C
Imprimatur Versaliis, die 26e Februarii 1952
M. Leiner

Procurez vous le fascicule : Prière à la Miséricorde Divine, consécration, chapelet, litanies, prières pour obtenir des grâces par l'intercession de Sœur Faustine.

PROPAGANDE DU SACRÉ-CŒUR
6, montée de l'Antiquaille

Gorzow (December 27, 1955) from an intestinal torsion. Fr. Sopoćko thought that her death was connected with the private vows she had made at the Jesuit church in Szczecin (April 12, 1953); she had offered up her life to God for the sake of priests.

In time, the number of faithful who had experienced various graces through Sr. Faustina's intercession while praying in the convent at Łagiewniki began to grow. They began to exert pressure on the congregation to initiate efforts in commencing Faustina's beatification process. Mother Michaela Moraczewska had talked to August Cardinal Hlond about the matter as early as January 9, 1947. He said: "Wait; it is not time yet. Gather documents, amass materials, so that you might have everything prepared when the time comes."

Mother Michaela, who took the primate's advice as an instruction, ordered the collection of data on Sr. Faustina, particularly about the graces that had been received through the mystic's intercession. In 1948, the superior general sent Sr. Bernarda Wilczek to Faustina's home area to collect information from those who knew her as Helen Kowalska.

The convent chronicler also collected accounts from those who had employed her as a domestic. The recollections of sisters who still remembered the deceased mystic were written down under oath between 1952 and 1965. The next superior general of the congregation, Mother Roza Klobukowska, asked the general of the Pallottine Order, Fr. Wojciech Turkowski, to appoint a postulator for the beatification process. Fr. Stanislaw Suwala became the postulator (May 22, 1951), and his deputy was Fr. Alojzy Zuchowski.

**SR. BERNARDETA**
Sopoćko, Fr. Michał Sopoćko's niece, was one of the first sisters of the Congregation of Sisters of Merciful Jesus.

**INFORMATION**
about Sr. Faustina and the Divine Mercy devotion, printed in France in 1952.

227

Meanwhile Fr. Andrasz managed to find another ally in his endeavors to spread the devotion. In 1951, the metropolitan of Kraków, Adam Cardinal Sapieha, gave permission for a public celebration of the Divine Mercy Feast in Łagiewniki. Shortly afterwards he granted a partial indulgence of seven years to all those who visited the Łagiewniki convent on that Sunday. It might have seemed that everything was on the right track for the Divine Mercy Feast to gain complete acceptance in the Church. Faustina's beatification also seemed to be just a question of time. But unexpected difficulties appeared.

In 1951 Archbishop Jalbrzykowski, who had heard Sr. Faustina's confessions in Vilnius many times before the war, issued an unfavorable opinion about the devotion as advocated by her. He submitted a statement, *On the Alleged Revelations—Visions of Sr. Faustina,* to an episcopal commission. He wrote: "Theologians are strongly opposed to elevating one attribute of God's perfection above another, since all are infinitely perfect. Fr. Sopoćko's reference to St. Thomas Aquinas is not justified and [is] groundless. ... For the above reasons I have categorically forbidden Rev. Prof. Sopoćko to publicize Sr. Faustina's quasi-visions or to propagate the devotion."

**ARCHBISHOP ROMUALD JAŁBRZYKOWSKI** was opposed to the Divine Mercy devotion in the forms prescribed by Sr. Faustina Kowalska.

The matter was referred to the Holy See for appraisal. At the same time, many critical opinions undermined the theological value of the Merciful Jesus image. The fact that many images—by various artists—although based on Sr. Faustina's vision—were to be found in many Polish churches increased the confusion. The problem of the conformity of the said paintings with liturgical and dogmatic norms even became the subject of the Polish episcopate's plenary conference of September 1953. The sharpest criticism came from Bishop Franciszek Bard. He claimed that some of the said works did not correspond to Church teaching, as they were based not so much on the revelations contained in Holy Scripture as on private visions whose authenticity had not been confirmed. Some of the Merciful Jesus images were removed from churches after that conference.

Fr. Sopoćko decided to defend the idea of the Merciful Jesus image. He intended to write a letter to Stefan Cardinal Wyszynski, but the primate had been arrested by the Communists. So he wrote to Bishop Michał Klepacz, the chairman of the Polish episcopate, asking him to look into the matter again. In his letter he argued that Eugeniusz Kazimirowski's canvas (painted in Vilnius) was in accord with the teaching of the Church, as it depicted Christ appearing before the apostles in the Upper Room and instituting the sacrament of reconciliation. The case for this was to have been the fact that Gospel excerpts about this event had been read in every church since the Council of Trent. In consequence of the letter, Fr. Sopoćko was instructed to come up with a completely new image that was based exclusively on the Gospel and not on Sr. Faustina's visions. So in 1954, he announced a competition that required artists to depict Christ instituting the sacrament of reconciliation in the Upper Room.

Adolf Hyła, who had until that point managed to paint over a hundred images of the Merciful Jesus for churches all over the country, categorically refused to take part in the competition. In his opinion, the preconditions of the whole enterprise were a compromise to which he could not agree. In a letter to Fr. Sopoćko, he wrote: "A compromise will be, among others, the very composition of the Merciful Christ image, which will simultaneously depict a scene from His life, as described in the Gospel, and details from Sr. Faustina's vision. But the result of this compromise will be a painting that will not depict the Gospel scene and one that will narrow the notion of Divine Mercy. After all, according to the Gospel [Jn 20:19–24], after the Lord Jesus had entered the Upper Room through the closed doors, He greeted the assembled disciples with the words 'Peace be with you', showed them the wounds in His hands and side, breathed the Holy Spirit upon them, and instituted the sacrament of reconciliation. In the painting, the floor and doors of the Upper Room will be depicted, while Christ Himself will be doing

**MOTHER MICHAELA MORACZEWSKA**, who, with the beatification process in mind, issued an instruction to gather information on Sr. Faustina (1948).

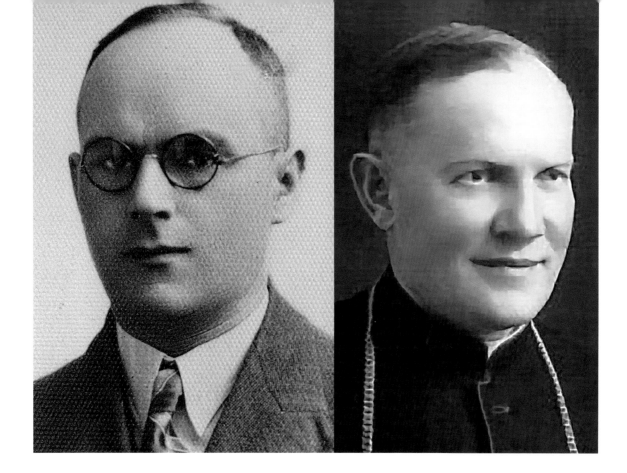

**LUDOMIR ŚLENDZIŃSKI,** the painter who won the Merciful Jesus painting competition.

**BISHOP MICHAŁ KLEPACZ** was chairman of the Polish Episcopal Conference from 1953 to 1956, when the primate, Cardinal Wyszyński, was under house arrest.

something else: He will be indicating the rays of Blood and Water gushing out of His side with His left hand, and His right will be raised in a gesture of blessing. The image also limits the notion of mercy as expressed in Sr. Faustina's vision, for it is narrowed down to just the mercy manifest in the sacrament of reconciliation."

On September 2, 1954, the commission—Bishop Stanislaw Rospond, Fr. Adam Bochnak, Fr. Kazimierz Figlewicz, Fr. Tadeusz Kruszyński, and Fr. Michał Sopoćko—announced the winner of the competition: Ludomir Ślendziński, from Vilnius. On October 5, 1954, his painting also received a positive opinion from the General Commission of the Polish episcopate under the chairmanship of Bishop Franciszek Bard. The commission regarded Ślendziński's work as worthy of imitation. But it stipulated that images of the Merciful Jesus could not be displayed at high altars and that public displays required the consent of the local bishop. Ślendziński's painting can be found in the chapel of the Congregation of the Sisters of Our Lady of Mercy (44 Hetmanska Street, Warsaw). There are two copies, one in a Bialystok parish church and the other in the Jesuit's Merciful Heart of Jesus sanctuary in Kalisz. Despite the episcopate's approval, Ślendziński's painting did not become as popular as Hyła's painting, which can be found in Łagiewniki.

**THE MERCIFUL JESUS** by Ludomir Ślendziński, who won the competition that was organized by Fr. Sopoćko in 1954.

**PROTOCOL** of the competition commission of June 30, 1954, evaluating the Merciful Jesus paintings.

231

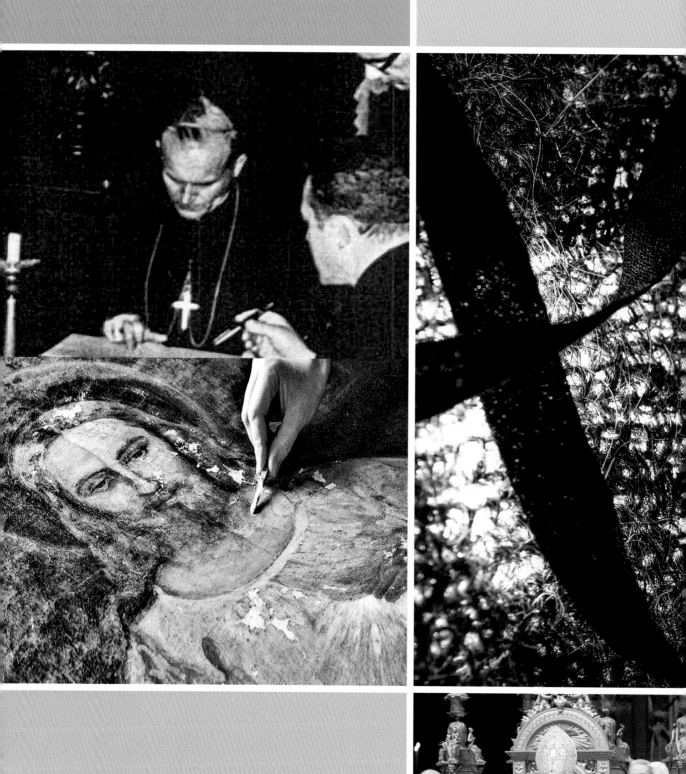

# Trial

— 1 —

1.

O miłości nieskończona, kazesz malować Oblicze Twej świętej
Twej, a ved stanieva mam zdroj miłosierdzia niepojęty.
Błogosławiem kto się zbliży do Twych promieni
A dana czasu w niego się zamieni.

O słodki Jezu, tu raczyłeś tron miłosierdzia Swego
Ku ucieczce i wspomaganiu człowieka grzesznego,
Z otwartego Serca jak ze zdroju czystego
Płynie pociecha dla duszy i serca skruszonego.

Niech dla Obrazu tego, cześć i chwała
Płynie z duszy człowieka nigdy nieustawa,
Niech z serca każdego cześć miłosierdziu Bożemu płynie
teraz i na wieki wieków i w każdej godzinie.

O Boże mój

Soły patrze w przyszłość, ogarnia mię trwoga,
Ale pocóż zagłębiać się w przyszłości;
Dla mnie jest tylko chwila obecna droga,
Bo przyszłość może w duszy mojej nie zagości.

Czas który przeszedł nie jest w mej mocy
By coś odmienić, poprawić lub dodać,
Bo tego nie dokazał ani mędrzec ani prorocy,
A więc co przeszłość w sobie zawarła na Boga zdać.

O chwilo obecna, ty do mnie należysz cała
Ciebie wykorzystać chcę ile tylko jest w mej mocy,
A chociaż jestem słaba i mała
Dajesz mi łaskę ...

... twoje
... płynie serce moje
... w każdą chwilę.

# CHAPTER 13

# Trial

At a time of disputes in Poland concerning images of the Merciful Jesus, Holy Office theologians in Rome were investigating whether Sr. Faustina's writings conformed to the teaching of the Church's Magisterium. Unfortunately, the Vatican experts relied on imprecise copies of the diary manuscript.

**ERRONEOUS TRANSLATIONS**
Mother Ksawera Olszamowska's inaccurate copies of Sr. Faustina's diary manuscript were the Holy See's basis in assessing Sr. Faustina's work.

Their author was Mother Ksawera Olszamowska, who—in good faith—corrected Sr. Faustina's work in her own way: she omitted many sentences or changed the meaning of some words. The omission of the pencil underlining, in the manuscript, of Jesus' words led to erroneous conclusions, for example, that Sr. Faustina was asking people to venerate her heart and not the Heart of Jesus. Mother Ksawera's inexact copies became in turn the basis for French and Italian translations. It was precisely on those translations that the Vatican experts had relied. As a result, the Sacred

Congregation of the Holy Office issued a decree (November 19, 1958), addressed to bishops and to superiors of religious orders, that ruled out the possibility of establishing a feast day in honor of God's mercy. The document stated that Sr. Faustina Kowalska's revelations were not of a supernatural nature, and in consequence of this, images and prayers based on her visions were to be withdrawn. Bishops were advised to be prudent in removing elements of the devotion from parishes. Moreover, the congregation instructed the Polish primate, Stefan Cardinal Wyszyński, to reprimand Fr. Michał Sopoćko severely, and to instruct him not to spread information about Sr. Faustina's alleged revelations.

Shortly afterwards, the mystic's former confessor was summoned before the primate, who read the Vatican decree to him. After a moment of silence, Fr. Sopoćko said: "I await my punishment." The cardinal said that the reprimand was a sufficient punishment in itself.

JEZU UFAM TOBIE

**MERCIFUL JESUS** by Adolf Hyła, painted for the church in Dzierżawy.

**ADOLF HYŁA'S** first painting was donated for the chapel in Łagiewniki in 1943 as a votive offering.

**ADOLF HYŁA"S PAINTING (ŁAGIEWNIKI)** is the best-known image of the Merciful Jesus. It is famous for the many graces associated with it.

237

But the Holy See's decision did not dispirit the stubborn priest. On the contrary, in a letter to the primate, he wrote: "I was glad that that which Sr. Faustina had foretold had come about." For in 1935, during a discussion with her spiritual director, she had a revelation as to the great obstacles the Divine Mercy devotion would face in the future. She told Fr. Sopoćko of the great suffering that was awaiting in connection with it. She said that there would come a time when it would seem as if the work had been utterly destroyed. Then God would act and convince people of the authenticity of the devotion. Sr. Faustina foretold that it would be a treasure discovered anew, one that had been in the Church for ages, but had remained forgotten. She repeated that before God came as a just Judge at the end of time, He wanted all to come to know Him as King of Mercy. She also told the priest that the triumph of Divine Mercy would come after they had both departed from this world. But first a hard trial had to come, during which Fr. Sopoćko would have the impression that all his efforts had ended in failure. She assured him that the said destruction would be but an apparent destruction, though the suffering would be very real. However, she could not say when that time of trial would come, or how long it would last.

On March 6, 1959, shortly after the publication of the decree, the Sacred Congregation of the Holy Office issued another document, a notification forbidding the propagation of the Divine Mercy devotion in forms communicated by Sr. Faustina. It ordered forbearance from propagating the devotion until there was a definitive decision about the matter. It left the issue of the Merciful Jesus images to the prudence of bishops; images that were already in use for the devotion could be left in place or removed, but bishops were advised not to display new ones.

The Vatican notification, issued by the Holy Office, was universally construed as the Holy See's official rejection of the devotion advocated by Sr. Faustina. As a result of that ruling, many images of the Merciful Jesus were removed from churches all over Poland. Adolf Hyła's painting in the church in Dzierzawy met such a fate; even the parish name was changed (from Divine Mercy to Sacred Heart of Jesus). Priests stopped giving homilies about the devotion. One could not talk openly about Faustina Kowalska. Her beatification process came to a standstill. New candidates did not flock to the Faustinians because parish priests, who regarded the order with suspicion, did not direct candidates there. Fr. Sopoćko, severely reprimanded by the Vatican, had to endure many tribulations. Even the Congregation of the Sisters of Our Lady of Mercy stopped distributing images, chaplets, and other prayers by Sr. Faustina.

**FOUNDATION STONE**. In 1950 Fr. Franciszek Jabloński laid the foundation stone for the Church of Divine Mercy in Dzierżawy, about five miles from Głogowiec, Sr. Faustina's home village.

**DIVINE MERCY CHURCH** in Dzierżawy. This church was consecrated by Bishop Antoni Pawlowski (1958). After the issue of the Vatican's notification critical of the Divine Mercy devotion, the church was renamed Church of the Sacred Heart of Jesus (1961).

The climate that then prevailed in the Church was one of the reasons it was difficult to get Sr. Faustina's message accepted. Fr. Andrzej Witko explained: "Before World War II, and even in the fifties, the Holy See took a critical stance with regard to all private revelations. Two special canons in the old Canon Law advised bishops to be extremely cautious with regard to such revelations. Moreover, Sr. Faustina, a simple, ordinary nun, theologically uneducated, had proposed 'shocking forms' of devotion. The idea of introducing a feast day in honor of God's mercy on the first Sunday after Easter caused the greatest difficulty, as that Sunday ended the Easter Octave; it crowned the most important liturgical celebrations in the Church." It was also not insignificant that some German and Lithuanian Catholic centers, who saw the devotion as a manifestation of Polish nationalism in the guise of popular piety, declared themselves against the proposed feast day. According to them the nationalism was evidenced by the rays in the image, which were associated with the white and red of the Polish national colors, and the claim that Poland was particularly beloved by Christ, as stated in Sr. Faustina's diary.

**NOVENA TO DIVINE MERCY** propagated after World War II by sisters from Łagiewniki.

239

Nowenna do Miłosierdzia Bożego

**FR. JULIAN CHRÓŚCIECHOWSKI, M.I.C.,** one of the most important apostles of Divine Mercy in the 20th century.

**METROPOLITAN OF KRAKÓW**
Archbishop Eugeniusz Baziak decided not to remove the Merciful Jesus image from the chapel in Lagiewniki.

The matter involving Fr. Julian Chróściechowski was another reason many of the hierarchy regarded the devotion with distrust. Fr. Sopoćko spoke of it in his memoirs: "In March 1948, Mr. Julian Chróściechowski, who later became a Marian Father, sent me a typescript about the development of the devotion of Divine Mercy for proofreading. I had to change most of it, and I also added the Church's teaching on Divine Mercy. In 1949 the Marian Fathers issued a brochure under my name (nota bene, without my consent). It was entitled *Divine Mercy—Humanity's Sole Hope*, and it was translated into various languages. Moreover, they added to the translations that the late August Cardinal Hlond had recommended the devotion on his deathbed, [probably] on the basis of information from Mother Ksawera, with whom Fr. Chróściechowski corresponded. Though His Eminence was on the whole favorably inclined toward the devotion, and even issued my treatise, *De Misericordia Dei Deque Eiusdem Festo Instituendo*, at his own expense, I did not know anything about his deathbed recommendation, and there was no mention of it in the Polish version of the brochure. In 1957 His Eminence Archbishop Baraniak, who had been the late Cardinal Hlond's secretary, read the note about the alleged recommendation in the Italian edition of the brochure, also under my name. He made a strong protest against it, stating that 'in all probability, it has all been made up,' as was

✚

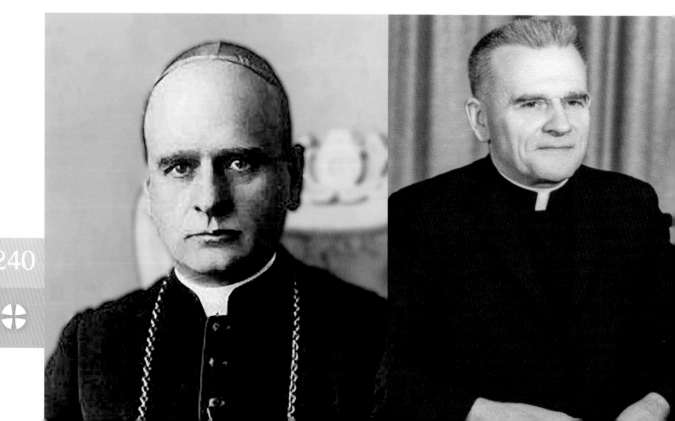

# FR. JULIAN CHRÓŚCIECHOWSKI, M.I.C.

**JULIAN CHRÓŚCIECHOWSKI, M.I.C.** (1912–1976) was one of those who contributed greatly to the Divine Mercy devotion being spread all over the world. After his law studies he attained a Ph.D. in law in 1938. He was active in the independence movement during the war and was arrested by the Germans. He miraculously escaped from Pawiak Prison – while returning to his cell for his picture of the Merciful Jesus, the other prisoners were driven away for execution without him. After the war he studied in Paris, Oxford, and London, but his desire to dedicate himself to the Divine Mercy apostolate remained. He wrote a treatise on the subject and sent it, from England, to Fr. Sopoćko in Poland, who was critical of it, but he sent it back with his own text on Divine Mercy. Chróściechowski, impressed by the text, shortly had it published in Great Britain. This promising lawyer abandoned his career and entered the Marian Order in Stockbridge, Massachusetts, where he dedicated himself to propagating devotion to Divine Mercy, coordinating the apostolate in countries in the Western Hemisphere. He carried on an extensive correspondence with Fr. Sopoćko, and sought his advice in many matters. He himself wrote and published a great deal on this subject. His best-known work is *A History of the Devotion to Divine Mercy in Our Day*, which he completed near the end of his life when he was seriously ill. The last thing he wrote was as follows: "Humanity, in turning directly to God for Mercy, will undoubtedly open the flood-gates of the Lord's pity upon the world. When humanity turns to the One who is Mercy Incarnate for pity, the era of Christ's peace shall reign on earth."

the prayer—supposedly arranged by Cardinal Hlond—for the beatification of Sr. Faustina, which Mother Ksawera had given to me."

The archbishop of Poznań, Antoni Baraniak, did not stop at that. On March 15, 1958, he sent a statement to bishops in Poland and abroad, saying that the devotion was based on fiction. Information about this reached the Sacred Congregation of the Holy Office, which was examining Sr. Faustina's revelations. The outcome of it all was that for many years Fr. Sopoćko was regarded as a liar—one who falsified history. No one knew that the real perpetrator of the confusion was Fr. Julian Chróściechowski. Sr. Ksawera Olszamowska maintained that she received a prayer for the beatification of Sr. Faustina from Cardinal August Hlond during a personal meeting with him. However, this was not possible to establish beyond doubt.

The sisters at Łagiewniki faced a dilemma with regard to the Holy See's ban of the devotion as advocated by Sr. Faustina; what were they to do with the

**MERCIFUL JESUS IMAGE**, by Eugeniusz Kazimirowski. After it had been in Belarus for 30 years it was conserved by Edyta Hankowska-Czerwińska.

Divine Mercy image that was in the side altar of their chapel, surrounded by numerous votive offerings and ceaselessly venerated by the faithful? Were they to continue to display it at the side altar for devotions to Divine Mercy, and by the high altar for the Divine Mercy Feast? Were they to conceal the image and abandon their tradition of solemn Masses on the third Sunday of every month, during which priests delivered homilies on God's mercy? The sisters turned to the metropolitan of Kraków, Archbishop Eugeniusz Baziak. It so happened that when the nuns were talking to the archbishop, the image was by the altar for a devotion. So the hierarch determined that the image was to stay where it was and that none of the ceremonies that had been observed until then were to be abolished. Thus the devotion was continually propagated at Lagiewniki. It was from there that, despite all sorts of setbacks, the fame of the extraordinary nun, through whose intercession numerous pilgrims obtained graces, spread throughout the world.

The devotion to Divine Mercy did not cease in Warsaw either, despite the Vatican notification banning devotions in forms advocated by Sr. Faustina. The devotions were connected with the Merciful Jesus image that was painted by Boleslaw Rutkowski (Częstochowa, 1953) for St. Florian's Cathedral in Warsaw. According to a prelate, Fr. Lucjan Swieszkowski, this Merciful Jesus image was the only one that was displayed in the capital for almost twenty years. Br. Józef—porter at Cardinal Wyszyński's palace —often came to pray before the image. It was Br. Józef who initiated devotions in the cathedral, often led by Polish bishops, on every fifth day of the month.

At this point it is worth mentioning the fate of the first Merciful Jesus painting, the work of Eugeniusz Kazimirowski, the only one that Sr. Faustina had seen. It had been in St. Michael's Church in Vilnius since 1937. In August 1948 the Communist authorities closed the church to turn it into a museum of architecture. The church's most valuable objects, including Kazimirowski's painting, ended up in the former Dominican Holy Spirit Church, where Fr. Jan Ellert was the parish priest. In 1956 Fr. Józef Grasewicz turned up there. He was Fr. Sopoćko's friend and a great advocate of the devotion. Fr. Ellert gave him the Merciful Jesus image. He took it to the little church in the village of Nowa Ruda, near Grodno, where he was the parish priest. The image of Christ, with the

**KAROL CARDINAL WOJTYŁA** signed the document ending the informative process concerning Sr. Faustina (September 20, 1967).

243

**CARDINAL KAROL WOJTYŁA**, metropolitan of Kraków, at Mass in the
chapel of the Congregation of the Sisters of our Lady of Mercy in Lagiewniki.

added inscription "Jesus, I trust in You", was hung high in the chancel, and people began to venerate it. Fr. Sopoćko's friend frequently gave homilies on God's mercy and also taught parishioners to recite the chaplet that Jesus had communicated to Sr. Faustina. The faithful did not stop venerating the image when the priest was moved to another parish in 1957. In 1970, the Communist authorities closed the church in Nowa Ruda, and its interior decorations were taken to the nearby church in Porzecz. The image was not taken because it was hung too high. Hence the inhabitants of the little village in Soviet Belarus continued to go to the church for many years to beg God for mercy before that extraordinary image.

Karol Wojtyła was a man whose destiny was particularly interwoven with that of Sr. Faustina Kowalska and her mission. He became the temporary administrator of Kraków in 1963, after the death of Archbishop Baziak, and was appointed metropolitan archbishop by Pope Paul VI in 1964. As Sr. Beata Piekut recalled: "In 1964 I approached Archbishop Wojtyła with a request for him to discern—during his stay at the Vatican—if it was the right time and climate to begin Sr. Faustina's beatification process." The metropolitan gladly agreed. He decided to talk to the prefect of the Sacred Congregation of the Holy Office, Alfredo Cardinal Ottaviani, during the third session of Vatican Council II. He asked him whether the negative notification of 1959 concerning Sr. Faustina excluded the possibility of a beatification process. "Not only was I allowed, but I was instructed to commence Sr. Faustina's process as quickly as possible, while witnesses were still alive", Archbishop Wojtyła related years later. On his return to Kraków, the metropolitan gave instructions that Sr. Faustina's diary was not to be made available to anyone, even to priests, and that no excerpts from it were to be quoted anywhere. At the same time, he ordered prayers to be written and distributed for Sr. Faustina's beatification.

On August 22, Karol Wojtyła wrote: "They have been bombarding me to commence the process, so I have passed the whole matter over to the suffragan bishop, Julian Groblicki." Two months later (October 21) Bishop Groblicki, delegated by the metropolitan of Kraków, solemnly commenced the informative process in the Kraków Archdiocese on the life and virtues of Sr. Faustina Kowalska. Archbishop Wojtyła wanted Sr. Beata Piekut to be the postulator, but at that time women could be neither process postulators nor notaries, as those functions were solely entrusted to priests. So the metropolitan appointed a Franciscan, Fr. Izydor Borkiewicz, as the postulator, and he made Sr. Beata Piekut his deputy. The chairman of the tribunal was Fr. Józef Szczotkowski, and the promoters of the Faith were the Resurrectionist

**CATHEDRAL OF ST. FLORIAN**, Warsaw, where the Divine Mercy devotion developed despite the Holy Office's negative opinion.

245

Fr. Jerzy Mrowczynski and the Michaelite Fr. Walerian Moroz; the judges were Fr. Stanislaw Dabrowski, Fr. Ludwik Piechnik (Jesuit), Fr. Anzelm Kubit (Franciscan), and Fr. Bonawentura Kadeja (Piar); the notaries, Fr. Augustyn Dziedziel (Salesian), Fr. Antoni Dabija (Jesuit), and Fr. Stefan Marszowski. During the tribunal's seventy-five sessions, forty-five witnesses were questioned, and the mystic's writings were collected. On November 25, 1966, the nun's mortal remains were moved from a tomb in the convent cemetery to the chapel in Lagiewniki. The informative process, the Kraków Archdiocese stage, was concluded on September 27, 1967, during a solemn session chaired by Karol Cardinal Wojtyła.

Fr. Sopoćko's veracity was questioned during the process. It was recalled that concocted facts concerning prayers allegedly written by Cardinal Hlond were to be found in brochures in various languages issued under his name. The real cause of the confusion was explained by Fr. Chróściechowski: "The whole matter weighed heavily on my conscience, though I did not know about all of its consequences. I did not know, for example, that Fr. Sopoćko had received a severe reprimand from the Holy Office [1958] for his part in propagating the devotion, and for, among other things, propagating prayers that were attributed to Cardinal Hlond for Sr. Faustina's beatification, which indeed was not his work, but mine. In reality, if anyone deserved the severe reprimand, I did, for I did it on my own initiative; I did not consult him on the matter." During the process, when Fr. Sopoćko was accused of lying, Fr. Chróściechowski spoke in his defense and took all the responsibility on himself. On November 13, 1967, the Marian priest also submitted an explanation to the Sacred Congregation of the Holy Office that cleared Fr. Sopoćko of all the charges against him.

The process files were sent from Kraków to the Vatican, to the Sacred Congregation for the Causes of Saints, which inaugurated the beatification process on January 31, 1968. The postulator was a Jesuit, Fr. Antoni Mruk, a professor at the Gregorian University in Rome, and the vice-postulator was a Franciscan, Fr. Izydor Borkiewicz. The Sacred Congregation for the Causes of Saints, with the Holy Office notification in mind, maintained an exaggerated caution during the beatification process. A basic task was an examination and theological analysis of Sr. Faustina's writings, but particularly her main work, her diary. This was undertaken by Rev. Prof. Ignacy Różycki, who, for close to a quarter of a century, did not conceal his skeptical attitude towards the simple nun's professed revelations. In his opinion, Faustina "was a victim of hallucinations of the nature of hysteria, so not only her supposed revelations were devoid of any religious value, but at the

**CARDINAL ALFREDO OTTAVIANI**, prefect of the Holy Office, standing to the right of Pope Pius XII.

**DURING VATICAN II**
Archbishop Karol Wojtyła and Cardinal Alfredo Ottaviani discussed Sr. Faustina.

247

**SR. BEATA PIEKUT**, the vice-postulator for Sr. Faustina's beatification process.

**BISHOP JULIAN GROBLICKI**, at Cardinal Wojtyła's request, supervised the course of Sr. Faustina's process.

same time, and thereby, the heroism of her life—it was a lost cause." But one day he decided to read the diary to reassure himself as to his decision. The more he immersed himself in the mystic's writings, the more smitten he was by the depth, insight, and precision of her theological formulations. When he had finished reading the deceased nun's sixth notebook, he declared: "Sr. Faustina's sanctity is truly heroic, while her revelations have all the hallmarks of supernatural origin." When he shared his impressions with Archbishop Wojtyła, the latter instructed him to make a meticulous theological analysis of Sr. Faustina's diary. Even Fr. Różycki himself did not notice how his analysis grew into a 500-page treatise (in French), in which he defended the authenticity and supernatural character of Sr. Faustina's revelations. Another Church censor wrote a similar review.

However, theologians were not of one mind with regard to Sr. Faustina's message. Her diary led some to the conviction that the author was admittedly a pious person, but hysterical, overreactive, and subject to delusions. A "battle about Faustina"—a discussion on the authenticity and Catholicity of her revelations—ensued in Polish theological circles. Rev. Prof. Wincenty Granat was the best known of her critics; he was an out-

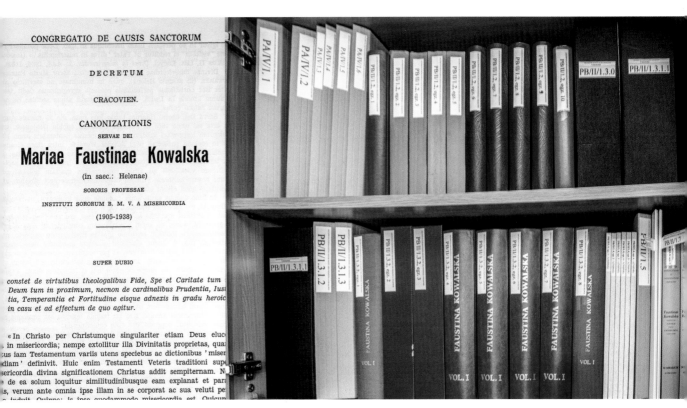

CONGREGATIO DE CAUSIS SANCTORUM

DECRETUM

CRACOVIEN.

CANONIZATIONIS
SERVAE DEI

# Mariae Faustinae Kowalska

(in saec.: Helenae)
SORORIS PROFESSAE
INSTITUTI SORORUM B. M. V. A MISERICORDIA
(1905-1938)

SUPER DUBIO

constet de virtutibus theologalibus Fide, Spe et Caritate tum
Deum tum in proximum, necnon de cardinalibus Prudentia, Iusti-
tia, Temperantia et Fortitudine eisque adnexis in gradu heroic
in casu et ad effectum de quo agitur.

«In Christo per Christumque singulariter etiam Deus eluc
, in misericordia; nempe extollitur illa Divinitatis proprietas, qua
:us iam Testamentum variis utens speciebus ac dictionibus ' miser
idiam' definivit. Huic enim Testamenti Veteris traditioni sup
sericordia divina significationem Christus addit sempiternam. N
e de ea solum loquitur similitudinibusque eam explanat et par
.s, verum ante omnia ipse illam in se corporat ac sua veluti pe

standing theologian of dogma and vice-chancellor of the Catholic University of Lublin. According to him, the forms of the devotion advocated by Sr. Faustina were unacceptable: "God's mercy is one of His attributes, and were we to venerate it through a separate feast day it would also be fitting—he argued—to establish yet other feast days to venerate God's other attributes; but such a stance would obscure God's unity and lead to the danger of polytheism." Fr. Różycki responded to the charges. He wrote: "God is not only wise, but is Wisdom; He is not only omnipotent, but is Omnipotence; in relation to the world, He not only reveals His providence, but is Providence; He not only loves us, but is Love; He is not only merciful, but is Mercy. So, Wisdom, Providence, Omnipotence, Love, and Mercy, which are ipso facto God, have the right, on our part, to veneration and adoration."

But Fr. Granat directed the most serious charges against the Divine Mercy Chaplet. The following part of the chaplet particularly roused his opposition: "Eternal Father, I offer You the Body and Blood, Soul and Divinity of Your dearly beloved Son, our Lord, Jesus Christ, in atonement for our sins and those of the whole world." This eminent dogmatist thought that the above formulations contained serious theological errors.

**DOCUMENT**
from Sr. Faustina
Kowalska's
canonization
process.

**DOCUMENTATION**
on the life of
Sr. Faustina, collected
for her beatification
process.

Firstly, the Son's Godhead is the same as the Father's, so it cannot be offered to the eternal Father. Secondly, one cannot offer up the Godhead at all. Thirdly, it cannot be an atonement for sins, as God forgives sins, so it is not an atonement offering.

Fr. Różycki responded to Fr. Granat's charges by accusing him of an erroneous equation of two notions: "Godhead" and "divine nature"; the Council of Trent had already, in its dogmatic formula on the Real Presence of Christ in the Eucharist, stated that Jesus' eucharistic Godhead is not synonymous with His divine nature, common to the three Persons. For in the context of the Eucharist, Godhead strictly denotes only the Divine Person of Jesus. Besides, the same formula appeared in the prayer dictated by an angel to the children during the Fatima revelations in 1916. It refers to the words of St. Paul, who, in his Letter to the Ephesians, wrote that Christ "gave Himself up for us, an offering and sacrifice" (cf. Eph 5:2). So, in reciting the Divine Mercy Chaplet we act like priests who offer up the Son to the Father as a sacrifice, with His whole Godhead and humanity. We thereby participate in the common priesthood, to which the Church calls us.

Fr. Sopoćko put forward similar arguments when he polemicized with Fr. Granat: "In the Incarnation, two natures, divine and human, were united in the

**CORRESPONDENCE** between Fr. Michał Sopoćko and Cardinal Wyszyński concerning the Feast of the Divine Mercy.

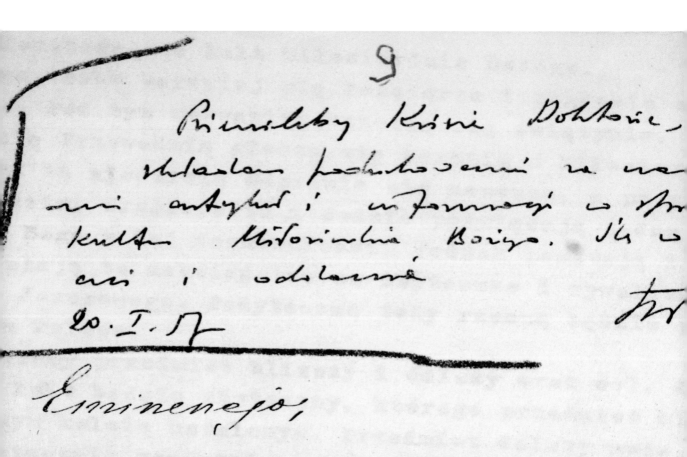

Person of the Son of God, in such a way, essentially and forever, that human nature has not even its own existence, while it owes its being to the Pre-eternal Word. In view of this, in the Holy Mass the Redeemer offers Himself to His Father (as we do), that is, His whole being, as a man, and so, both His humanity and His Deity."

Over the course of time the opinions of Fr. Sopoćko and Fr. Różycki prevailed in theological discussions. In November 1977, Cardinal Wojtyła put a question to the Congregation for the Doctrine of the Faith with regard to the possibility of revising the memorable notification of 1959, which banned the devotion to Divine Mercy in the forms advocated by Sr. Faustina. The Vatican dicastery acceded to the request and promised to examine the matter again. The letter of the Polish primate (Stefan Wyszyński) to the Holy See helped to up the resolution of the matter. On April 15, 1978, the Congregation for the Doctrine of the Faith withdrew the ban.

Unfortunately, Fr. Sopoćko did not live to see this. He had died at the age of eighty-seven (February 15, 1975) at the convent of the Missionary Sisters of the Holy Family in Bialystok. After being relieved of his work as a professor at the seminary in Bialystok, and after his retirement in 1962, he devoted the last dozen or so years of his life to pastoral work at the chapel on Poselska Street. When he sensed death approaching, he decided to find someone from among his former students—later theological lecturers—to continue his mission of spreading the devotion in honor of God's mercy. But he did not find anyone who had an adequate understanding of the matter. The best source of his thinking in the last years of his life turned out to be his diary. On January 1, 1967, he made the following entry: "New year, the 79th of my life, and the 53rd of my priesthood, in which I have said about 19,200 Masses. If, after each of them, I had become better and more pleasing to the Father of mercy, I would undoubtedly have gone far in perfecting myself. But I unfortunately did little in that direction. I did not overcome myself, deny myself to the extent the Lord required of me. Hence I feel a void within me, remorse for wasting so many of God's graces. Though I experienced very difficult conditions throughout my life, I did not take advantage of all my opportunities to become ever humbler, more mortified, and ever less covetous. I do not know how long I shall remain in this vale of tears . . . ; whatever occurs, I resolve to spend the last days of my life in the fear of God. Knowing my weaknesses, I trust only in my Savior's mercy: Jesus, I trust in You!"

**REV. PROF. WINCENTY GRANAT** was the rector of the Catholic University of Lublin and the best known of the theologians who were critical of the devotion to the Divine Mercy.

251

# Blessed

# CHAPTER 14

# Blessed

Thanks to Fr. Ignacy Różycki's positive opinion, Cardinal Pietro Palazzini, the prefect of the Sacred Congregation for the Causes of Saints, was able to sign the decree that allowed the continuation of Sr. Faustina Kowalska's beatification process (June 19, 1981). The first official edition of her diary was issued two months earlier.

**CROSS** above the entrance to the Divine Mercy Spirituality Center in Rome.

It was published in Rome in 1981. That edition, in Polish, was the basis for editions in other languages, including one in Italian, which was useful during the beatification process. Archbishop (later Cardinal) Andrzej Deskur, Pope John Paul II's friend and trusted associate, agreed to write the foreword. He emphasized that he recommended Sr. Faustina's diary because "this document of Catholic mysticism is of exceptional value not only for the Polish Church, but also the universal Church." There is no doubt that the hierarch could not have imagined that Faustina's diary would not only become the world's

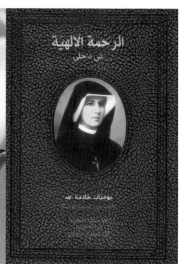

most widely read and influential Christian masterpiece of twentieth-century mystical literature, but also the most frequently translated and best-selling work of Polish literature. As to the number of foreign-language translations and sales, Sr. Faustina's *Diary* has surpassed the works of other Polish authors, including Henryk Sienkiewicz, Wladyslaw Reymont, Ferdynand A. Ossendowski, Stanislaw Lem, and Ryszard Kapuscinski. Only the works of John Paul II can equal *Diary* in popularity and circulation.

In his foreword to the first edition of *Diary*, Archbishop Deskur pointed to the many points of contact between the Polish mystic's message and the Polish pope's second encyclical, *Dives in Misericordia* (*Rich in Mercy*), which Pope John Paul II announced at the Vatican on November 30, 1980. In the encyclical, the Holy Father theologically deepened the Divine Mercy devotion proclaimed by Sr. Faustina. He wrote that "mercy constitutes the fundamental content of the messianic message of Christ and the constitutive power of His mission." It is manifested when it "restores to value, promotes and draws good from all forms of evil existing in the world and in man." The culminating point of Christ's Paschal Mystery is the revelation of God's mercy. "The Cross is the most profound condescension of God to man and to what man—especially in difficult and painful moments—looks on as his unhappy destiny." Pope John Paul II also called on Christians to imitate Christ in the work of mercy and to forgive each other: "Society can become 'ever more human' only when we introduce . . . the moment of forgiveness, which is so much the essence of the Gospel. Forgiveness demonstrates the presence in the world of the love which is more powerful than sin." He indicated that, particularly in our times, the Church cannot cease to proclaim this

**SR. FAUSTINA'S *DIARY*** is the world's best-selling Polish work.

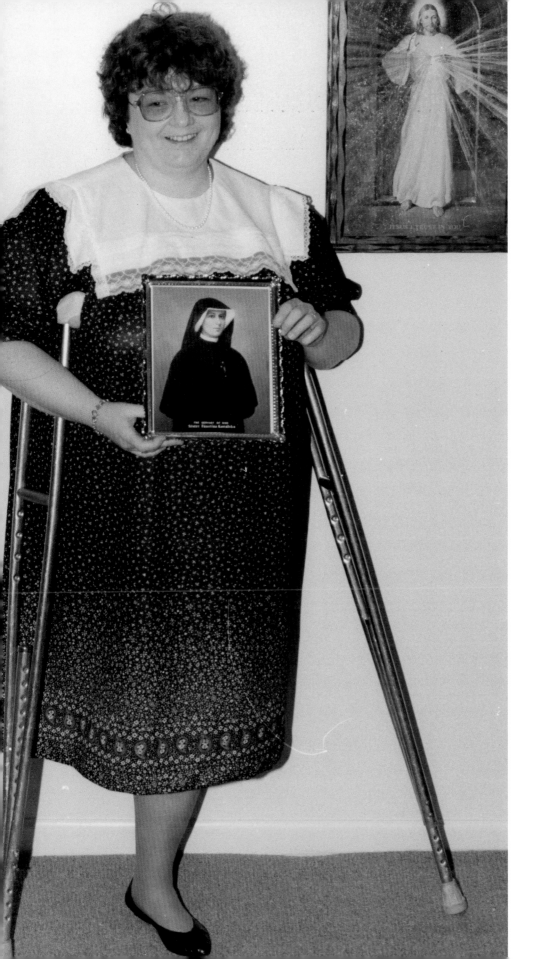

**MAUREN DEEGAN'S** medically inexplicable cure was the miracle that led to Sr. Faustina's beatification.

TU SEI SACERDOTE PER SEMPRE

message. "The more the human conscience succumbs to secularization, loses its sense of the very meaning of the word 'mercy,' moves away from God and distances itself from the mystery of mercy, the more the Church has the right and duty to appeal to the God of mercy with 'loud cries.' " The papal encyclical occasioned the growth of interest in God's mercy among theologians all over the world; special conferences and retreats began to be organized, and books written.

Franciszek Cardinal Macharski, the metropolitan of Kraków, was a great promoter of the devotion. In 1985 he entered the Divine Mercy Feast (first Sunday after Easter) in the liturgical calendar of his archdiocese. Some Polish bishops did likewise. In 1995, Pope John Paul II, at the request of the Polish episcopate, introduced this feast in every diocese in Poland.

The devotion to Divine Mercy also began to revive in Lithuania. It was under Soviet occupation, but after Mikhail Gorbachev had assumed power in Moscow, it was possible to sense clearly a decline in religious oppression. Perestroika occasioned that people stopped being afraid of Communist repressions and began to fill churches again. Hence three Polish priests in Lithuania—Jozef Grasewicz, Tadeusz Kondrusiewicz, and Aleksander Kaszkiewicz—decided to move Eugeniusz Kazimirowski's Merciful Jesus image to Vilnius. This was not easy, as the inhabitants of Nowa Ruda (Belarus), where the painting was to be found, were so attached to the image that they would not have agreed to its being moved elsewhere. There was also the real danger that the local authorities, when aware of the plans to move the painting, might well have wanted to seize and destroy it. So the priests decided to act in complete secrecy. First, they commissioned Maria Szocik to paint an exact copy of Kazimirowski's Merciful Jesus image. Next, they formed a group of five trusted people. In 1986, on a certain autumn evening, they set off for Nowa Ruda. There, in the abandoned church, under the cover of darkness, the conspirators replaced the Merciful Jesus image with a copy. The local inhabitants who went to the church the next day did not notice the change.

Meanwhile Kazimirowski's painting was taken to Vilnius and hung in the former Dominican Holy Spirit Church (1987). The parish priest was the aforementioned Fr. Aleksander Kaszkiewicz, who became a great promoter of the devotion. In 1991, Pope John Paul II nominated him bishop of Grodno. He chose "Jesus, I trust in You" as his motto and placed the rays of Divine Mercy, emanating from Christ's Heart, on his coat of arms. The image remained in the Holy Spirit Church until 2005, when it was moved under dramatic circumstances.

Meanwhile the beatification process was running its own course. The next stage was the preparation of the informative process summary, which was undertaken by

**JOSÉ CARDINAL SARAIVA MARTINS,** prefect of the Sacred Congregation for the Causes of Saints, during Sr. Faustina's canonization.

**CHURCH OF SANTO SPIRITO IN SASSIA,** Rome. Pope John Paul II established the Divine Mercy Spirituality Center there in 1994.

259

**POSITIO,**
that is, the account of Sr. Faustina Kowalska's life that arose during her beatification process.

**MEDICAL DOCUMENTATION**
of Mauren Deegan, an American, who was inexplicably healed in Łagiewniki.

Msgr. Luigi Giuliani, a lawyer of the Roman Rota. He completed his work on November 27, 1948. The relator, Fr. Michał Machejek, a Discalced Carmelite, was solicitous about an appropriate preparation of the positio, that is, the thorough study of the life and virtues of Sr. Faustina, which was required for the beatification process. A miracle through her intercession, that is, a scientifically inexplicable intervention, was needed for her beatification. This came about through the cure of an American, Maureen Digan. First, there were diocesan processes, one in Kraków, where the miraculous cure had occurred, then one in Boston, the diocese from which she came, and finally one in Rome. On March 7, 1992, Pope John Paul II promulgated the decree about Sr. Faustina's heroic virtues and, on December 21, a decree about the miracle through her intercession.

How did the said cure come about, which the Holy See officially acknowledged as miraculous? Maureen Digan herself related:

"I suffered from a swelling of the legs from the age of fifteen. Between the ages of fifteen and twenty I had over fifty operations and treatments. I was in and out of the

be used in both home and clinic.
...ple to operate, reliable.
...ssure easily controlled.
...ves adjustable to fit any
...lling condition.

**...cations**

...YMPHATIC DISORDERS:
...genital lymphedema,
...ondary lymphedema.
...ENOUS DISORDERS: Painful
...cose veins, chronic venous
...fficiency, ulcus cruris.
...YSFUNCTION OF THE
..."SCLE PUMP": Paralysis of
...ower limbs, long standing
...cular inactivity.
...REVENTION OF DEEP VEIN
...ROMBOSIS DURING AND
...ER OPERATIONS.
...ortant: To be used only in
...ordance with physicians'
...ructions.

**...traindications**

...te infection of the affected limb.
...ompensated cardiac failure.

**...hod of Operation**

...pha press is a pneumatic device
...h acts physiologically on the
...cted limb. Pressure is exerted by
...e-controlled overlapping sacs
...n a sleeve which is fitted to the

Before treatment

Before treatment

During treatment

During treatment

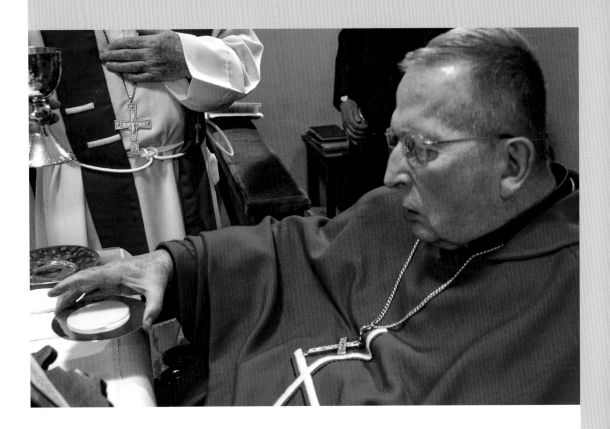

# CARDINAL **ANDRZEJ MARIA DESKUR**

**CARDINAL ANDRZEJ MARIA DESKUR** (1924-2011) wrote the foreword to the first edition of Faustina Kowalska's *Diary*. He was of Polish nobility with French roots. During the Nazi occupation he clandestinely studied law, and then, after the war, theology in Kraków and Fribourg, where he gained a Ph.D. He was ordained in France in 1950, and two years later he began work at the Vatican. He carried out many functions in the Holy See, for example, he was a referent (official) undersecretary, secretary, and president of the Pontifical Council for Social Communications (formerly the Pontifical Commission for Cinematography, Radio, and Television). During Vatican II he was one of the experts and a secretary of the Council. He received the title of Honorary Chamberlain and Prefect of the Papal Household. In 1974 he became titular bishop of Tene. Andrzej Maria Deskur was an old friend of Karol Wojtyla. During the conclave that elected John Paul II, Bishop Deskur was in the Gemelli Hospital in Rome after a stroke. He was the first to visit the newly elected pope. He offered up the suffering connected with his illness for the intentions of Pope John Paul II. Because of his illness Bishop Deskur had to use a wheelchair to get about. He became an archbishop in 1980 and a cardinal in 1985. Despite health problems he worked for many Vatican institutions. He died in 2011 at the age of eighty-five, and was interred in the crypt of the John Paul II Shrine in Łagiewniki, Kraków.

**CARDINAL ANDRZEJ DESKUR** was a close friend of Pope John Paul II. He lived in Rome for many years and had many functions in the Holy See. He wrote the foreword to the first publication of *Diary* in 1981.

## METROPOLITAN
## OF KRAKÓW
Franciszek Cardinal
Macharski was
a keen promoter
of the devotion to
Divine Mercy from
1979 to 2005.

hospital for over a period of ten years. My stays in the hospital lasted from one week to twelve months. I had a spine operation at the age of nineteen, which left me paralysed from the hips down for two years. When I was twenty, I had my first amputation. The disease in the rest of my leg became so serious that it had to be amputated right up to my hip.

"Bob, my husband, a man of great faith and prayer, felt that he should take his family, my ill son and me, to Poland. He went to Eden Hill, Stockbridge, and asked Fr. Seraphim Michalenko if he could accompany us on the journey to Poland. Fr. Seraphim, who was occupied with matters about Sr. Faustina in the USA, received permission from his superiors, and so we set off on the arduous journey to Kraków.

"On March 28, 1981, I went to confession in Kraków. I suppose it was my first good confession for many, many years. I felt closer to the Lord Jesus and Sr. Faustina, but not quite close enough. That evening, March 28, we prayed at Sr. Faustina's graveside, particularly for a cure. Still in a spirit of incredulity, I said to Sr. Faustina: 'All right, Sr. Faustina, do something with it.' And the pain subsided, the swelling went down. I thought that it was a sign of a nervous breakdown, as I did not believe in miracles. I stopped taking medicine, and I stuffed a napkin into my shoe so that no one might

notice that I did not have a swelling. From that time my illness vanished completely. I had seen four doctors, who told me that it was an incurable illness, that there were no known cases of remission, and that no medicine was effective.

"Our Lord chooses whomever He desires. I thank Him with my whole heart for my cure, which will be of help in the beatification of Sr. Faustina. What we can read in her *Diary* is true: 'The greater the misery of souls, the more right they have to My mercy.'"

Pope John Paul II beatified Sr. Faustina Kowalska in Rome on April 18, 1993. Many years earlier she wrote of her path to beatification in her diary. During a vision she saw a great number of people gathered at Łagiewniki—in the chapel, outside it, and in the street. They all wanted to get inside, but were unable to do so as such a large number of people surrounded it. There were a lot of consecrated people near the altar, both priests and nuns. It was announced that someone would shortly take their place on the altar. She then heard a voice saying that this was a reference to her. So she went out toward the chapel, and suddenly everyone began to throw whatever they could get hold of at her—stones, mud, sand, brooms—so that she hesitated to go on. But the voice kept on

**SR. FAUSTINA'S** beatification and canonization took place in Rome (April 18, 1993, and April 30, 2000, respectively).

**BEATIFICATION AND CANONIZATION** painting of Sr. Faustina.

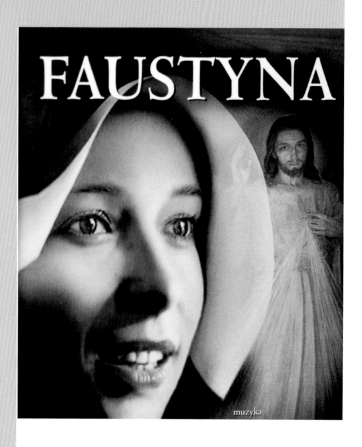

FAUSTYNA

muzyka

## JERZY ŁUKASZEWICZ'S FILM

**JERZY ŁUKASZEWICZ'S** 1994 film, *Faustina*, contributed to the popularization of the Divine Mercy message to a great degree. Based on a biography of the beatified nun, it became a cultural and religious event in Poland. Over 500, 000 watched it in cinemas; later it was repeatedly shown on various TV stations. Dorota Segda played the title role and was voted the best Polish actress of 1996 by the readers of the monthly magazine *Film*. Krzysztof Wakuliński, as Fr. Sopoćko, and Wojciech Kilar for the music, also received good reviews. Dorota Segda mentioned that she had never encountered convent life before the film, hence she did not know how to play the role of a nun. So she decided to go to Łagiewniki. The first nun she approached was extraordinarily joyful; she simply radiated happiness. Such is Faustina in the film – cheerful, smiling, and happy.

summoning her, so she pushed through the crowd. When she entered the chapel, those inside attacked her: nuns, superiors, pupils, and parents. They all tried to hit her with whatever they could find. So Sr. Faustina made her way to the altar as quickly as she could so as to avoid the blows. The moment she took her allotted place, the reaction of all those gathered changed. All of a sudden the very same people now began to hold out their arms to her, asking for graces. The mystic did not bear any grudge against them. What is more, she felt love and gratitude toward them, as their attacks had forced her to take her place on the altar more quickly. She then felt a surge of happiness, and heard a voice: "Do whatever you wish, distribute graces as you will, to whom you will and when you will" (*Diary*, 31). Then the vision instantly disappeared.

At the April 18 service, Pope John Paul II beatified five people: Ludovico of Casoria, Paula Montal Fones of St. Joseph of Calasanz, Stanisław Kazimierczyk, Angela Truszkowska, and Faustina Kowalska. During the beatification ceremony in St. Peter's Square, the Holy Father gave a homily in which, among other things, he said: "I salute you, Sr. Faustina. Beginning today the Church calls you Blessed,

**SR. FAUSTINA'S** mission "continues and is yielding astonishing fruit", said Pope John Paul II, referring to the nun's words, written in 1934: "I feel certain that my mission will not come to an end at my death, but just begin."

265

especially the Church in Poland and Lithuania. O Faustina, how extraordinary your life! Precisely you, the poor and simple daughter of Mazovia, of the Polish people, chosen by Christ to remind people of this great mystery of Divine Mercy! You bore this mystery within yourself, leaving this world after a short life, filled with suffering. However, at the same time, this mystery has become a prophetic reminder to the world, to Europe. Your message about Divine Mercy was born almost on the eve of World War II. Certainly you would have been amazed if you could have experienced upon this earth what this message meant for the suffering people during that hour of torment, and how it spread throughout the world. ... Today you experience it at its very source, which is your Christ, 'dives in misericordia' ".

" 'I clearly feel that my mission does not end with death, but begins', Sr. Faustina wrote in her diary. And it truly did! Her mission continues and is yielding astonishing fruit. It is truly marvellous how her devotion to the Merciful Jesus is spreading in our contemporary world and gaining so many human hearts! This is doubtlessly a sign of the times—a sign of our twentieth century. The balance of this century which is now ending, in addition to the advances which have often surpassed those of preceding eras, presents a deep restlessness and fear of the future. Where, if not in Divine Mercy, can the world find refuge and the light of hope? Believers understand that perfectly."

Over four months after Sr. Faustina Kowalska's beatification, Pope John Paul II went to Lithuania on his first pilgrimage. On September 5, 1993, during his stay in Vilnius, he visited Holy Spirit Church, where he prayed before Eugeniusz Kazimirowski's painting of the Merciful Jesus. The pope was accompanied by the archbishop of Moscow, Tadeusz Kondrusiewicz, who, seven years earlier, as an Ostra Brama curate, was one of those who had organized the transfer of the painting from Nowa Ruda to Vilnius. The pope devoted his homily to the necessity of mutual cooperation between Poles and Lithuanians and also entrusted relations between the neighboring nations to the recently beatified nun. He said to the faithful assembled in the church: "Sr. Faustina was 'one of you' for many years. Also, in an atmosphere of great piety, this church houses the holy image of the Merciful Jesus, Whose cult she propagated. My dear brothers and sisters, strive to be imitators of that infinitely trustful love for the Most Holy Trinity. Learn from Bl. Sr. Faustina, from this humble and faithful servant of God, how to be a child—a son or daughter—of the Heavenly Father in all circumstances, how to remain a disciple of the Word Incarnate as well as a docile instrument in the hands of the Holy Spirit, Life-Giver and Comforter. May Bl. Faustina intercede for each one of us, and may she teach us always to fix our eyes on celestial eternity, putting God—as she did—in the center of our lives."

**OSTRA BRAMA CHAPEL**, where Pope John Paul II prayed during his pilgrimage to Lithuania in 1993. He visited the former Soviet republic shortly after the fall of Communism. For many of the local Catholics it was the first opportunity for many years to manifest their religious freedom. Pope John Paul II then visited Latvia and Estonia.

**LETTERS OF GRATITUDE**
for graces
received at the
intercession of Sr.
Faustina flow into
Łagiewniki from
the whole world.

A feature film, *Faustina*, shot in 1994, and directed by Jerzy Lukaszewicz, greatly contributed to the popularization of the message about the Divine Mercy. It is based on a biography of the beatified nun, and its showing became a cultural and religious event in Poland. Over half a million people watched it in cinemas. It was also repeatedly shown by various television channels. The title role was played by Dorota Segda, who was chosen by the readers of *Film*, a monthly magazine, as the best Polish actor of 1996. Krzysztof Wakulinski, as Fr. Sopoćko, and Wojciech Kilar, the composer of the music, also received good reviews. Dorota Segda recalled that she had never encountered convent life before and did not know how to play a nun. To get to know how to do so, she decided to go to Łagiewniki. The first sister she approached was extraordinarily joyful and quite simply radiated happiness. The actress then understood what her heroine was to be like. Such is Faustina in Lukaszewicz's film—cheerful, smiling, and happy.

In 1992, Franciszek Cardinal Macharski elevated the chapel of the Congregation of the Sisters of Our Lady of Mercy in Łagiewniki to the status of a shrine. It has become the center of the devotion that was initiated by Sr. Faustina. Great numbers of pilgrims began to come to Łagiewniki, and the small convent premises could barely accommodate them. So it became necessary to build a new basilica, as well as a pastoral-social base for the faithful. The Foundation of the Divine Mercy Shrine was set up in 1996 to raise funds. The project, the basilica and surroundings, was undertaken by Professor Witold Ceckiewicz, from Kraków. Pope John Paul II, during his pilgrimage to Poland, went to Łagiewniki on June 7, 1997. He signed his name under the model of the project and prayed in the chapel before Hyla's Merciful Jesus image.

During his homily there, Pope John Paul II said: "There is nothing that man needs more than Divine Mercy—that love which is benevolent, which is compassionate, which raises man above his weakness to the infinite heights of the holiness of God. In this place we become particularly aware of this. From here, in fact, went out the Message of Divine Mercy that Christ himself chose to pass on to our generation through Bl. Faustina. And it is a message that is clear and understandable for everyone. Anyone can come here, look at this image of the Merciful Jesus, His Heart radiating grace, and hear in the depths of his own soul what Bl. Faustina heard: 'Fear nothing, I am with you always' (*Diary*, 586). And if this person responds with a sincere heart: 'Jesus, I trust in You', he will find comfort in all his anxieties and fears. In this 'dialogue of abandonment', there is established between man and Christ a special bond that sets love free. And 'there is no fear in

love, but perfect love casts out fear' (1 Jn 4:18). The Church rereads the message of mercy in order to bring the light of hope more effectively to this generation at the end of the millennium and to future generations. The Church unceasingly implores God for mercy for everyone."

A decision Pope John Paul II made in 1994 testifies to the importance he attached to the Divine Mercy message: he decided to establish the Divine Mercy Spirituality Center in Rome as a pastoral and evangelizing center based on Sr. Faustina's message. He chose the Santo Spirito in Sassia Church, close to St. Peter's Basilica. The church has been immemorially connected with the neighboring hospital, where many Christians—doctors, nurses, chaplains, volunteers—can in practice show mercy to the sick and the suffering. When visiting the church on April 23, 1995, Pope John Paul II acknowledged: "It is very significant and timely that precisely here, next to this very ancient hospital, prayers are said and work is done with constant care for the health of body and soul."

**OFFERINGS OF THANKSGIVING** at the Divine Mercy Shrine in Łagiewniki are at times of a developed form.

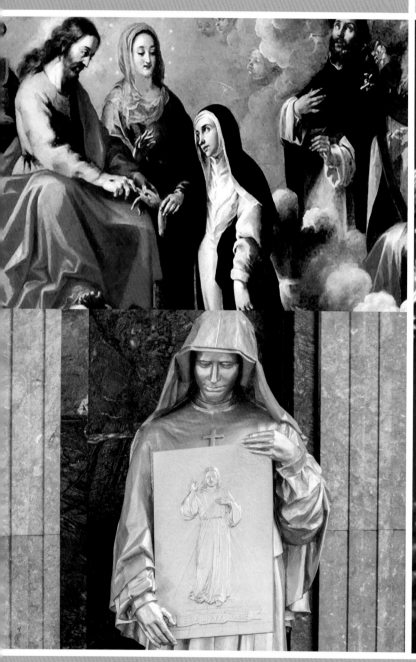

*Joannes Paulus II*

# Saint

# Saint

After Sr. Faustina's beatification, the devotion to Divine Mercy gathered momentum throughout the world. Information about favors received through the intercession of the Polish nun began to pour in from all corners of the world. After the Holy See's examination of another miracle, the healing of an incurable illness, Pope John Paul II decided to canonize Bl. Faustina Kowalska, to recognize her as a saint of the Catholic Church. Ronald Pytel, an American priest of Polish descent, took part in the canonization Mass; he himself had been miraculously healed.

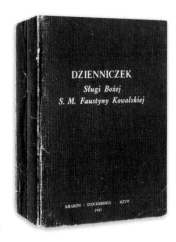

**SR. FAUSTINA'S DIARY**. First edition of 1981.

**A SCULPTURE** of St. Faustina at the Basilica of Our Lady of Sorrows, Queen of Poland, Old Licheń.

273

**CORRESPONDENCE,** in many languages, to the shrine in Łagiewniki, relates many accounts of favors received at Sr. Faustina's intercesssion.

274

Here is Fr. Pytel's story:

"On November 16, 1999, doctors—at the invitation of the Sacred Congregation for the Causes of Saints—examined my case and accepted that the immediate cure of my badly damaged left ventricle was medically inexplicable. On December 9, a Vatican commission of theologians confirmed that it was a miracle, and attributed it to the intercession of Bl. Sr. Faustina Kowalska. Later there was a commission of cardinals, and on December 20, the decree about the miracle was promulgated in the presence of the Holy Father, John Paul II.

"My name is Father Ronald Pytel, and I am the pastor of Holy Rosary Church in Baltimore, Maryland. Our parish church is the Archdiocesan Shrine for Divine Mercy. … I have been a priest for twenty-six years. I was ordained at Holy Rosary Church, which is my home parish. I am of Polish ethnic background. My parents were born in America, but my grandparents came from Poland.

"As a young boy, I remember seeing the image of Divine Mercy in our school with the inscription 'Jezu, ufam Tobie!' It was not until 1987, however, that I first became very well acquainted with the devotion to Divine Mercy and the chaplet. …

"Throughout the winter and spring of 1995, I was suffering from what seemed like a cold and allergies. Eventually, it seemed like I had developed bronchitis. I could not get my breath when going up a flight of stairs, and I was constantly coughing. I made an appointment with a local general medical doctor who confirmed that I was suffering from allergic bronchitis. He also said, however, that my heart murmur, which I knew I had had since I was a boy, seemed extremely exaggerated, and he made an appointment for me to have a Doppler echocardiogram.

"The echocardiogram was taken on June 7, 1995. It showed that my aorta had stenosis, that a calcium dome had formed over the valve, and that I was getting only about 20 percent blood flow through the valve; some was backwashing. In essence, I was in cardiac heart failure.

On June 8, I had an emergency appointment with Dr. Nicholas Fortuin, an eminent cardiologist from the world-renowned Johns Hopkins Hospital in Baltimore. Dr. Fortuin is considered one of the best cardiologists in the United States. Dr. Fortuin read the echocardiogram and confirmed the stenosis of the aortic valve. He prescribed medication and sent me home for complete bed rest while he arranged for a surgical team to perform surgery at Johns Hopkins Hospital.

"On the morning of June 14, … Father Larry Gesy took me to Johns Hopkins Hospital at 6:30 A.M. On the way to the hospital, Father Larry said to me, 'Don't worry, Ron, this is all about Divine Mercy.' I underwent my heart surgery at the

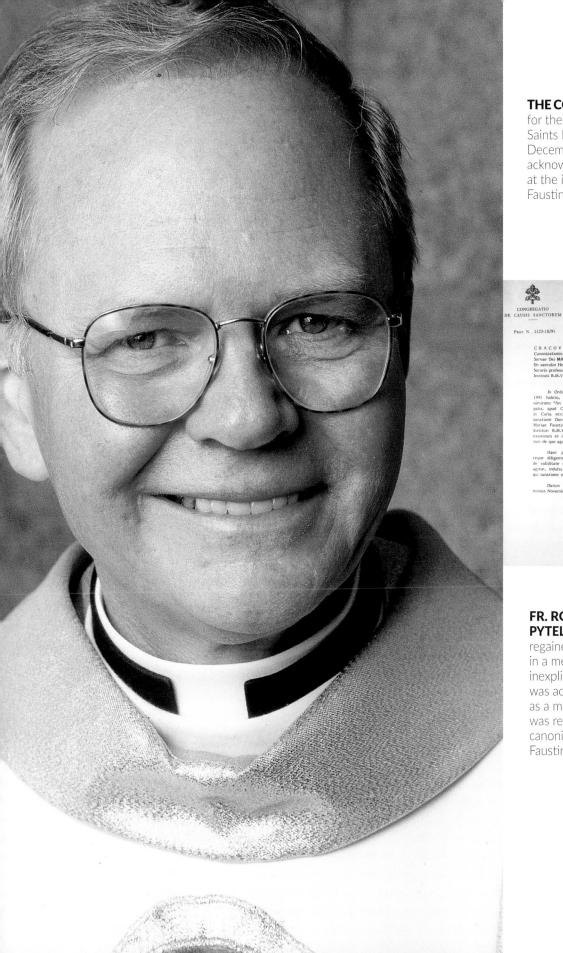

**THE CONGREGATION** for the Causes of Saints Decree of December 16, 1991, acknowledging a miracle at the intercession of Sr. Faustina.

**FR. RONALD PYTEL** regained his health in a medically inexplicable way. This was acknowledged as a miracle, which was required for the canonization of Bl. Faustina Kowalska.

SW. SIOSTRA FAUSTYNA

JEZU UFAM TOBIE

...USTYNY

**CHAPEL IN ŁAGIEWNIKI.** Reliquary and small casket contain St. Faustina's remains.

**MAIN ALTAR** in the chapel of the Congregation of the Sisters of Our Lady of Mercy in Łagiewniki.

beginning of the novena, before the Feast of the Sacred Heart of Jesus. Included in the things that I packed for the hospital stay was the diary of Blessed Faustina. Even though I did not like the thought of cardiac surgery, I was at peace. I just knew all would be fine.... During my recovery, I read the diary of Blessed Faustina whenever I could. I also prayed the chaplet every day.

"After the surgery had been performed, Dr. Peter Green, the surgeon, met with Fr. Larry Gesy and told him that, prior to the operation, I had suffered serious damage to the left ventricle of my heart. Since the valve had so much stenosis, the left ventricle was trying to push blood that was not going through the valve; if the surgery had not been performed, I would not have lived much longer. ...

"Gradually during July and August, I regained some weight and strength. I visited Dr. Fortuin in August. After the examination, ... Fr. Larry discussed my situation at length with Dr. Fortuin, who said that he did not know what kind of life I would be able to resume. He did not think that I would resume any normal schedule. He also said I was uninsurable. My longevity was certainly shortened, and Dr. Fortuin's prognosis was not optimistic. The damage to the left ventricle was quite serious. The situation had been pushed to the maximum before surgery. I had indeed been in congestive heart failure, which was masked by what I thought were allergies and bronchitis. Fr. Larry was startled and shocked by this information. He gradually shared the prognosis with me.

"I returned to the parish in early September. I was, however, on a restricted schedule. On October 5, we celebrated an all day vigil before the Blessed Sacrament

**A GROUP** of pilgrims on the Divine Mercy pilgrimage from Warsaw to Kraków.

277

**QUOTES FROM** Sr. Faustina's *Diary* can even be seen on shirts.

**BASILICA AND CONVENT**
by night.
Basilica and convent of the Sisters of Our Lady of Mercy at the Shrine of Divine Mercy in Łagiewniki, Kraków.

with prayers, Chaplet of Divine Mercy, Rosary, and talks on our Lord's Gift of Mercy. The day concluded with a concelebrated Mass. All of this was in preparation for the Holy Father's visit to Baltimore on October 8th.

I was the celebrant of the Mass. I spoke about trust and how I felt the Lord was touching me with his mercy. Physically, I was feeling and looking somewhat better. That evening, a group of individuals who have a ministry entitled Our Father's Work prayed over me for continued healing. Blessed Faustina was invoked to join in the prayer, and I venerated a first class relic of Blessed Faustina. . . . I felt as though I were paralyzed as the healing ministry and my parishioners gathered around me and prayed.

"Later that evening, I realized that I had forgotten to take my heart medication. I took the medication around midnight, and was relaxing before going to bed. I began to have chest discomforts when I took a deep breath. Up until this time, I had no chest pains except from the incision in the chest after surgery. This was something new. I felt that I probably had been too active that day.

"[Some time later], I realized that the pain was the strongest after I took the heart medication. The next day, I did not take the medication, and there was no pain. I called Dr. Fortuin and told him of the problem. I felt that the heart medication, Zestril, which he had prescribed for me, caused the problem. Dr. Fortuin told me that this was the best possible medication for my heart condition and that I had already tolerated the

medication for two months with no reaction. He told me, however, that if I felt that my body was telling me something, to try alternating between a half dosage and a full dosage to see if that helped and to call him in a week. The half dosage was better. The pain was less severe and dissipated more quickly. I called Dr. Fortuin and told him the results, and he told me to stay on the half dosage until my appointment with him in nine days.

"On November 9, I once again visited Dr. Fortuin for a scheduled appointment. After an initial examination, a Doppler echocardiogram was taken. Dr. Fortuin viewed the results of the test and then called me into his office. He stared at me in silence for what seemed like an eternity, and then he spoke. To the best of my recollection, these were his exact words: 'Ron, someone has intervened for you.' I asked, 'What do you mean?' He said: 'Your heart is normal.' I said 'What?' And he repeated, 'Your heart is normal.' I responded, 'Well, Dr. Green, the surgeon had suggested that you do an echo-cardiogram to see if the left ventricle was strengthening.' Dr. Fortuin said, 'No, no, we're talking normal. I was not at all optimistic about your condition. I can't explain it.' He continued, 'You have no restrictions; you are to take no medication except the coumadin, and I'll see you in a year.' I responded, 'A year?' He said, 'Yeah, a year. Your heart is normal.'

"... Upon leaving the doctor's office, I called Fr. Larry and told him what Dr. Fortuin had said. Fr. Larry's response was 'Well, I guess we got the miracle we prayed

**NATALIA GRZELAK,** Sr. Faustina Kowalska's younger sister, during the beatification ceremony (Rome, 1993).

**JÓZEFA JASIŃSKA,** one of St. Faustina's sisters, receiving Holy Communion from John Paul II at the beatification Mass, St. Peter's Square.

for.' In November of 1996, a formal tribunal was held in the Archdiocese of Baltimore to acquire sworn depositions from the doctors and other witnesses about the change in my health. On December 8, Fr. Seraphim Michalenko, M.I.C., vice-postulator for America, arrived in Baltimore. I should note that December 8, the Feast of the Immaculate Conception, was a favorite feast day of Blessed Faustina because the Blessed Mother had appeared to her on that day. On December 9, Fr. Seraphim went to the Baltimore tribunal where the documents were sealed and packaged. Then he, Fr. Larry, and I boarded a plane for Rome. The documents numbered over eight hundred pages in medical records and about five hundred pages of sworn depositions. . . .

"I know in my heart that Blessed Faustina put in a word with Jesus, and the love flowing from his heart touched mine and healed me. It's as simple as that."

Sr. Faustina Kowalska's canonization took place on April 30, 2000. She had written about this event sixty-three years earlier in her diary. On March 23, 1937, she had a vision of the canonization celebrations that took place in Rome and Kraków at the same time. Though she did not know of the invention of television, or of modern communications, she accurately described their application during those celebra-

**POPE JOHN PAUL II**, in the presence of Cardinal Macharski, looking at a model of the basilica at the Divine Mercy Shrine in Łagiewniki. He personally consecrated the shrine during a pilgrimage in 2002.

# FR. **SERAPHIM MICHALENKO, M.I.C.**

**FR. SERAPHIM,** one of the priests who has been of most service to the Divine Mercy apostolate in the English-speaking world, was born in 1930. He was brought up in Adams, Massachusetts, where he came to know the Marian Fathers, including Fr. Józef Jarzębowski, M.I.C., from whom he first came to know of Sr. Faustina and her mission. He entered the Marian Order and devoted himself to propagating the devotion to Divine Mercy. He did this for over fifty years, until his death in 2021, as a theologian, writer, preacher, and retreat leader.

Fr. Seraphim prepared and published the Polish edition of Faustina's *Diary*. The Marian Fathers published *Diary* and numerous publications in English and Spanish under his supervision. He became vice-postulator during Sr. Faustina's canonization process. He was a witness to the miracle that opened the way to her beatification. He was also the rector of the National Shrine of Divine Mercy in Stockbridge, Massachusetts. In 1966, he established the John Paul II Divine Mercy Institute (Stockbridge). He wrote many books and publications on the message revealed to Sr. Faustina and consulted on numerous films on the subject. English-speaking Christians know him from his frequent appearances on EWTN (Mother Angelica's TV station), where he spoke on Divine Mercy for years, and from numerous conferences and missions in various countries in the Western Hemisphere and Asia.

tions. Faustina described how she suddenly became aware of God's presence, and that all of a sudden she found herself in two places at the same time: in the papal chapel in Rome and in the chapel in Łagiewniki. She was unable to explain this, but she saw the course of the solemnity at both places at the same time.

She saw that the Kraków chapel was festively decorated and packed with the faithful. The Blessed Sacrament was exposed on the high altar. Joy emanated from those present, and many were granted the graces that they had besought.

The same celebration was also held at St. Peter's Basilica, led personally by the Holy Father, and assisted by a large number of clergy. Sr. Faustina suddenly saw St. Peter, who stood between the altar and the pope, saying something to the Holy Father. She could not hear what St. Peter said to his successor, but saw that he had understood everything.

Suddenly clergymen appeared around her, whom she did not know. They told her that they had to examine her writings. They conversed with her and asked her questions, but she sensed that they were trying to humiliate her. Then Christ Himself stood in her defense, answering the priests, and gave them to understand what they did not comprehend.

Later, the mystic saw two rays—as in the Merciful Jesus image—emanate from the Blessed Sacrament and spread all over the world. It all lasted for but a moment, though it seemed as if a whole day had passed.

At a certain moment Sr. Faustina saw Jesus standing on the chapel altar in Łagiewniki. He appeared as depicted in the Divine Mercy image. She noticed that He was not visible to those gathered in the chapel. He looked with great kindness upon everyone, particularly the pope and the priests.

Sr. Faustina was suddenly raised up and placed on the altar next to Christ. She felt full of happiness and heavenly peace. Jesus leaned toward her and asked her what she desired. Glory and veneration for His mercy, she replied.

That prophecy, which Sr. Faustina entered in her diary in March 1937, was fulfilled in April 2000. The canonization celebrations took place in two places at the same time: at the Vatican, with the participation of the Holy Father, and at the convent in Łagiewniki, Kraków. Vast crowds participated in the celebrations, as in the vision. There was not only a spiritual link between the two gatherings, but also a literal one. The sounds and pictures were transmitted in both directions, thanks to which the pilgrims in St. Peter's Square were able to observe the celebrations in Kraków, and those in Łagiewniki could watch the live transmission from the Vatican. The announcement of Sr. Faustina's canonization evoked enthusiasm

**MERCIFUL JESUS IMAGE**, Stockbridge. Painted by Marie Gama in Mexico in 1945. It was commissioned by Fr. Józef Jarzębowski, M.I.C.

# SHRINE IN **STOCKBRIDGE**

**THE APOSTOLATE** of Divine Mercy and the National Shrine of the Divine Mercy run by Marian priests in Stockbridge, Massachusetts, USA, is still the most important center for promoting the Divine Mercy in the western hemisphere. The Apostolate, which embarked on its mission in 1942 in Washington, D.C., gained momentum two years later after moving to new quarters in Stockbridge. The Marian Helpers Center, established there, began the Apostolate's publishing work, cultivating worship not only among the multilingual peoples of the United States, but also in the many countries of origin of US citizens around the world.

In the late 1940s and early 1950s, the Apostolate published the Divine Mercy chaplet, images of the Merciful Jesus, and booklets on Sr. Faustina's message in several hundred thousand copies. The priests who contributed most to the flourishing mission were Fr. Joseph Jarzębowski, MIC (who brought the message to the USA), Fr. Julian Chróściechowski, MIC (author and publisher of materials on the Divine Mercy message) and Fr. Władysław Pełczyński, MIC (who bought the property in Stockbridge and founded the Divine Mercy Apostolate and the Association of Marian Helpers, with hundreds of thousands of members and its own publishing center).

In 1959, when the Holy Office prohibited the propagation of Sr. Faustina's visions, the Marian Fathers conformed to the decree. However, they did not cease to proclaim the mercy of God, though they based their teaching on the Bible and on Church tradition and not on the Polish mystic's visions. When the Holy See revoked the decree in 1978, the Marian Fathers embarked again on the promotion of Divine Mercy through other media: from brochures and books, to radio and television programs, to films and phonograph recordings. The initiator of most of these endeavors was Fr. Seraphim Michalenko, MIC. Under his supervision, Sr. Faustina's *Diary* was also published in various languages, including Polish in 1981, English in 1986, and Spanish in 1996.

In 1994, the Divine Mercy Shrine in Stockbridge, which was established in 1950 next to the publishing center, was elevated to the status of a national shrine by the US episcopate. Ever since its inception, it has propagated the message and devotion to the Divine Mercy on the American continent. Numerous pilgrims from home and abroad have been coming to it for years. Its importance is highlighted by the fact that the chaplet prayer and the annual celebration of the Feast of the Divine Mercy are broadcast daily from this place by the largest Catholic television station in the USA (EWTN – Mother Angelica Television).

285

**U.S. NATIONAL DIVINE MERCY SHRINE.**
The Divine Mercy Shrine in Stockbridge, Massachusetts, is run by the
Marian Fathers and attracts pilgrims from all over North America.

**POPE JOHN PAUL II** among nuns from the Congregation of the Sisters of Our Lady of Mercy during his visit to Kraków in 1997.

in both places. It was estimated that 70,000 pilgrims from all over the world took part in the Kraków celebrations, led by Bishop Kazimierz Nycz, and 150,000 in the canonization in Rome.

In his canonization homily, Pope John Paul II said: "Today my joy is truly great in presenting the life and witness of Sr. Faustina Kowalska to the whole Church as a gift of God for our time. By divine Providence, the life of this humble daughter of Poland was closely linked with the history of the twentieth century, the century we have just left behind. In fact, it was between the First and Second World Wars that Christ entrusted His message of love to her. Those who remember, who were witnesses and participants in the events of those years and the horrible sufferings they caused for millions of people, know well how necessary was the message of mercy.

"Jesus told Sr. Faustina: 'Mankind will not have peace until it turns with trust to My mercy' (*Diary*, 300). Through the work of the Polish religious, this message has become linked for ever to the twentieth century, the last of the second millennium and the bridge to the third. It is not a new message but can be considered a gift of special enlightenment that helps us to relive the Gospel of Easter

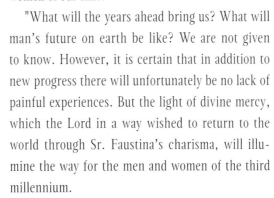

more intensely, to offer it as a ray of light to men and women of our time.

"What will the years ahead bring us? What will man's future on earth be like? We are not given to know. However, it is certain that in addition to new progress there will unfortunately be no lack of painful experiences. But the light of divine mercy, which the Lord in a way wished to return to the world through Sr. Faustina's charisma, will illumine the way for the men and women of the third millennium.

"However, as the apostles once did, today too humanity must welcome into the upper room of history the risen Christ, Who shows the wounds of His Crucifixion and repeats: Peace be with you! Humanity must let itself be touched and pervaded by the Spirit given to it by the risen Christ. It is the Spirit Who heals the wounds of the heart, pulls down the barriers that separate us from God and divide us from one another, and at the same time, restores the joy of the Father's love and of fraternal unity."

In a later part of the homily, the Holy Father said: "Sr. Faustina's canonization has a particular eloquence: by this act I intend today to pass this message on to the new millennium.

"I pass it on to all people, so that they will learn to know ever better the true face of God and the true face of their brethren.

"In fact, love of God and love of one's brothers and sisters are inseparable, as the First Letter of John reminds us: 'By this we know that we love the children of God, when we love God and obey his commandments' (5:2). Here the apostle reminds us of the truth of love, showing us its measure and criterion in the observance of the commandments.

**POPE JOHN PAUL II** at prayer before the Merciful Jesus painting (Łagiewniki, 1997). He prayed here 60 years earlier when he worked at a nearby chemical factory (Solvay, in Borek Fałęcki) during World War II.

287

# MYSTICAL MARRIAGE

**CHRIST'S BELOVEDS:**
St. Catherine of Siena, St. Bridget of Sweden, and St. Veronica of Giuliani.

**SR. FAUSTINA'S** mystical marriage to Christ has its counterparts in the history of Christian spirituality. History knows of female mystics who were spiritually betrothed to Jesus. According to masters of spiritual life, such a marriage is the most perfect expression of spousal love between the Creator and the creature.

The following women, among others, had such a mystical experience: St. Catherine of Siena, St. Bridget of Sweden, and St. Veronica Giuliani. The best known case, however, is that of St. Catherine of Alexandria. The Infant Jesus appeared during one of her visions and put a mystical marriage ring on her finger. This scene became an inspiration for many painters, for example, Hans Memling, Lucas Cranach, and Lorenzo Lotto.

"It is not easy to love with a deep love, which lies in the authentic gift of self. This love can only be learned by penetrating the mystery of God's love. Looking at Him, being one with his fatherly heart, we are able to look with new eyes at our brothers and sisters, with an attitude of unselfishness and solidarity, of generosity and forgiveness. All this is mercy!

"To the extent that humanity penetrates the mystery of this merciful gaze, it will seem possible to fulfil the ideal we heard in today's first reading: 'The community of believers were of one heart and one mind. None of them ever claimed anything as his own; rather everything was held in common' (Acts 4: 32). Here mercy gave form to human relations and community life; it constituted the basis for the sharing of goods. This led to the spiritual and corporal 'works of mercy'. Here mercy became a concrete way of being a 'neighbor' to one's neediest brothers and sisters.

"Sr. Faustina Kowalska wrote in her diary: 'I suffer great pain at the sight of the sufferings of others. All these sufferings are reflected in my heart. I carry their torments in my heart so that it even wears me out physically. I would like all pains to fall upon me so as to bring relief to my neighbor' (*Diary*, 1039). This is the degree of compassion to which love leads, when it takes the love of God as its measure!

"It is this love which must inspire humanity today, if it is to face the crisis of the meaning of life, the challenges of the most diverse needs and, especially, the duty to defend the dignity of every human person. Thus the message of divine mercy is also implicitly a message about the value of every human being. Each person is precious in God's eyes; Christ gave His life for each one; to everyone the Father gives His Spirit and offers intimacy.

"This consoling message is addressed above all to those who, afflicted by a particularly harsh trial or crushed by the weight of the sins they committed, have lost all confidence in life and are tempted to give in to despair. The gentle face of Christ is offered to them; those rays from His heart touch them and shine upon them, warm them, show them the way and fill them with hope. How many souls have been consoled by the prayer 'Jesus, I trust in You', which Providence intimated through Sr. Faustina! This simple act of abandonment to Jesus dispels the thickest clouds and lets a ray of light penetrate every life."

At the end of his homily Pope John Paul II addressed the saint directly: "And you, Faustina, a gift of God to our time, a gift from the land of Poland, to the whole Church, obtain for us an awareness of the depth of divine mercy; help us to have a living experience of it and to bear witness to it among our brothers and sisters. May your message of light and hope spread throughout the world, urging sinners

**STATUE OF OUR LADY,** the congregation's patron, above the main altar at the Divine Mercy Shrine in Łagiewniki, Kraków.

289

to conversion, calming rivalries and hatred, and opening individuals and nations to the practice of brotherhood. Today, fixing our gaze with you on the face of the risen Christ, let us make your prayer of trusting abandonment our own and say with firm hope: Christ Jesus, I trust in you!"

The momentousness of what had happened in St. Peter's Square on April 30, 2000, was not limited to Sr. Faustina's canonization. For on that day Pope John Paul II fulfilled Jesus' wish, contained in the Polish mystic's diary. He established in that Jubilee Year a new Church feast day—Divine Mercy Sunday. The pope spoke to the faithful about it: "It is important then that we accept the whole message that comes to us from the word of God on this Second Sunday of Easter, which from now on will be called Divine Mercy Sunday [throughout the Church]. In various readings, the liturgy seems to indicate the path of mercy which, while re-establishing the relationship of each person with God, also creates new relations of fraternal solidarity among human beings. Christ has taught us that 'man not only receives and experiences the mercy of God, but is also called to practice mercy toward others: 'Blessed are the merciful, for they shall obtain mercy' (Mt 5: 7) (*Dives in Misericordia*, no. 14). He also showed us the many paths of mercy, which not only forgives sins but reaches out to all human needs. Jesus bent over every kind of human poverty, material and spiritual.

"His message of mercy continues to reach us through His hands, held out to suffering man. This is how Sr. Faustina saw and proclaimed Him to people on all the continents when, hidden in her convent at Łagiewniki in Kraków, she made her life a hymn to mercy."

In the Congregation for Divine Worship and the Discipline of the Sacrament document of May 5, 2000, we read: "The Holy Father, John Paul II, has graciously instructed that the term 'Divine Mercy' be added to the Roman Missal, that is, after the heading: Second Sunday of Easter. At the same time he has prescribed that the liturgy of that Sunday is to always be based on texts from the Roman Missal and the Liturgy of the Hours According to the Roman Rite." The congregation announced that Pope John Paul II's instructions were to be carried out "irrespective of any counter directive whatsoever." Thus was fulfilled Jesus' wish, which He expressed to Sr. Faustina for the first time in Plock (February 22, 1931). Christ, in subsequent revelations, determined not only the place of the feast in the liturgical calendar, but also the motive and purpose of the feast, the way it was to be prepared and celebrated, and the promises connected with it. The promises are indeed exceptional. The most important of them is the grace of "complete remission of sin and punishment".

**MERCIFUL JESUS.** This painting was on a wall in St. Anne's in Warsaw during John Paul II's first pilgrimage to Poland in 1979, when he had a meeting with the youth. It is now in the Sisters of Loreto chapel in Rembertów, Warsaw.

It is linked with the reception of Holy Communion on that day after a good confession (confession need not be on the same day, but the soul must be free from attachments to sin). Also necessary is a spirit of devotion to God's mercy; that is, an attitude of trust in God and an active love of neighbor.

But the establishment of the Divine Mercy Feast in 2000 was not automatically synonymous with a recognition of all the graces associated with it. That did not come about until June 29, 2002, when the Holy See published another document concerning the new feast. Archbishop Luigi de Magistris, on behalf of the Apostolic Penitentiary, issued a decree—"eternally binding"—where we can read:

"To ensure that the faithful observe this day with intense devotion, the Supreme Pontiff himself has decreed that this Sunday be enriched by a plenary indulgence, as will be explained below. . . .

"A plenary indulgence is granted under the usual conditions (sacramental confession, Eucharistic communion, and prayer for the intentions of the Supreme Pontiff) to those of the faithful who, on the Second Sunday of Easter, or Divine Mercy Sunday, in any church or chapel, in a spirit that is completely detached from

**COMMUNAL PRAYER.**
Nuns from the Congregation of the Sisters of Our Lady of Mercy at the Divine Mercy Shrine, Kraków–Łagiewniki.

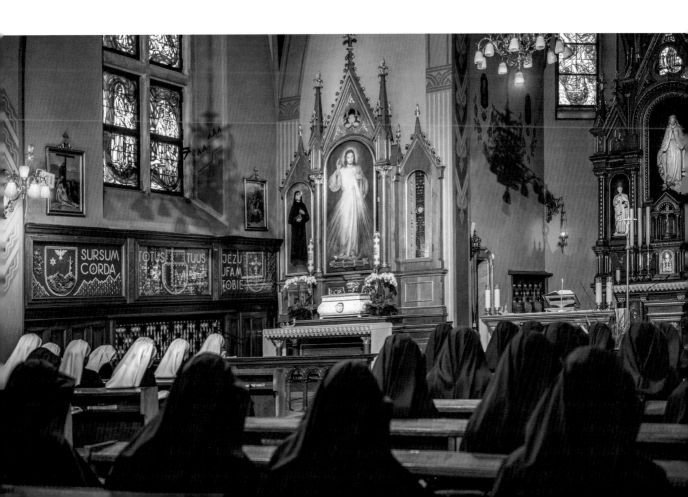

**A MERCIFUL JESUS** image was displayed at St. Anne Church, Warsaw, during Pope John Paul II's first pilgrimage to Poland, in 1979.

sin, even a venial sin, take part in the prayers and devotions held in honor of Divine Mercy, or who, in the presence of the Blessed Sacrament, exposed or reserved in a tabernacle, recite the Our Father and the Creed, adding a devout prayer to the merciful Lord Jesus (e.g., 'Merciful Jesus, I trust in You!').

"A partial indulgence is granted to those of the faithful who, at least with a contrite heart, recite an approved invocation to the merciful Lord Jesus.

"In addition: sailors working on the vast expanse of the sea; the countless brothers and sisters, who, because of war disasters, political events, local violence, and other such causes have been driven out of their homeland; the sick and those who nurse them, and all who for a just cause cannot leave their homes or who carry out an activity for the community which cannot be postponed, may obtain a plenary indulgence on Divine Mercy Sunday, if totally detesting any sin, as has been said before, and with the intention of fulfilling, as soon as possible, the three usual conditions, will recite the Our Father and the Creed before an image of Our Merciful Lord Jesus and, in addition, recite a devout invocation to the Merciful Lord Jesus (e.g., 'Merciful Jesus, I trust in You').

"If the above is impossible, then, on the same day, people may obtain the plenary indulgence if they are spiritually united with those carrying out the prescribed practice for obtaining the indulgence in the usual way, and if they offer up a prayer, their suffering, illnesses, and difficulties to the merciful Lord, resolved to fulfil the three conditions prescribed to obtain the plenary indulgence as soon as possible."

Rev. Prof. Ignacy Rożycki, who had elaborated the theological basis of God's mercy, noticed that there were two complementary attitudes at the heart of the devotion: trust in God and mercy toward one's neighbor. As is evident in Faustina's diary, trust is man's first and most appropriate response to the merciful love of God. Christ told Sr. Faustina: "The graces of My mercy are drawn by means of one vessel only, and that is— trust. The more a soul trusts, the more it will receive. Souls that trust boundlessly are a great comfort to Me, because I pour all the treasures of My graces into them. I rejoice that they ask for much, because it is My desire to give much, very much. On the other hand, I am sad when souls ask for little, when they narrow their hearts" (*Diary*, 1578). Trust is not an isolated virtue in Sr. Faustina's writings, nor a pious feeling, but an overall, open attitude toward God. A merciful attitude toward others is the other element that is essential for a proper devotion to God's mercy. Jesus told Sr. Faustina: "I demand from you deeds of mercy, which are to arise out of love for Me. You are to show mercy to your neighbors always and everywhere. You must not shrink from this or try to excuse or absolve yourself from it" (*Diary*, 742). But these acts of mercy—deeds, words, and prayers—must arise out of love of God, and not from natural charity or philanthropy.

**LOW RELIEFS** of Pope Benedict XVI and Pope John Paul II (in the convent complex) commemorating their visits to Łagiewniki.

293

# Spark

# Spark

The decree on the Divine Mercy Feast indulgences was issued almost two weeks after Pope John Paul II's visit to Poland. It was the last pilgrimage of the very ill pope to his country. During it, he entrusted his spiritual testament to his countrymen. He first made his way to Łagiewniki, to consecrate the new Divine Mercy Basilica on August 17, 2002.

**CONSTRUCTION** of the two-tiered basilica, crowned by a 233-foot tower, took three years (1999–2002).

**SECOND WORLD CONGRESS** on Divine Mercy, Łagiewniki, 2011.

He then recalled: "I often came here, particularly during the occupation, when I worked at the nearby Solvay chemical factory. I remember to this day the road that led from Borek Falecki to Debniki. I walked along this road in clogs, going to work on various shifts. . . . Could one have imagined that that man in clogs would one day consecrate the Divine Mercy Basilica in Łagiewniki?"

## PLAQUE COMMEMORATING
the consecration of the basilica by Pope John Paul II in 2002.

## MOTHER OF MERCY.
A copy of the Virgin Mary, Mother of Mercy, image from Ostra Brama at the Basilica of Divine Mercy in Łagiewniki.

During the homily at the basilica, Pope John Paul II said:

"As we dedicate this new church, we too can ask the question that troubled King Solomon when he consecrated the Temple of Jerusalem as the house of God: 'But will God indeed dwell on the earth? Behold, heaven and the highest heaven cannot contain you; how much less this house which I have built!' (1 Kg 8:27). Yes, at first glance, to bind certain 'places' to God's presence might seem inappropriate. We must never forget that time and space belong to God in their entirety. Yet even though time and the entire world may be considered his 'temple', God has chosen certain times and places to enable people to experience in a special way His presence and His grace. Impelled by their sense of faith, people journey to these places, confident that there they will truly find themselves in the presence of God.

**OVER 2,000** believers, from 270 countries, at the World Congress on Divine Mercy in Kraków (2011).

**IN SOME
POLISH TOWNS**
and cities there is
communal prayer
at 3 P.M., the
Hour of Mercy, as
here in Mokotow,
Warsaw.

"In this same spirit of faith I have come to Łagiewniki to dedicate this new church. I am convinced that this is a special place chosen by God to sow the grace of His mercy. I pray that this church will always be a place where the message of God's merciful love is proclaimed; a place of conversion and repentance; a place for the celebration of the Eucharist; a fountain of mercy; a place of prayer and of constant appeals for mercy for ourselves and for the whole world. . . .

"I firmly believe that this new church will always be a place where people will come before God in spirit and truth. They will come with the trust that accompanies all those who humbly open their hearts to God's merciful love, to that love which is stronger than even the greatest sin. Here, in the fire of divine love, human hearts will burn with desire for conversion, and whoever looks for hope will find comfort."

Pope John Paul II not only consecrated the basilica. He did something that was much more momentous—namely, he entrusted the world to God's mercy: "How greatly today's world needs God's mercy! In every continent, from the depth of human suffering, a cry for mercy seems to rise up. Where hatred and the thirst for revenge dominate, where war brings suffering and death to the innocent, there the

**PASSING ON THE DIVINE MERCY SPARK,** in the form of lanterns with the images of Merciful Jesus, Sr. Faustina, and Pope John Paul II. These were used on April 27, 2014, the Feast of the Divine Mercy, as well as the canonization of Pope John Paul II.

 **WORLD CONGRESS** on Divine Mercy, Łagiewniki, 2011.

grace of mercy is needed in order to settle human minds and hearts and to bring about peace. Wherever respect for life and human dignity are lacking, there is need of God's merciful love, in Whose light we see the inexpressible value of every human being. Mercy is needed in order to ensure that every injustice in the world will come to an end in the splendor of truth.

"Today, therefore, in this shrine, I wish solemnly to entrust the world to Divine Mercy. I do so with the burning desire that the message of God's merciful love, proclaimed here through St. Faustina, may be made known to all the peoples of the earth and fill their hearts with hope. May this message radiate from this place to our beloved homeland and throughout the world. May the binding promise of the Lord Jesus be fulfilled: from here there must go forth 'the spark that will prepare the world for [His] final coming' (cf. *Diary*, 1732).

**PERPETUAL ADORATION CHAPEL**.
The Blessed Sacrament in the shrine chapel, Łagiewniki. There has been ceaseless prayer here –before the Blessed Sacrament – since Pope John Paul II's death; the spiritual fulfillment of the pope's testament.

303

"This spark needs to be lighted by the grace of God. This fire of mercy needs to be passed on to the world. It is in the mercy of God that the world will find peace and mankind will find happiness! I entrust this task to you, dear brothers and sisters, to the Church in Kraków and to Poland, and to all the votaries of the Divine Mercy who will come here from Poland and from throughout the world. May you be witnesses to mercy!"

So Pope John Paul II left the Poles his spiritual testimony during his last visit to his country: he entrusted them with the task of proclaiming God's mercy to the whole world. At the same time, he referred to Jesus' prophecy, contained in Sr. Faustina's *Diary*, that out of Poland will come "the spark that will prepare the world for [His] final coming."

Before he said that, many commentators thought that the "spark" might be Pope John Paul II himself or Sr. Faustina. But from what the Holy Father said, it appears that it is rather the message of Divine Mercy.

In conclusion, the pope said a prayer entrusting the world to God's mercy:

God, merciful Father,

**MULTITUDES OF PILGRIMS** come to Łagiewniki every year, particularly on the Feast of Divine Mercy.

in Your Son, Jesus Christ, You have revealed Your love

and poured it out upon us in the Holy Spirit, the Comforter.

We entrust to You today the destiny of the world

and of every man and woman.

Bend down to us sinners,

heal our weakness,

conquer all evil,

and grant that all the peoples of the earth

may experience Your mercy.

In You, the Triune God,

may they ever find the source of hope.

Eternal Father,

by the Passion and Resurrection of Your Son,

have mercy on us and upon the whole world!

Amen.

Many commentators drew attention to the extraordinary spiritual bond that linked Sr. Faustina with Pope John Paul II. For years, Karol Wojtyła's activities

were closely interwoven with the message about Divine Mercy, which—as the pope emphasized—was not solely an expression of a specific piety, but the very heart of Christianity. It is not a coincidence that his last book, *Memory and Identity*, published in 2005, has a chapter devoted to mercy: "The Mystery of Mercy". He wrote that, despite the spread of evil in the world, "The whole of the twentieth century was marked by a special action of God, the Father that is 'rich in mercy.' " Pope John Paul II's death, on the evening of April 2, 2005, sealed the mission that linked the Polish pope with the Polish mystic. Just before departing from this world, the Holy Father managed to participate in the Mass—his last—that coincided with the liturgical commencement of the Divine Mercy feast.

It might seem that all the misunderstandings and conflicts connected with Sr. Faustina's legacy were a thing of the past. But that is not quite so. In September 2005, under quite dramatic circumstances, Eugeniusz Kazimirowski's painting was moved from the Church of the Holy Spirit (Vilnius) to the nearby Church of the Holy Trinity. In March 2004, the Vilnius metropolitan, Audrys Cardinal Juozas Bačkis, issued a decree on the transfer of the Merciful Jesus image from the former Dominican church. The decision met with the displeasure of the Polish community in Lithuania, as the Church of the Holy Spirit was the main Polish pastoral center in

**TURIN SHROUD**. It is still a mystery as to how Jesus' image came to be depicted on the shroud (opposite page). Also mysterious are the faces on the Veil of Manoppello and on the Merciful Jesus image of Kazimirowski's painting (below).

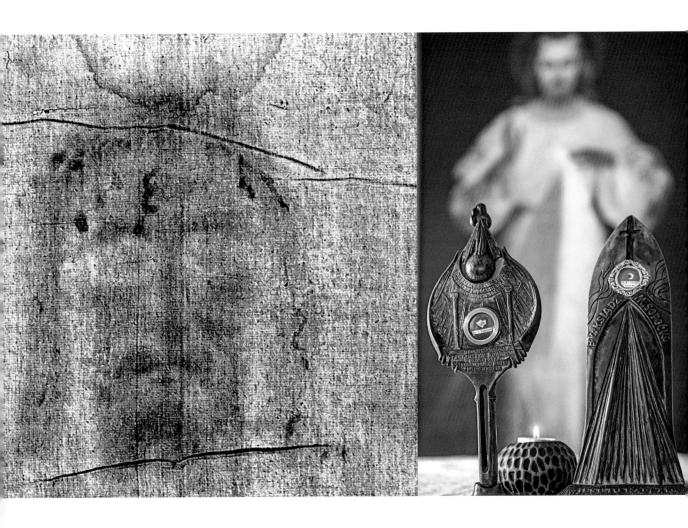

Vilnius. Over ten thousand people signed an open letter to Cardinal Bačkis, request-ing that he leave the painting where it was. The representatives of twenty-five Polish organizations in Lithuania appealed to the metropolitan—if he considered the Church of the Holy Spirit to be unsuitable for displaying the famous image of Christ—to find a place in Vilnius that was worthy enough and accessible to the faithful from all over the world. According to the representatives of the Polish minority, the Church of the Holy Trinity did not fulfil those conditions, as it was too small to become a pilgrimage center, a shrine on a European scale.

Many Poles in Lithuania received the cardinal's decision with bitterness, as, in their opinion, it had features akin to the unfavorable stance of the Lithuanian authori-ties with regard to the Polish minority. They complained that nobody had even con-sulted them about the controversial matter. As a result, the parishioners of the Church of the Holy Spirit decided not to allow the painting to be moved. They kept watch over the painting day and night. That lasted for eighteen months—until September

**RELIQUARIES.**
Faustina Kowalska's and Blessed Michał Sopoćko's in the convent of the Congregation of the Sisters of the Merciful Jesus, Vilnius.

307

# VALE
# OF MERCY

**OF THE MALE RELIGIOUS ORDERS,** it is the Pallottines who, apart from the Marians, have done most in propagating the devotion to Divine Mercy throughout the world. Their main center, devoted to this mission, is the Vale of Mercy, just to the west of Jasna Góra in Częstochowa. In 1947, the Pallottines took over an area where there had once been a brick factory. They built a house and a chapel wherein they had Adolf Hyla's painting of Merciful Jesus at the main altar. Two years later, Bishop Teodor Kubin blessed the center.

The Vale of Mercy center has ceaselessly practiced the devotion to Divine Mercy, in the forms recommended by Sr. Faustina, even from 1959 to 1978, when the Holy See ban was in force. In 1952, the parish of Divine Mercy was established. When Primate Stefan Wyszyński visited the parish in 1965 he instructed the Pallottines to continue their work and to deepen the devotion theologically. So it is not surprising that congresses and symposiums began to be organized at the Vale of Mercy, at one of which Fr. Michał Sopoćko lectured.

In 1992, because the center was attracting masses of pilgrims, Archbishop Stanislaw Nowak issued a decree that established the Pallottine's church as a Sanctuary of the Divine Mercy. The Pallottines practice mercy daily, giving free meals and medical aid to the needy.

**THE VALE OF MERCY** (close to the Jasna Góra basilica, Częstochowa) is attracting more and more pilgrims.

28, 2005. That day, a group of men, directed by Fr. Vaidasa Vaisvilasa, barged into the church. They took the painting by force and, in passing, ill-treated several female parishioners who were guarding the painting. Shortly afterwards Kazimirowski's painting was located in the Church of the Holy Trinity, which, by virtue of Cardinal Bačkis's decision, became the Divine Mercy Shrine.

The history of the devotion has still not come to an end. It is very likely that many surprises still await us. For example, one of them may well be connected with the discovery by a German Trappistine, Sr. Blandina Paschalis Schömer. This nun is famous for her recognition of congruities between the Shroud of Turin and the Veil of Manoppello, which she identified as a burial linen from Christ's tomb and, at the same time, as St. Veronica's veil. Using reference points, and eventually superimposing life-sized slides, she illustrated that the two images matched. (It is not yet known how these two images arose, for no scientist has been able to establish how someone possibly could have painted them.) Later, the German mystic took an interest in Kazimirowski's painting. She superimposed the Vilnius Merciful Jesus image on the Manoppello and Turin images. It turned out that the painting also matched these images. Sr. Blandina was surprised by her own discovery. But something else amazed her yet more: "Faustina wrote down a prophecy from Jesus in her diary: 'Before I come as the Just Judge, I am coming first as the King of Mercy' (*Diary*, 83). I profoundly believe that the Manoppello image depicts God's kind face. That defenseless face is the fulfillment of Faustina's prophecy."

Pope John Paul II's successor, Cardinal Joseph Ratzinger, Benedict XVI, went to Poland on one of his first pilgrimages. He arrived at the Divine Mercy shrine in Łagiewniki on May 27, 2006. He prayed before St. Faustina's relics and the Merciful Jesus image. In the basilica, he met eight hundred sick and handicapped, as well as their caregivers. In a short address to the faithful, the pope said, among other things: "We encounter two mysteries: the mystery of human suffering and the mystery of Divine Mercy. At first sight these two mysteries seem to be opposed to one another. But when we study them more deeply in the light of faith, we find that they are placed in reciprocal harmony through the mystery of the Cross of Christ. As Pope John Paul II said in this place: 'the Cross is the most profound bowing down of the Divinity toward man. ... The Cross is like a touch of eternal love on the most painful wounds of humanity's earthly existence' (August 17, 2002). Dear friends, you who are sick, who are marked by suffering in body or soul, you are most closely united to the Cross of Christ, and at the same time, you are the most eloquent witnesses of God's mercy. Through

**POPE BENEDICT XVI**
visited Łagiewniki
in May 2006.

**PAINTING**
of Blessed Michał Sopoćko,
Divine Mercy Shrine,
Białystok.

309

**ATOK IN 2001**, Bishop John Ozga (Doume Diocese, Cameroon) entrusted a parish in Atok (Cameroon) to the Marian Fathers, requesting that they organize a Divine Mercy apostolate there. On April 18, 2004, the Feast of Divine Mercy, he consecrated the Divine Mercy Sanctuary in Atok. Hundreds of pilgrims went to the ceremony on foot.

you and through your suffering, He bows down toward humanity with love. You who say in silence: 'Jesus, I trust in You' teach us that there is no faith more profound, no hope more alive, and no love more ardent than the faith, hope, and love of a person who in the midst of suffering places himself securely in God's hands. May the human hands of those who care for you in the name of mercy be an extension of the open hands of God."

On September 28, 2008, the solemn beatification of Fr. Michał Sopoćko took place in Białystok. He had died in 1975, not living to see the rehabilitation of the devotion in honor of God's mercy. After the Vatican had recognized Sr. Faustina's message, this theologian's works were referred to more and more. His beatification process commenced at the diocesan level in 1987, and at the Vatican level in 1993. In 2004, Pope John Paul II promulgated the decree on Fr. Sopoćko's heroic virtues, and then a decree about the miracle attributed to his intercession. Thereby the beatification of Sr. Faustina's confessor, whose relics repose at the Divine Mercy Shrine in Białystok, became possible. The homily was given by the metropolitan of Kraków, Cardinal Stanisław Dziwisz. He emphasized that the turning point in the life of Bl. Michał Sopoćko came when he met St. Faustina: "He became the bridge between the 'Secretary' of God's mercy and the whole Church community, to which the message was addressed." Fr. Sopoćko

**STATUE OF CHRIST** was designed so that the rays are in fact stairs that lead into a little chapel. Numerous pilgrims thus, as if, enter into Jesus' Heart.

**EL SALVADOR**, on the island of Mindanao, in the Philippines, is one of the two most important centers of devotion to Divine Mercy in Asia.

**A GRAND PROCESSION**
passed through the streets
of Vilnius on May 8, 2016,
on the occasion of the
Divine Mercy National
Congress being held in
the city. Cardinal Piero
Parolin, Secretary of State
of the Holy See, headed
the procession. The faithful
carried an original painting
by Eugeniusz Kazimirowski
and recited the Divine
Mercy Chaplet along the
way. The ceremony was
broadcast by Lithuanian
state television.

**THE PROCESSION** in Vilnius walked a two-kilometer route: from the Lithuanian Seimas (parliament) to the Cathedral of St Stanislaus and St Vladislaus.

endeavored to fulfil the role of a mediator, despite all sorts of adversities, to the end of his life. The cardinal noted that Fr. Sopoćko not only spoke about mercy, he also strived to bear witness to it in his life, being solicitous about the weakest, the poor and the needy, and also the so-called dregs of society.

Looking back on Sr. Faustina's mission, one can say that it ended in success, though it seemed to be presumptuously daring. The veneration of God's mercy, which was virtually unknown to Catholics in the middle of the twentieth century, is now one of the most rapidly spreading forms of devotion in the Christian world. All forms of the devotion—those that Jesus instructed Faustina to propagate—have spread throughout the world: the image of the Merciful Jesus is at present the best-known image [of Jesus] in the world; the chaplet is one of the most popular Catholic prayers; more and more people adore Christ during the Hour of Mercy; and the Holy See has officially entered the Divine Mercy Feast in the liturgical calendar, which Jesus promised Faustina in a revelation.

That which seemed to be her most painful failure, and the source of her greatest affliction, the new congregation, also became a victory for Sr. Faustina. The saint's last vision with regard to the congregation showed its varied forms, that is, its three "aspects", though one in fidelity to the main message. That vision is undoubtedly in accord with the missionary movement based on the message about God's mercy.

**THE KNIGHTS OF COLUMBUS**, participating in the 2016 Divine Mercy National Congress in Vilnius, carried the image of the Merciful Jesus first; then it was carried by other groups.

313

# MISERICORDIN

### ON NOVEMBER 17, 2013,

Pope Francis, after saying the Angelus, began to encourage the faithful that had gathered in St. Peter's Square to take a special medicine.

"Now I would like to recommend a medicine to you. Some of you may be wondering: 'Is the pope a pharmacist now?' It is a special medicine which will help you to benefit from the Year of Faith, as it soon will come to an end. It is a medicine that consists of 59 threaded beads; a 'spiritual medicine' called Misericordin. A small box containing 59 beads on a string. This little box contains the medicine, and will be distributed to you by volunteers as you leave the Square. Take them! There is a rosary, with which you can pray the Chaplet of Divine Mercy, spiritual help for our souls and for spreading love, forgiveness, and brotherhood everywhere. Do not forget to take it, because it is good for you. It is good for the heart, the soul, and for life in general!"

On leaving St. Peter's Square, pilgrims were given Misericordin by members of the Swiss Guard and sisters of the Missionaries of Charity, as well as by the papal almoner, Archbishop Konrad Krajewski. It was he who had shown Pope Francis the unusual medicine that had been concocted by a deacon, Błażej Kwiatkowski, who, before entering a seminary in Gdańsk, had studied pharmacy.

When the pope became acquainted with the prescription, he began to laugh and decided to distribute the medicine to the faithful in St. Peter's Square. So the Vatican produced 25,000 packets of medicine, which also contained papal rosaries. Thus the Divine Mercy message took on another form.

**THE PAPAL ALMONER**, Archbishop Konrad Krajewski, with sisters of the Missionaries of Charity during the distribution of Misericordin in St. Peter's Square, Rome.

**POPE FRANCIS** – a great devotee of the Divine Mercy – initiated the distribution of Misericordin to pilgrims.

**ON SATURDAY, JULY 30, 2016,** Pope Francis met for an evening prayer vigil at the Divine Mercy Sanctuary in Kraków.

# YEAR OF MERCY

**AT ST. PETER'S BASILICA IN ROME**, on March 13, the second anniversary of his election, Pope Francis announced the Extraordinary Jubilee of Mercy: from December 8, 2015 – the Feast of the Immaculate Conception and the 50th anniversary of Vatican II – to November 20, 2016, the Solemnity of Our Lord Jesus Christ, King of the Universe. The president of the Pontifical Council for the Laity, Cardinal Stanisław Ryłko, stated that this extraordinary period was proclaimed so that people might discover the merciful countenance of God the Father.

One of the most important events of the Jubilee is the World Youth Day in Kraków – the main center for the dissemination of the Divine Mercy message. Cardinal Stanisław Dziwisz, the host of this mass Church event, said familiarity with St. Faustina's and St. John Paul II's spiritual legacy can bring about a deepening of people's faith and many vocations.

Pope Francis also established new indulgences for the Jubilee Year. In addition to that, on Ash Wednesday he sent out over 1,100 missionaries of mercy to all the continents, that is, priests who can absolve people of sins that hitherto the pope alone could absolve.

**POPE FRANCIS** in front of the tomb of Sister Faustina and the image of the Merciful Jesus in the chapel in Łagiewniki.

**DIVINE MERCY CONGRESS**
for countries of the African Great Lakes region (Central Africa) in 2010 at the shrine in Kabuga, in the diocese of Kigali, Rwanda.

It is made up of both old and new religious orders, fraternities, associations, apostolates, communities, and individuals. It is worth mentioning a few initiatives: first and foremost, Sr. Faustina's mother-convent, the Congregation of Sisters of Our Lady of Mercy; the Congregation of the Sisters of the Merciful Jesus, founded by Fr. Sopoćko; the Pallottine Fathers, the Marian Fathers, and the Felician Sisters in the United States; the Association of the Apostles of Divine Mercy in Kraków; the hermitages centered on Divine Mercy in Slovakia; the Community of the Sisters of the Handmaids of Divine Mercy in Rybno, Poland, where the sisters wear white habits and red capes. We must not forget about the new shrines and missionary and pastoral centers where the devotion that was advocated by St. Faustina is cultivated. They are to be found throughout the world, and some of them have become famous for extraordinary graces and have become pilgrimage centers—for example, the Kana Marian Formation Center, conducted by the Marian Fathers, near Kibeho in Rwanda, where there is a statue of the Merciful Jesus which stands over sixteen feet high, the work of a Mexican woman, Gogi Farias. One could mention many more places. They all form a movement concentrated on the mystery of God's mercy, a movement desirous of propagating the mystery throughout the world in various ways and of worshipping God in the forms the Lord Jesus Himself communicated to Sr. Faustina.

The Philippines is one of the countries where the devotion is thriving in particular. Sr. Faustina's message reached the Philippines in the 1940s through the Marian Fathers in the United States. The devotion has spread so much that road traffic in many Philippine towns virtually comes to a standstill every afternoon at three o'clock; people pray, venerate the moment of Christ's death on the Cross, and take

advantage of the Hour of Grace. Two of the best known centers of the devotion are in Manila, the capital, and in El Salvador, on the island of Mindanao. In El Salvador, the lay members of a prayer group bought land and erected a fifty-foot-tall statue of the Merciful Jesus. The huge figure quickly became one of the country's main pilgrimage centers.

Stanley Villavicencio, from the island of Cebu, did a great deal in spreading the devotion in the Philippines. He had apparently died on March 2, 1993, at a hospital in Chong Hua. The death certificate had been issued, and a coffin, in which he was to be exposed in the chapel, had arrived at the hospital. The funeral preparations were interrupted by Villavicencio himself—he suddenly got out of his hospital bed. The nurses who witnessed the event ran out of the ward in panic. His doctor entered a seminary and became a Jesuit. Villavicencio related that, during the time that he was thought to be dead, he had a vision of the Merciful Jesus, Who told him about God's mercy.

Stanley Villavicencio is not the only person who has experienced supernatural intervention. Every year brings examples of specific aid for those who have entrusted themselves to God's mercy or who prayed for St. Faustina's intercession. the Divine Mercy Shrine in Łagiewniki is visited by one and a half to two million pilgrims every year. Many of them have described the graces they received there in the visitors' book. The testimonies speak of those who were, for example, healed of an incurable disease or saved from committing suicide; the sisters estimate that pilgrims yearly leave about one million testimonies on cards and in books. This is not only an eloquent testimony to the power of God's mercy, but also a harbinger of our destiny, which is happiness and love throughout eternity.

**WORLD YOUTH DAY IN SYDNEY** (2008) was patronized by, among others, St. Faustina. Young people spread the Divine Mercy message in the streets of the city.

317

# Tribunal of Mercy

# CHAPTER 16

# Tribunal of Mercy

The mystery of Divine Mercy runs through Karol Wojtyła's and Faustina Kowalska's twentieth-century destinies like a gold thread. It is through them that the modern world is able to discover anew the essence of the Christian message, the message about God's merciful love for every person.

**POPE JOHN PAUL II** died on April 2, 2005, on the eve of the Feast of the Divine Mercy. He made his last public appearance on March 30. John Paul II was raised to the Glory of the Altars—beatified and canonized—on the day of the Feast of the Divine Mercy that he himself had established.

**POPE FRANCIS** opens the Holy Door in St Peter's Basilica in Rome, initiating the Extraordinary Jubilee Year of Mercy on 8 December 2015.

This truth has always been present in the Church, but in recent centuries it seems to have been pushed, pastorally and catechetically, into the background by other elements of Church teaching. Now, in the light of Divine Mercy, the Church is interpreting Holy Scripture anew, discovering God's merciful love in the sacraments.

Divine Mercy is not abstract, emotional, or sentimental. It always manifests itself in the realities of human life, in the most painful and difficult matters. One has always been able to experience it in the Church from the very beginning: in the confessional, in the sacrament of reconciliation, which Jesus called the

321

**POPE JOHN PAUL II** in Szczecin, 1991. He blessed Andrzej Kurzawski's Merciful Jesus painting.

"tribunal of mercy". As Benedict XVI observed, the main element of the sacrament is "a personal meeting with God, the Father of goodness and mercy. Sin is not at the very heart of sacramental liturgy, but God's mercy, which is infinitely greater than all our sins."

Sr. Faustina's *Diary* is full of entries devoted to the sacrament of reconciliation. She wrote down what Jesus told her of the transformation that can be accomplished in a person precisely through meeting God in the confessional: "Were a soul like a decaying corpse so that from a human standpoint, there would be no [hope of] restoration and everything would already be lost, it is not so with God. The miracle of Divine Mercy restores that soul in full" (*Diary*, 1448).

Christ, however, complained that many people closed themselves to His mercy and rejected the possibility of forgiveness and the healing of wounds inflicted by

**DEVOTION
TO SR. FAUSTINA**
is also present in the
Orthodox Church. Her
relics can be found in
a Romanian church in the
center of Bucharest. The
faithful there emphasize
that there is nothing in
her message that might
arouse controversy, and
there are many elements
that appeal to them.

323

sin. "I am speaking to them through their remorse of conscience, through their failures and sufferings, through thunderstorms, through the voice of the Church. And if they bring all My graces to naught, I begin to be angry with them, leaving them alone" (*Diary*, 1728). It is precisely these people that He warns: "Oh, how miserable are those who do not take advantage of the miracle of God's mercy! You will call out in vain, but it will be too late" (*Diary*, 1448).

Sr. Faustina, like other masters of the spiritual life, has left us specific advice as to the attitude we ought to assume in going to the sacrament of reconciliation:

First, she advised complete sincerity and openness. Even the best confessor could not help if a soul were to be insincere. Moreover, a lack of sincerity and openness exposed one to spiritual danger.

Second, one needs to be humble. Without it one will not be healed. The opposite attitude is pride, which plunges one into darkness.

Third, it is necessary to be obedient. Without it confession cannot be fruitful, even if the Lord Jesus Himself were to be the confessor.

Jesus told Faustina that the sacrament of reconciliation is a personal encounter with Him: "Just as you prepare in My presence, so also you make your confession before Me. The person of the priest is, for Me, only a screen. Never analyze what sort of a (89) priest it is that I am making use of; open your soul in confession as you would to Me, and I will fill it with My light" (*Diary*, 1725). He also said: "As you will act toward your confessor, so I will act toward you. If you conceal something from him . . . I too will hide Myself from you, and you will remain alone" (*Diary*, 269).

The mystic wrote that confession filled her with calm, and a feeling of gratitude toward the Holy Trinity for the incomprehensible miracle of mercy that occurs in the sacrament. She emphasized that she profited from the sacrament in two ways: through inner healing and through spiritual growth. Thanks to the sacrament, she could cleanse her soul and come ever closer to God.

So the message of God's mercy has a real dimension—a personal meeting with God in sacramental confession, where one experiences forgiveness and reconciliation. This demonstrates that every man is, of his nature, weak and that everybody needs support from God. The confessional is a place where God's mercy triumphs over every weakness, over every sin and evil.

**MERCIFUL JESUS** icon in the Greek-Catholic Church of the Dormition of Our Lady, Warsaw.

**DIVINE MERCY SPIRITUALITY CENTER** near the Vatican attracts pilgrims from all over the world.

RELIKWIE ŚW. SIOSTRY FAUSTYNY